Sheryl Lindsell-Roberts

New Rules
for Today's Workplace

Houghton Mifflin Harcourt
Boston   New York

The inclusion of any word or phrase in this book is not an expression
of the Publisher's opinion as to whether or not it is subject to
proprietary rights. No word in this book is to be regarded
as affecting the validity of any trademark.

Visit our website: www.hmhbooks.com

Library of Congress Cataloging-in-Publication Data

Lindsell-Roberts, Sheryl.
  New rules for today's workplace / Sheryl Lindsell-Roberts. -- 1st ed.
    p. cm.
  Includes index.
  ISBN 978-0-547-42808-6
  1. Online social networks. 2. Business communication. 3. Virtual
work teams--Management.
  I. Title.
  HM742.L56 2011
  650.0285'6754--dc22

                                    2010041006

Manufactured in the United States of America
Book design by Joyce C. Weston

PowerPoint is a registered trademark of Microsoft Corporation.

Author photograph by Jon Roberts; "Word from Sheryl" icon
photograph by Jon Roberts; "Hot tip" icon photograph by Don
Farrall/Photodisc Green/Getty Images; "Reminder" icon photograph
by Stockdisc/Getty Images.

1 2 3 4 5 6 7 8 9 10 -EB - 15 14 13 12 11 10

Dedicated to three generations of Lindsells

Baby Boomer (that's me)

I bought my first computer when I got my second book contract. The manual wasn't user-friendly (manuals haven't gotten much better since then), and I struggled with the word processor. Every time I turned on the computer my palms became sweaty, my heart raced, my blood pressure rose, my hair curled, and my language degenerated. My poor sons felt like running out the door because I turned into a person they didn't recognize. (I was something like the Incredible Hulk, only I didn't turn green and bulk up.) Ultimately, they remembered that they wanted to remain in my will, so they came to my rescue.

Generation X (my sons, Marc and Eric)

When Marc (an architect) designed my home in the early 90s, he presented me with computer-generated plans and hand-drawn sketches of what the outside and some of the rooms would look like. It was hard to envision because some of the rooms had 27-foot beamed ceilings. Several years later he began using a highly sophisticated computer program for architects that lets clients "walk through the rooms." When I first saw some of his work on this program, I felt like a cavewoman looking at fire for the first time. It was incredible; the next best thing to standing in the room and looking around.

I had become accustomed to having Eric email me wonderful pictures of Brooke, my little granddaughter. All of a sudden the pictures stopped coming. When I questioned Eric, he told me that he's posting everything on Facebook, and if I wanted to see pictures of Brooke, I'd have to join Facebook and view them there. "That's no way to treat your mother," I told him. "If you don't start emailing pictures, I'm going to move in." I guess he decided not to call my bluff because he sent a few pictures. I did, however, join Facebook (and I didn't move in).

Generation Y (my granddaughter, Brooke)

When Brooke was five years old, she expressed curiosity about an item on a table in my office. It's an old, portable typewriter with a cover that I bought at an antique store a number of years ago. I keep the lid open as a showcase (bookcase) for many of the books I've written. I explained to Brooke that people used to type on typewriters such as this one. She looked puzzled and asked, "Where's the monitor?" *Yes, times have changed!*

Contents

Acknowledgments

To Chris Leonesio, Vice President, Managing Editor, Reference, at Houghton Mifflin Harcourt, who continues to be my champion. And to Catherine Pratt, who has worked *patiently* with me on my past four books. I not only meet my deadline but usually send my manuscript in somewhat early. However, I am a writer and instrument of change and send Catherine new versions of chapters regularly until the book goes into production. It's somewhat like adding last-minute spices to a recipe before you serve a gourmet meal. Catherine always accepts these late additions with a smile—or at least I think so. (I can't see her.)

To my colleagues and the companies (in order of their appearance) whose contributions added immensely to the depth of content in this book:

Intel Corporation
Mark Tetrault, 2M Architecture
Dave McKeon, Game On!
Margot Rutledge, KidsWin
Ned Gulley, MathWorks
Emily Greenwood, EKG Networking
Martin Lieberman, Constant Contact
Bobby DiMarino, Roche Bros.
Cathy Browne
Cisco Systems
Simerpreet Kaur
Eric Bloom, Manager Mechanics
American Society for Training & Development
Dave Yakonich, Boston Scientific
Julia Young, Facilitate.com

Nancy Settle-Murphy, Guided Insights
ON24
Bard Williams, TiVo
Charlie Sidoti, OneBeacon Insurance
Hal Tugal, Barry Controls
Candace Toner, Biomatters, Ltd.
Mary Ellen Eagan, Harris Miller Miller & Hanson
Jeff Teisch, Brown Brothers Harriman
Tom Gardam, Pegasystems
Suzanne Bates, Bates Communications

And to everyone who came to the US from other countries and allowed me to share their inspiring, genuine, and sometimes amusing stories. A few asked to remain anonymous because of the sensitive nature of their stories, so I used first names only. Thank you to Jurgen, Robin, Ari, Suzie, Brigitte, April, Jianyao, Aman, Robert, Simon, Muhammad, Nalini, Keiko, Marita, Akram, John, Tony, and Claudio.

And last, but certainly not least, to my clients, who always inspire me and contribute immensely to my professional growth. I'm so grateful to all of you for your ongoing support and confidence in me.

When you're through changing, you're through.
—Bruce Fairchild Barton, American author
and advertising executive

Introduction

Virtual is the conversation in today's rapidly changing international workplace—virtual workers, virtual teams, virtual classrooms, virtual meetings, virtual networks, virtual trade shows, virtual interviews, virtual offices, virtual office assistants, and more.

Because of this trend, outstanding communications skills are more essential than ever. People are working at a faster pace, they're doing more with fewer resources, and they're dealing with constant change. Competition in many industries has become global, and the pace of innovation in products and services has accelerated. This has increased information access and flow for workers and managers. If you look back over the last 30 years (and that's merely a flash in time), you realize how much has changed. We've gone from . . .

Lifestyle
- 9-to-5 → 24/7
- jet setters → cyber-surfers
- office workers → virtual workers
- single skill set → lifelong learning
- shopping malls → amazon.com, craigslist, and eBay
- brick and mortar → virtual workplaces
- security → risk taking
- status quo → constant change
- national → global
- homogeneous → heterogeneous
- lifers → job hoppers

Technology

- electric typewriters → high-speed computers
- radios → MP3 players
- encyclopedias → wikipedias
- wired → wireless
- letters → email, IM, and texting
- rotary phones → smartphones
- kilobytes → terabytes
- local data storage → clouds

Today's workplace continues to be about rapid-fire changes in technology. Don McLaughlin, Chief Learning Officer at Cisco Systems, asked his 20-something-year-old son, "What's the leading edge in technology?" His son replied, "Dad, I'm too old. Talk to someone in high school because they use technology dramatically differently from the way I use it."

Flashback (early 1980s)

Max Hosh is packing up his office. He's retiring from the 9-to-5 job he's had with Marric Corporation for nearly 45 years. His father worked for Marric, and Max joined the company right after graduating from college. Max started in the mailroom and worked his way up to Director of Corporate Affairs.

Max had been managing a team of 20 men who have been with the company for most of their careers. All of them have cubicles outside Max's office, and he's been looking forward to seeing them each morning. Ethel, Max's personal secretary, was Max's right arm. After taking dictation from Max each morning, she'd return to her typewriter and neatly type up all of Max's memos, letters, and other documents. Ethel also took care of Max's appointments, screened his calls, and did a myriad of other things to make his day run more smoothly. Max doesn't want to retire, but he's 65 and it's time. "Although I won't miss having to put on a suit and tie each morning," he thought, "what will I do with the rest of my life?"

Flash forward (21st century)

The alarm goes off at 2:30 AM. "Oh, no," mumbles Alice Hosh (Max's granddaughter) as she stumbles from bed to make a quick cup of coffee.

During the afternoon Alice had gotten a text from her manager in China informing her of a conference call at 3:00 AM, EST. She was up until midnight preparing for the meeting and consoles herself that at least she's gotten a couple hours' sleep.

Since graduating from college nearly ten years earlier, Alice has been with three different start-up technology companies. She's always looking for her next opportunity and the next level of technology. Alice works virtually. She has a dedicated office in her home with technology connections to the mother ship, including a webcam for teleconferencing. She has a smartphone that gives her the ultimate in mobility so she can work and be available 24/7. Although Alice dreads these occasional middle-of-the-night meetings, they're offset by having flexible hours and being able to work from home in her sweatsuit with her dog curled up next to her chair.

This book is for you if you . . .

- Manage virtual workers (telecommuters) or work virtually.
- Struggle with the challenges of the multigenerational and cross-cultural workforce.
- Are hankering to reap the rewards of the social networking/social media phenomena.
- Want to be a productive facilitator for virtual learning and meetings.
- Need to understand the new lingo.

Icons in this book

Scattered throughout this book you'll find the following icons (somewhat like road signs) to help you find tips, things to remember, notes from me, and cross-references.

Hot tip. This may be a time saver, life saver, frustration saver, or just about anything relevant to the information at hand.

Reminder. This is akin to tying a string around your finger so you won't forget something important, such as packing your umbrella during monsoon season.

Word from Sheryl. This is an opportunity to share "war stories" from my own experience or my clients' experiences.

 Cross-reference. This directs you to a related topic.

This book abounds with real-life stories from people and companies in the business world who are very successful at what they do. You can learn from their numerous tips and best practices. Please look for their names in the Acknowledgments.

A word about gender

Which word doesn't belong: *aunt, brother, cousin, father, grandfather, grandmother, mother, nephew, niece, sister, uncle*? The answer is *cousin* because it's the only gender-neutral term.

I searched for a gender-neutral term for my books to avoid getting into the clumsy *he/she* or *him/her* pronouns, but I couldn't find one. So I tossed a coin, and here's how it landed: I use the male gender in the even-numbered chapters and the female gender in the odd-numbered chapters. (If this offends you, I apologize.)

Sheryl Lindsell-Roberts, MA

P.S. Keep this book for easy reference. Don't share it. You may never get it back!

Part One

Going Social

UNLESS YOU'VE been hiding in a cave and haven't had contact with the outside world, you've undoubtedly heard the buzz about social media and social networking. This phenomenon has dramatically changed the way people connect. Remember the "six degrees of separation," the theory that everyone in the world is connected to everyone else by no more than six links? Consider this: If you have 100 connections on LinkedIn, and each of those connections has 100 connections, you'll be two links away from 10,000 connections. If each of those 10,000 connections has 100 connections, you'll be three links away from 1 million connections. That's powerful!

The difference between PR and social media is that PR is about positioning, and social media is about becoming, being, and improving.

—Chris Brogan, President of New Marketing Labs, a media marketing agency

Chapter 1

Build the Buzz with Social Networking and Social Media

In this chapter

- *Include "the socials" as part of your marketing strategy*
- *Build the buzz*
- *Publish great content*
- *Generate a social media policy*
- *It's all about interactivity*
- *Pick the sites that are right for you*

Imagine this . . . You're trying to extend the reach of your business. You sit in your office day after day, week after week, month after month, making cold calls. Nobody visits. Nobody calls. So you try a new strategy. You become active in your local chamber of commerce, several professional organizations, and face-to-face networking groups. You meet new people in your geographic community. You get a few phone calls. People you meet start to visit your website. And you have extended the reach of your business.

Now add to the mix . . . You become active in several of the popular social networking sites such as LinkedIn, Twitter, and Facebook. You blog. You publish articles on Ezine. You post videos on YouTube. You do a few podcasts. You meet new people from all over the world. All of a sudden there's a hubbub of activity on your website. Your phone is ringing constantly. You have dramatically extended the reach of your business. And, best of all, you're getting new clients.

Ezine

Ezine is short for *electronic magazine*. Go to http://ezinearticles.com to become a contributing member at no cost. Read through the guidelines you'll receive, submit an original article of 250 to 5,000 words, and wait one week to learn if your article has been accepted. Once you've been published, you enhance your credibility, get exposure to hundreds of thousands of readers, build your brand, become known as an expert, and drive traffic to your website.

As businesspeople, you have one thing in common—you want to make money selling your products and services. To reach beyond your regional areas, you have to let your markets know you exist. You also have to gain access to people and businesses who wouldn't hear of you through traditional marketing venues.

That's where social networking and social media add tremendous value. They open the world so you can participate in networks no matter where you are or where they are. What's the difference between social networking and social media?

- **Social networking** occurs when a group of like-minded people interact online to share interests or concerns, collaborate, give and seek advice, and offer one another assistance or support. Popular social networking sites for business include LinkedIn, Twitter, and Facebook, to name just a few. (These are the three social networking sites highlighted later in this chapter.) There are also a vast number of closed social networks, such as sites for organizations, sites connecting you with former classmates, and others.

- **Social media** are the online tools that enable people to communicate and share information, such as blogs, chats, videos, bookmarks, wikis, podcasts, email, IM, and more.

 I'm breaking blogs into a separate chapter because there's a lot to share. Check out Chapter 2, "I Blog, Therefore, I Am."

Include "the socials" as part of your marketing strategy

Make social networking and social media *part* of your overall marketing strategy. They don't operate in a vacuum, and they can't be a stand-alone marketing strategy. Other marketing and networking channels are still

Email Marketing · Press Releases · Professional Organizations · Build · Facebook · Ezine Articles · $ · LinkedIn · YouTube · Relationships · Twitter · Blogs and Wikis · Podcasting · FTF Networking and Mastermind Groups

central to your business. Combined, they build relationships that lead to increased revenue.

Think of your social network as a way to introduce yourself; your blog as a way to strengthen your brand and position yourself as the expert; and your website as a way to sell yourself, your products, and your services.

Build the buzz

Amass raving fans so they follow you all over. Be authentic and straight-forward and let people know you. Establish your brand, claim your name, build your profile, include your photo, provided valuable contacts. Build it, cultivate it, and they will come.

Establish your brand. Establish your brand so people see you all over and recognize you. Your brand can include your name, company name, or however you want to be identified. Use the same name (or username) on all the social networks you join so when they're categorized by the search engines, they all point to you.

Tell your story. If you were to write a story about yourself or your busi-ness, how would that story read? If you were to paint a picture of your-self or your business, what would that painting look like? If you were to sculpt a statue of yourself or your business, what would that sculpture look like? Consider using expressions such as

- I'm a lot like you because . . .
- If you're like most of my clients/customers, . . .
- I started my business by . . .

Include a photo. Include a professional-looking photo of yourself and use the same photo on all your sites. It will build consistency and make you seem more trustworthy. If you have a common name, the picture will identify you.

 Don't display a photo with your arms crossed. Crossed arms can be interpreted as a defensive barrier blocking out the outside world.

Articulate what differentiates you from your competitors. Regis McKenna, best known for helping start several firms in Silicon Valley during the '70s and '80s with his own marketing firm, believes that "the more alike two products [or services] are, the more important their differences become." Don't just say you provide outstanding service. Everyone says that, so it's become a tedious expression. If your service is truly outstanding, what makes it so?

- Are you the least expensive?
- Do you provide greater value?
- Do you offer a special or unique service?
- Are you the first?
- Are you an industry leader?
- What have you invented?
- What have you written?
- What special or unique programs have you developed or offered?

Identify the people or groups you want to associate with and reach. Take a page from Barack Obama's playbook. Obama has been referred to as the social media president, and for good reason. During his 2008 campaign, Obama and his campaigners "spread the word" using Twitter, Myspace, blogs, and other social media outlets to reach their target audience of young people. This connected him closely with followers, rallied his supporters and influencers, and helped him to raise funds in unprecedented ways.

Before the election Obama had tapped into more than 3 million young voters on Facebook, nearly a million friends on Myspace, and hundreds of thousands of followers on Twitter. And this doesn't take into account other splinter groups such as Students for Obama, Florida (and other states) for Obama, Women for Obama, and the like.

Obama used "pull marketing" and created interactive content. This pulled readers into his content to let them feel he cared. His Democratic-primary opponent Hillary Clinton used "push marketing." She pushed information in front of readers with no interaction. That gave the impression she didn't care. John McCain didn't bother showing up. Many people say that Obama's social media blitz helped him to gain traction and ultimately win the election. Although you may not be running for office, let social media help you to be a winner in business.

Make your sites keyword rich. When you identify keywords, you help people to find you. Think of the words you would use if you were searching for yourself. For example, in mine I use keywords such as *writing, business writing, technical writing, coaching, email, presentations, workshops, facilitation, marketing, marketing communications, marcomm, email, email communications,* and *communications.*

 Write for spiders. Spiders, also called web crawlers, are computer programs that "crawl" around the web collecting information. Spiders are used to create indexes used by search engines. The spiders will retrieve the locations of pages and sites based on keywords. Do a search on SEO Book (SEO stands for *search engine optimization*) to find many resources helping you identify keywords for your profession or industry. Your web developer should also be able to help.

 Search Google Wonder Wheel to learn how you can view relevant search results and Yahoo! Answers to learn what people are searching for.

Claim your name. Claim your name on all the sites you want to join. Here are some suggestions:

- If you have a common name such as James Smith, you'll find it's probably taken. Try some variations such as SmithJames, James-Smith2, James.Smith, JSmith403, and other combinations.
- If you have a long name, such as I do, think of something that identifies you. For example, I use sherylwrites as my web address because Sheryl Lindsell-Roberts & Associates is too long for people to type. My full name doesn't even fit into the character constraints

of Twitter. It reads Sheryl Lindsell-Robe. Therefore, my branded name is sherylwrites.

Go to http://www.namechk.com and you'll see a listing of all the major social networking and social bookmarking websites. Follow the directions to see if the name you want is available. Claim your name, and use it consistently to establish your brand.

Personalize your site. You can personalize your site by adding your name to the end of the URL:

> www.Linkedin.com/YourName
> www.Facebook.com/YourName
> www.Twitter.com/YourName

Build your profile. Your profile is what you want visitors to know about you. Be careful what you include, however. If you've ever watched police shows on TV, you're familiar with Miranda rights: "You have the right to remain silent. Anything you say can and will be used against you. . . ." This is true on social networks as well. Following are tips on how to build your profile and distinguish yourself from the crowd in a positive way:

- **Don't just post your name.** Tell your story. Include your experiences, abilities, and what you want people to know about you.

- **Select your words carefully.** Use lots of adjectives, lively words, and the active voice. Note that on Twitter you have only 140 characters. Use them prudently.

- **Create a memorable tagline.** This is a short, clever sentence that makes your business more memorable. The one I use is *You make more dollars when you make more sense*™. There are people who don't remember my name, but they remember my tagline.

- **Generate an elevator pitch.** Imagine you're in an elevator with someone you've been anxious to meet, and you have 30 seconds to relay your message. It should include who you are, what your business does, and why you're unique. The last part is critical.

- **Briefly detail your skills and experience.** Include industry buzzwords, particular abilities, and passions.

- **Provide social proof.** Ask colleagues, clients, and managers for a brief write-up (testimonial) attesting to your abilities and performance. This adds lots of credibility and makes you authentic.

Here's what my LinkedIn profile looks like:

Sheryl Lindsell-Roberts

Principal at Sheryl Lindsell-Roberts & Associates
Greater Boston Area

→ Contact Sheryl Lindsell-Roberts

→ Add Sheryl Lindsell-Roberts to your
network

Current •	**Principal at Sheryl Lindsell-Roberts &** **Associates**
Education •	Montclair State University
Recommended	5 people have recommended Sheryl
Connections	111 connections
Industry	Professional Training & Coaching
Websites •	My Company
•	My Blog
•	YouTube: Email Etiquette

Public profile powered by: **Linked** in

Create a public profile: **Sign In** or **Join Now**

View Sheryl Lindsell-Roberts's full profile:

• See who you and **Sheryl Lindsell-Roberts** know in common
• Get introduced to **Sheryl Lindsell-Roberts**
• Contact **Sheryl Lindsell-Roberts** directly

View Full Profile

Sheryl Lindsell-Roberts's Summary

For nearly 25 years Sheryl has been Principal of Sheryl Lindsell-Roberts & Associates, a business writing and marketing firm helping clients to maximum productivity and profitability. As an award-winning business writer, business/technical writing workshop facilitator, coach, and speaker, Sheryl is considered an expert in the field of business writing.

ABOUT THE FIRM

Sheryl and her team work with large and small companies, academic institutions, and government agencies to increase revenue through strategic business/technical writing and marketing. Clients typically call Sheryl Lindsell-Roberts & Associates for all their business writing needs because they're frustrated by their company's poorly written business documents or they're troubled by lost revenue due to ineffective and inconsistent marketing messages.

BUSINESS WRITING WORKSHOPS AND COACHING

Sheryl continues to receive rave reviews from long-standing clients. Several of the workshops are being offered as virtual sessions as well as classroom sessions.

· Write It So They'll Read It™
· Emails That Mean Business
· What I Forgot From Ms. Grump's English Class™
· Laser Sharp Technical Writing™
· Storyboarding: The Key to Influential Presentations

MARKETING AND GENERAL BUSINESS WRITING

Sheryl's company has produced proposals, brochures, websites, videos, manuals, technical papers, and many other tyes of business documents that have helped companies to close multi-million-dollar contracts. Most recently, she wrote a proposal that helped an architectural firm close a $70 million school contract.

BOOKS PUBLISHED AND NATIONAL RECOGNITION

Sheryl has appeared on television and radio networks throughout the United States. She's been featured and quoted in THE NEW YORK TIMES and in magazines such as CONTINENTAL AIRLINES, PROFIT, HOME BUSINESS, CIO, and others. Sheryl has written 23 books related to business writing, several of which were part of the... FOR DUMMIES series.

Sheryl Lindsell-Roberts's Specialties:

Comprehensive business writing and marketing, business writing workshops, technical writing workshops, presentation workshops; email workshops; business writing coaching, and more.

Name Search:

Search for people you know from over 75 million professionals already on LinkedIn.

First Name	Last Name
(example: Jeff Weiner)	

Search

> ### Build your followers, friends, fans, and connections carefully.
>
> The key is quality, not quantity. Once you put yourself out there, you'll get lots of invitations to be a follower (on Twitter), a friend or a fan (on Facebook), or a connection (on LinkedIn). Connect only with people you know and trust. You *are* judged by the company you keep.

Monitor the buzz. Sign up for a Google Alert and create an alert for your own name or your company's name. When the name appears, you'll be notified. On Twitter, go to TweetBeep.com to find out when someone else is talking about you. You must be on top of the buzz so you can address damaging information. Here are two examples:

In October 2006, Stonyfield Farm issued an online rebuttal to allegations arising from an article in *BusinessWeek* about the growing demand for organic food. Stonyfield CEO Gary Hirshberg stated, "The story generated a surprising amount of Internet activity which included some gross misconceptions and falsehoods about our company and our practices. So I'd like to take this opportunity to set the record straight." He strongly spelled out Stonyfield's position and asked members of the public to visit the Stonyfield website and share their views. In so doing, he debunked the allegations and averted further damage.

Domino's Pizza wasn't on top of its buzz, and it nearly spelled disaster for the company. In April 2009 two employees at a Domino's in Houston, Texas, uploaded footage to YouTube showing themselves doing unsavory things with ingredients. Within days every newspaper and television news channel was showing these objectionable acts. Although the employees were fired, this became a major public relations disaster for Domino's, who didn't hear of the incident until it went public. The company's reputation was damaged, and Domino's quickly stepped up its own social media presence to turn this incident around.

Publish great content

Publish content that's informative and valuable to your readers. No one wants to read a tweet that says "I'm stuck on the tarmac at O'Hare Airport."

What to include. Include timely tips, industry trends, links to interesting articles or sites, and anything else your readers will find informative and valuable. Don't include too much about your products or services. This isn't a sales venue.

 Post regularly—daily, weekly, or in whatever pattern you establish. This will help people to know that you're reliable and organized. Also, they'll know when to expect your posts.

Get the most out of your content. To get the most mileage from your content, create links to your blog, podcasts, videos, presentations, e-books, news releases, website, other networking sites, and anything else you're broadcasting. Here are a few other things you can do to get the most from your content:

- **Syndicate.** In other words, share your content through social media channels.

- **Establish media relationships.** Journalists are always looking for good material and want to develop relationships with people they trust. Call publications in your area to get yourself started. Offer to write an article. Offer an interview. Show you're a subject-matter expert. Sites to consider are https://twitteringjournalists.pbwicki .com and http://mediaontwitter.pbwiki.com.

- **Create a blog that contains articles with educational content.** To learn more, check out Chapter 2, "I Blog, Therefore, I Am."

- **Volunteer your knowledge.** Join an online community and engage in meaningful conversations.

- **Interview thought leaders.** Leverage the brands and names of others to build your reputation. Post the interviews on your website or blog.

- **Create an online community.** This has the potential to grow from early interest to long-term loyalty. Check out http://www.ning.com. It's a great website for creating communities.

- **Copy something relevant one person said and send it to your followers.** In this way you strengthen relationships. In the Twitter world, this is known as retweeting. Make sure you give credit to the source.

Generate a social media policy

It's estimated that more than 90 percent of all companies report using at least one form of social media for business. Today's companies are rapidly jumping online for marketing and advertising. Employees also have their own online personas. Many employers are cracking down (and in some cases forbidding) employees from using social networking sites at the workplace. They're concerned about security breaches, loss of trade secrets, reduced productivity, and damaged reputations.

Now that the workplace extends beyond the traditional brick and mortar 9-to-5, social networking and social media sites are hard to control. Company guidelines for social media may not be able to prevent damage to your company's reputation, but they may be able to lessen it. Your guidelines should dovetail with other company policies about written communication. Following are the guidelines Intel has established:

Intel Social Media Guidelines

These are the official guidelines for social media at Intel. If you're an Intel employee or contractor creating or contributing to blogs, wikis, social networks, virtual worlds, or any other kind of social media both on and off intel.com—these guidelines are for you. We expect all who participate in social media on behalf of Intel to be trained, to understand and to follow these guidelines. Failure to do so could put your future participation at risk. These guidelines will continually evolve as new technologies and social networking tools emerge—so check back once in a while to make sure you're up to date.

When You Engage

Emerging platforms for online collaboration are fundamentally changing the way we work, offering new ways to engage with customers, colleagues, and the world at large. It's a new model for interaction and we believe social computing can help you to build stronger, more successful business relationships. And it's a way for you to take part in global conversations related to the work we are doing at Intel and the things we care about.

If you participate in social media, please follow these guiding principles:

- Stick to your area of expertise and provide unique, individual perspectives on what's going on at Intel and in the world.

- Post meaningful, respectful comments—in other words, no spam and no remarks that are off-topic or offensive.

- Always pause and think before posting. That said, reply to comments in a timely manner, when a response is appropriate.

- Respect proprietary information and content, and confidentiality.

- When disagreeing with others' opinions, keep it appropriate and polite.

- Know and follow the Intel Code of Conduct and the Intel Privacy Policy.

Rules of Engagement

Be transparent. Your honesty—or dishonesty—will be quickly noticed in the social media environment. If you are blogging about your work at Intel, use your real name, identify that you work for Intel, and be clear about your role. If you have a vested interest in something you are discussing, be the first to point it out.

Be judicious. Make sure your efforts to be transparent don't violate Intel's privacy, confidentiality, and legal guidelines for external commercial speech. Ask permission to publish or report on conversations that are meant to be private or internal to Intel. All statements must be true and not misleading and all claims must be substantiated and approved. Product benchmarks must be approved for external posting by the appropriate product benchmarking team. Please never comment on anything related to legal matters, litigation, or any parties we are in litigation with without the appropriate approval. If you want to write about the competition, make sure you know what you are talking about and that you have the appropriate permission. Also be smart about protecting yourself, your privacy, and Intel Confidential information. What you publish is widely accessible and will be around for a long time, so consider the content carefully.

Write what you know. Make sure you write and post about your areas of expertise, especially as related to Intel and our technology. If you are writing about a topic that Intel is involved with but you are not the Intel expert on the topic, you should make this clear to your readers. And write in the first person. If you publish to a website outside Intel, please use a disclaimer something like this: "The postings on this site are my own and don't necessarily represent Intel's positions, strategies, or opinions." Also, please respect brand, trademark, copyright, fair use, trade secrets (including our processes and methodologies), confidentiality, and financial disclosure laws. If you have any questions about these, see your Intel legal representative. Remember, you may be personally responsible for your content.

Perception is reality. In online social networks, the lines between public and private, personal and professional are blurred. Just by identifying yourself as an Intel employee, you are creating perceptions about your expertise and about Intel by our shareholders, customers, and the general public—and perceptions about you by your colleagues and managers. Do us all proud. Be sure that all content associated with you is consistent with your work and with Intel's values and professional standards.

It's a conversation. Talk to your readers like you would talk to real people in professional situations. In other words, avoid overly pedantic or "composed" language. Don't be afraid to bring in your own personality and say what's on your mind. Consider content that's open-ended and invites response. Encourage comments. You can also broaden the conversation by citing others who are blogging about the same topic and allowing your content to be shared or syndicated.

Are you adding value? There are millions of words out there. The best way to get yours read is to write things that people will value. Social communication from Intel should help our customers, partners, and co-workers. It should be thought-provoking and build a sense of community. If it helps people improve knowledge or skills, build their businesses, do their jobs, solve problems, or understand Intel better—then it's adding value.

Your responsibility: What you write is ultimately your responsibility. Participation in social computing on behalf of Intel is not a right but an opportunity, so please treat it seriously and with respect. If you want to participate on behalf of Intel, take the Digital IQ training and contact the Social Media Center of Excellence. Please know and follow the Intel Code of Conduct. Failure to abide by these guidelines and the Intel Code of Conduct could put your participation at risk. Contact social.media@ intel.com for more information. Please also follow the terms and conditions for any third-party sites.

Create some excitement. As a business and as a corporate citizen, Intel is making important contributions to the world, to the future of technology, and to public dialogue on a broad range of issues. Our business activities are increasingly focused on high-value innovation. Let's share with the world the exciting things we're learning and doing—and open up the channels to learn from others.

Be a leader. There can be a fine line between healthy debate and incendiary reaction. Do not denigrate our competitors or Intel. Nor do you need to respond to every criticism or barb. Try to frame what you write to invite differing points of view without inflaming others. Some topics— like politics or religion—slide more easily into sensitive territory. So be careful and considerate. Once the words are out there, you can't really get them back. And once an inflammatory discussion gets going, it's hard to stop.

Did you screw up? If you make a mistake, admit it. Be upfront and be quick with your correction. If you're posting to a blog, you may choose to modify an earlier post—just make it clear that you have done so.

If it gives you pause, pause. If you're about to publish something that makes you even the slightest bit uncomfortable, don't shrug it off and hit 'send.' Take a minute to review these guidelines and try to figure out what's bothering you, then fix it. If you're still unsure, you might want to discuss it with your manager or legal representative. Ultimately, what you publish is yours—as is the responsibility. So be sure.

Moderation Guidelines

Moderation is the act of reviewing and approving content before it's published on the site. Intel does not endorse or take responsibility for content posted by third parties. It is preferred that all content be posted by registered users of a site in accordance with accepted terms and conditions and a code of conduct.

Intel Content: We do not moderate content we publish. This means we allow our blog authors to post directly without approval, as long as they have taken the required trainings.

Anonymous Content: Anonymous content is defined as content submitted as a comment, reply, or post to an Intel site where the user has not registered and is not logged in to the site. For anonymous content, we require moderation on all submissions. Authors of the originating content and space moderators are required to review the content for approval or deletion before the content can be published.

Registered Content: Registered content is content submitted as a comment, reply, or post to an Intel site where the user has registered and is logged in to the site. We do not require moderation of registered content before the content is published to the site. Registered content is directly published and content is moderated post-publishing.

Intel strives for a balanced online dialogue. When we do moderate content, we moderate using three guiding principles.

The Good, the Bad, but not the Ugly. If the content is positive or negative and in context to the conversation, then we approve the content, regardless of whether it's favorable or unfavorable to Intel. However if the content is ugly, offensive, denigrating and completely out of context, then we reject the content.

Last updated: May 2009
Reprinted with permission of Intel Corporation

It's all about interactivity

I'd be remiss if I didn't start this section by saying that social networking isn't a magic bullet, and it's not fairy dust. It can take up your time 24/7 if you allow it to, yielding little or no return. Some people are investing large amounts of money to have marketing or public relations firms design exhaustive social media strategies. Others are designing their own tactical plans. Still others are dipping their toes in slowly. *The key is to determine what you want social networking to do for you and/or your business and develop a strategy that will meet those needs.* Remember, in today's workplace, it's all about interactivity.

 Most important of all, don't lose sight of face-to-face or telephone networking. Electronic social networking will never take the place of interpersonal connections. Let social networking be your way of determining the people or companies with whom you want to have more personal relationships.

Many people still think of social media and social networking as a means for people with idle time to broadcast every brain cramp they have. But today's companies are using social media strategically to promote dialogue, get customer feedback, learn what customers are saying, share news and updates, and much more. The socials are the least expensive and most far-reaching public relations and marketing channels available because they . . .

- Provide better search engine optimization.
- Create more traffic.
- Engage customers and make them advocates of your brand.
- Track who's talking about you and what they're saying.
- Reach global markets.
- Build trust between you and your customers or clients.
- Turn your business (and you) into a resource for others.

Here's how some companies and professions are using social media to amplify brand awareness and communicate with customers (and potential customers) in ways never before thought possible:

Ford Motor Company. Ford is an example of a leading-edge organization establishing a strong social media presence. Ford's strategy is "to humanize the company by connecting customers with Ford employees and with each other when possible, providing value in the process." Ford is out there and personalized on http://facebook.com/ford, http://youtube .com/ford, http://delicious.com/fomoco, http://twitter.com/ford, among many other sites. Ford also has Twitter accounts for its vehicles: @Ford Fiesta, @FordCustService, @FordTaurus, @FordTrucks, and others. Key executives at Ford use Twitter to promote dialogue with customers and potential customers.

Dell. As reported by Marisa Taylor in *The Wall Street Journal* (November 19, 2009), Dell said it had sold "more than $3 million in PCs and accessories through Twitter promotions and other activity on the microblogging service."

Kraft Foods. Kraft queried the online community to learn how people make choices about snacks. The company learned that people don't want to diet or deprive themselves; they want to control how much they eat. That spawned the idea for the 100 Calorie Packs, which has been a financial windfall for Kraft.

IKEA. Go to IKEA's website to decorate a room. Click on "Ask Anna!" and you bring up a dialogue box with a customer service representative, a smiling avatar who blinks and tilts her head. She welcomes you with the message, "I'm Anna, IKEA USA's Automated Online Assistant." If you want to redo your kitchen, for example, Anna will take you to the kitchen page and you can download a kitchen planner.

Starbucks. As reported by Emily Bryson York in *Advertising Age* (November 18, 2009), "the brand [Starbucks] is going big in social media . . . having learned that its consumers want to participate in a variety of ways. So Starbucks is pulling back from its Thanksgiving TV buys of the past two years to focus on where its customers already spend time online and drive them into stores."

Southwest Airlines. Southwest set up an "online water cooler" with postings from pilots and ticket agents to the flying public. The airline was investigating whether to adopt a policy of assigned seating to replace its first-come, first-served seating policy. More than 600 people swarmed the site. The consensus was, "If it ain't broke, don't fix it," says Paula Berg, who runs Southwest's site. "People who fly us all the time already know how the system works."

Naked Pizza. Naked Pizza, one of the newest kids on the block offering healthy pizza, turned to Twitter to launch its restaurant chain. The company posted 1 to 15 times a day and put up billboard ads with the Twitter logo. Naked Pizza Cofounder Jeff Leach organized mailings with the company's Twitter contact information instead of its own phone number. According to reports, the return on investment (ROI) was tremendous. The company's first Twitter-only promotion resulted in 15 percent of total sales, with 90 percent of those being new customers. Nearly 70 percent of customers who called in said, "I'm calling from Twitter."

Medical community. The medical profession is embracing Twitter, Facebook, and YouTube to bring patients into operating rooms and provide patient education. For example, dermatologists have been sharing medical and product information on Twitter. Surgeons have used Twitter to explain blow-by-blow steps of an operation to remove a kidney tumor. Doctors are writing blogs on the latest medical techniques. And another doctor has been using Twitter to keep families informed of patients' progress during operations.

Journalism. Where does our news come from? Recent surveys have shown that more than half of all reporters and editors use social media as sources for reporting and producing stories.

Pick the sites that are right for you

Decide how social networking will align with your business goals and how you want to manage it. Many people spend too much time doing social networking and get very few (if any) results. As mentioned earlier, step in with your big toe rather than jumping in with both feet.

The following are three key reasons businesses are using social networking: to make money, develop relationships, and form partnerships. Here are a few things to keep in mind for any site:

- **Think in terms of quality, not quantity.** As mentioned, you don't need to have 10,000 people in your social networking circles. This isn't a numbers game. It's about establishing your brand and growing your business strategically.

 Accept invitations only from people you know and trust. If you get an invitation to join from someone you don't know well, check out that person first. Check her website. Ask others on your site about her. Have a phone conversation. If in doubt, don't include her.

- **Decide if you want to have business and personal accounts.** Don't merge the two. Use a business account to keep customers up to date on product offerings, sales, events, conferences, white papers, a recent blog post, a professional book you recommend, recent projects, tips, and more. Use a personal account for letting people know what you're reading in your leisure time, hobbies you enjoy, and the like.

- **Be careful what you post.** People have been disqualified from potential jobs, denied admission to colleges, and lost jobs because of postings that reflected poorly on them.

 Check out Chapter 3, "Get Ready, Get Set, Get a Job" to learn how the social networking sites are helping to pair job opportunities and job candidates.

LinkedIn

In 2002, LinkedIn started in the living room of its cofounder Reid Hoffman, and it has matured into the leading business to business (B2B) site for professional networking. Use LinkedIn to increase your visibility, make connections, expand your search engine ranking, gauge the health of a company, post and view events, ask for advice, give answers, and much more.

Write a vibrant profile. While the importance of filling in a profile may seem like a no-brainer, it's amazing how many people leave their profiles blank or include only a few sketchy lines. Don't miss this opportunity to establish yourself and your brand. Following are a few tips, some of which may be a review from earlier in this chapter:

- Customize your URL to include your name.
- Write as if you're speaking to the people/companies you're looking to attract. Don't just post a resume.
- Include your relevant career history and interests.
- Use headlines with keywords to help search engines find you.
- Include information about past employers.
- Get several strong recommendations. (Offer them to others as well.)
- Add links you're trying to promote such as your website, blog, and postings on YouTube.
- Fill in the summary field with your critical skills and career-related keywords.
- Join groups relevant to your profession and join the conversations. (This can generate lots of unwanted email, so be selective.)
- Include a professional-looking photo.

 If you have a name that's commonly misspelled (such as Jon, rather than John), put the varied spelling or spellings into the summary sheet of your profile. In that way, people looking for you with another spelling will be able to find you. If you've been known by another name, reflect that in your profile. For example, if you changed your name after getting married, you may write "Barbara Smith (nee Grayson)" or "Barbara Smith, also known as Barbara Grayson."

Establish your base of connections. Building your social network increases your ability to find and be found. Search for people from networking groups, former companies, or colleges or universities you attended, customers, clients, and any others you want in your social network. When you connect with someone, you also have access to that person's connections.

 Here are a few tips about connecting:

- When you send an invitation to connect, include a short, personalized message, rather than sending the default message.
- Don't feel obliged to accept invitations from people you don't know well. Once again, it's about quality, not quantity.
- If you want to remove a connection, you can do so without that person being notified.

Create a company page. If you own or operate a small business, create a company page in addition to creating a profile. Company pages are a powerful research tool to help people find and explore potential companies to work for or do business with. Become one of those companies.

Join group and association conversations. Join associations relevant to your business. You can opt to receive updates of posts and become part of the conversation. This is a wonderful way to extend your exposure and become better known.

Use SlideShare. SlideShare is the largest community for sharing presentations. Use SlideShare to showcase your resume, portfolio, sales and marketing presentations, promotional contests, and anything else that will communicate your story visually. Upload your presentations to SlideShare, LinkedIn, and Facebook, and have a valuable triad.

Ask and answer questions. Perhaps you need to find a new hire with specific skills, take a poll, or get some free market research. Get answers from like-minded people you know and trust. Conversely, answer questions. Whether you work for a large company or small company, you're a consultant, or you're a single shingle, answering questions is a great way to establish your credibility. This puts you in front of your peers and colleagues as a person who's knowledgeable, it builds your reputation, and it helps strengthen your profile in the search engines. You can also expect to make a few connections through each activity.

Create regular network updates. Create updates once or twice a week. Include a tip, link, project you're working on, event you attended, or anything else that may be of interest to your connections. This brings you to their attention in Google searches.

Post events and check events. LinkedIn Events is one of the site's most underutilized features. When you're looking for an interesting conference, trade show, meeting, webinar, or networking opportunity, check LinkedIn Events. The site posts events by type, topic, industry, location, and date. You can receive event recommendations that match your specific business needs based on your LinkedIn profile and view lists of attendees.

- When you sponsor or participate in an event, create an event for yourself or your organization.
- When you attend an event, post it on your LinkedIn site to enhance your professionalism.

Here are a few additional tips for using LinkedIn:

- Add your LinkedIn address to your email signature block.
- Read the profiles of leaders at companies you want to connect with. Learn about their initiatives and needs.
- Target people you may want to hire. (My colleague was recruited on LinkedIn, even though he wasn't in the job market. He got a great job with a 25 percent pay increase.)
- Go through your business cards and contact your first-degree connections.

Twitter

If you've been sitting on the sidelines thinking that Twitter is a tsunami of mindless nonsense, think again. This successful social networking site has become the latest pulsating heart of real-time Internet. What started out as a micro-messaging service that captured the imagination of everyone from techies to cable news networks and from athletes to Hollywood stars has grown into a vibrant business community bringing people together in ways they never thought possible. Even the American Red Cross uses Twitter to exchange minute-to-minute information about local disasters including statistics and directions.

Create a discreet handle. Your handle is the name you'll use. Be certain it's something you won't be ashamed of sharing with the world. Many years ago when people used citizens band radios (and there are many of you who may remember CBs), people used all sorts of funny, lewd, and crude handles. Maybe they weren't appropriate, but they were strictly between you and the person you were hailing. On Twitter, you share your handle with the entire cyberworld. Be discreet.

Generate a 140-character profile. What's the first thing you check when deciding whether to follow someone? Her profile. Statistics show that Twitter accounts that have profiles attract nearly 10 times as many followers as accounts that don't have profiles. Decide if you want people to find you by your name, career, company, industry, or location. Use this virtual real estate wisely and select the words or phrases that best represent you.

Twitter limits you to 140 characters on all messages, so how do you send a long link? Go to http://tinyurl.com to shorten any link. Just put in the long URL and "tiny it." In the following example, both URLs take you to the same place.

A word from Mark Tetrault, M. Arch., CGBP, Principal, 2M Architecture

"LinkedIn has proven to be an invaluable extension of my business. It helps me to stay in touch easily with many professionals that I work with, even those I work with on occasion. I find that when I'm in touch more regularly—even virtually—there's a greater chance that a new business lead or opportunity will come up. And many new opportunities have already surfaced. I've also become reacquainted with many of my former Harvard University colleagues who've settled in California. That's leading to additional friendships as well as new business.

"While it's sometimes an effort to manage relationships consistently in the daily rush of business, LinkedIn's interface and tools take a lot of guesswork out of the process. For entrepreneurs and small businesses that don't have the luxury of an in-house marketing department, LinkedIn provides an easy and professional means of keeping your business visible to a lot of decision-makers. Group affiliations and conversations among professionals serve to strengthen connections and the feeling of being part of your business community. We never know where the next business lead will come from. In an industry such as architecture that relies heavily on personal recommendations, LinkedIn is an invaluable tool for introductions and connections."

Long version (252 characters): http://chapters.astd.org/SiteDirectory/
CentralMassachusetts/Pages/Events/Chapter%20Events/EventDescriptions.
aspx?Event = 8&recur = &ParentUrl = /Pages/Events/Chapter%20Events/
ChapterCalendar.aspx&ID = http://chapters.astd.org/SiteDirectory/Central-
Massachusetts
Tiny version (26 characters): http://tinyurl.com/ydkc7kt

Know what to tweet about. Make your tweets interesting and informative (nobody cares if you overslept or ate oatmeal for breakfast). Tweets may include an event you're attending, something you observed, a book you read, something from your blog or someone else's blog, links followers may find interesting, jobs to fill, (retweeting) what someone else said, a tip, a link to your blog, a link to a YouTube video, and more. Remember that everything you say is public. Don't include anything you wouldn't want your boss or your grandmother to read.

- Engage people by asking questions, conducting polls, and making your page a place to connect followers.
- Retweet as a great way to get involved in the Twitter community.

Government agencies are realizing a tremendous cost savings using Twitter. They relate critical information about road closures, water-main breaks, missing pets, and other happenings. Many agencies are sending e-newsletters with details of events in the area. Police departments use social media to broadcast arrests, disseminate information to the public, and post descriptions of criminal suspects. School districts use social media as a public relations tool to relate success stories of teachers and students, encourage attendance at school events, share information on sports teams, and more. Newscasters use Twitter to share the latest news, road conditions, and weather.

 To schedule tweets for automatic future posting, go to www.twuffer.com or www.socialsoomph.com/register. They're both free services. You can prepare your tweets in one batch and determine when you want them posted. Link your Twitter and LinkedIn sites and your posts will feed both.

Twitter do's

Following are a few more Twitter tips:

- Pay attention to who mentions you and decide if you want to follow them. This will grow your list of followers.
- If you want to let people know that your tweet is a reply to a specific user, set up your tweet as follows: @[username] [message].
- To send a message to one person only, set up your tweet as follows: d [username] [message]. (Think of the *d* as meaning *direct*.)
- When you receive a tweet you want to share with your followers, use the retweeting function. Place your cursor in the right side of the message, and you'll see an option to click on "retweet."
- Although many people think it's mundane to send tweets describing your whereabouts, such as "I'm on the train heading into New York City," followers may want to know you're in town.
- People attending trade shows and conferences are having lots of success meeting up with people via Twitter. Meet face-to-face with followers at these events via live tweeting.

Twitter taboos

Certain things will discredit you in the Twitter community:

- Tooting your own horn too loudly and too often; the network isn't a promotional tool. Too much self-promotion is akin to meeting

> ### A word from Dave McKeon,
> ### Managing Partner, Game On!
>
> "In 2008 I began challenging my business clients to leverage Web 2.0 and social media to increase their visibility. By mid 2009 it was apparent that not only had social media passed the tipping point, but if it wasn't part of your overall game plan you were seen as obsolete or old school. If you are a 'career changer,' you are at a distinct disadvantage if you aren't sending out Tweets. They can increase your visibility to recruiters looking for thought leaders in your field on Twitter. From a personal perspective, Twitter enables me to stay connected with thought leaders that I'd otherwise only see at conferences, if at all. It also helps me to foster credibility within my own network and increase my own network of followers. Like any asset, these tools need to be continually managed so they are working for you and not against you, and obviously integrated into your overall game plan."

someone face-to-face and talking about yourself. People will avoid you.

- Being too impersonal by setting up an automatic direct message. Use email for that purpose.
- Posting boring or mindless comments. That's the surest way to lose followers.
- Saying anything that can get you in trouble at work. That's happened more than you can imagine. And don't broadcast that you're looking for a new job—your manager may see the posting.

 If you have a lot of followers and opt to receive updates on your mobile phone, you may be barraged with text messages. And unless you have limited texting, you may notice a big jump in your bill.

 Many people feel that Facebook and Twitter confront us with more information overload. On the flip side, however, Facebook and Twitter are cleansing email excesses in one important way. When people send you emails on weekends and holidays, they expect immediate answers. Facebook and Twitter don't have that sense of immediacy. You can turn off your computer on weekends and holidays and simply return when you're ready as if there was no interruption.

Facebook

The idea for Facebook was conceived by Mark Zuckerberg while he was studying computer science and psychology at Harvard University. An avid computer programmer, he launched a trial balloon and within 24 hours had more than 1,200 Harvard subscribers. The network extended to other universities and is now a global Internet phenomenon, with more than 700,000 new people signing on each week.

Although Facebook began as a place for families and friends to share stories and photos, it has grown into a robust business site—especially popular for business to consumer (B2C). Savvy businesses are using Facebook to find new customers and clients, build online communities of fans, and mine for demographic information.

To avoid wasting time on Facebook, start by identifying your professional goals. Do you want to attract more customers or clients? Do you want to build brand awareness? Do you want to create a location for customer support?

One of the benefits of being on Facebook is that pages and groups (which are different from profiles) are indexed by Google and can show up on someone's search. So make your pages and groups keyword rich.

Following are some general tips for using Facebook:
- Disengage the email notifications, or you'll get an email every time a friend thinks of the word *Facebook*.
- Keep your chat off so you're not getting spammed. The little dot at the bottom of the screen to the left of the word *chat* means it's off.
- Syndicate your text by linking your Facebook page to your website, blog, Twitter, and LinkedIn.
- Include an ethical bribe such as a white paper, tip booklet, etc. (Big-name companies advertise for you to connect with them on Facebook. As a bribe, they offer discounts, coupons, and other enticing goodies.)

Don't advertise on any of your social networking sites that you'll be out of town. That's like putting a billboard outside your home or office announcing no one's there.

Create raving fans on Facebook pages. You can create only one profile, but you can create multiple pages. Create a page for each word or phrase that people would use to search for your products or services. For example, one of my pages is titled *Email Etiquette*. It includes a short blurb on how to generate a subject line that's as informational as a newspaper headline. People become *fans* on your pages, as opposed to *friends* on your profile.

In an article in *The New York Times* (Small Business section, November 11, 2009), Kermit Pattison says, "For most businesses, Facebook Pages [as distinct from individual profiles and Facebook groups] are the best place to start. Pages allow businesses to collect 'fans' the way celebrities, sports teams, musicians and politicians do. There are now 1.4 million Facebook Pages and they collect more than 10 million fans every day, according to the site." He suggests some basic rules: "Buy-buy-buy messages won't fly. The best practitioners make Facebook less about selling and more about interacting. Engage with fans and critics. Listen to what people are saying, good and bad. You may even pick up ideas for how to improve your business. Keep content fresh. Use status updates and newsfeeds to tell fans about specials, events, contests or anything of interest."

Some companies are using Facebook very creatively to gain a following. For example, a local credit union advertised on Facebook that if it got 1,000 friends it would donate $1,000 to charity.

Attract members on Facebook groups. Groups attract members. Groups are interactive and provide a forum for conversations. Following are a few tips for putting your best *face* forward with pages and groups:

- Initially, ask your friends and family to become fans and members. Then your pages and group can grow organically by word of mouth

- Let your pages reflect the flavor of your business. A crafts store should have a different flavor from a law office.

A word from Margot Rutledge, Executive Director, KidsWin

"I'm the Executive Director of KidsWin, an organization offering tools and strategies to help children realize their value and reach their potential (while having fun). I originally created a social networking site on Ning and found that people would join me on the site but wouldn't return. So I decided to go to where the people are already—and that's Facebook. I started a group to encourage participation and active discussions among members.

"I am encouraged by the initial growth and active participation in the KidsWin group. In just a short time my group has driven traffic to my company store on my website and I'm reaching and helping more kids, which is the intent of my business."

- Include photos and videos to add visual interest.

- Use Facebook data to analyze your customer demographics.

- When in groups, respond to people's comments, so they don't think you're ignoring them. That's all part of the group interaction.

Be mindful of Facebook's disadvantages. "All Facebook, the Unofficial Facebook Resource," a blog started by Nick O'Neill, revealed that in December of 2009 Facebook was costing companies about $350 billion a year in lost productivity. With the number of Facebook users increasing by the minute, that number will grow exponentially. Social networking sites pose problems for schools as well, where students often use the sites to bully others.

If your teenage or college-age children don't want you to friend them, that's normal. They consider Facebook their space, and don't want parental oversight. If your children (or grandchildren) do allow you to be a friend, it's *uncool* to intrude on their dialogue. You can send messages via the "Inbox" that appears at the top of your screen, which is much like sending an email.

As a little aside, there's even social networking for furry friends. On Dogbook, for example, owners show off their pets, connect with other dog owners, set up play dates, locate dog parks, and find the latest products. When Dogbook launched an app in early 2010, it got 800,000 downloads in the first two weeks. There's also Catbook, Horsebook, Rodentbook, Fishbook, and any other *book you can imagine.

As valuable as social networking is, there's inherent danger. Cyberterrorists are targeting social networking sites. These attacks (via viruses, programs known as Trojans, and malware) have already started. Primary targets are Twitter and Facebook. LinkedIn is also vulnerable because the site provides hackers with what are effectively corporate directories that can be reverse-engineered to garner the email addresses of potential victims. Many pundits believe these attacks will continue to escalate and become more sophisticated.

My colleague was the recipient of such an attack. The Facebook page of his business account (infected with a virus) was sent to all his friends, with added obscene language and lewd photographs. Once my colleague became aware of the attack, he had Facebook deactivate his account. However, the damage was done. Here are a few things you can do to help protect yourself:

- Be careful of where you post and what you post.
- Don't accept as a friend or connection anyone you don't know and trust.
- Pay attention to the security pop-up warnings. We get so many, we've become desensitized and often disregard them.

Additional Resources

- **Google Wave** is a free personal communication and collaboration tool that was designed to merge the capabilities of email, IM, wikis, and social networking. It has a grammar checker and can be translated into 40 languages.
- **Google Reader** is a free web-based aggregator. It shows you the latest updates on your favorite sites, all in one place. You can share content, create your own tags, and manage streams of news.
- **Google Alerts** are email updates that automatically notify you of the latest news on topics of your choice.
- **OnlyWire** is a free service that allows you to submit your latest web content simultaneously to a variety of social bookmark sites.
- **SlideShare** is a free launching service that lets you upload PowerPoint or Open Office presentation files and share them online through a YouTube-like interface.
- **Delicious** is a free social bookmarking web service for storing, sharing, and discovering web bookmarks.

Chapter 2

I Blog, Therefore, I Am

In this chapter

- *Big businesses are blogging*
- *Get started*
- *Develop high-quality content*
- *Hello, world. Here I am!*
- *Make money from your blog*
- *Remember your blogging manners*
- *How companies benefit from blogs*

No longer are blogs merely teenage musings on life; they can be powerful and career-changing. If you have any doubts, read the book *Julie & Julia* by Julie Powell, or rent the movie. Julie's rise to prominence started with a blog. She decided to cook all 524 recipes (within one year) from Julia Child's cookbook *Mastering the Art of French Cooking*. At the end of each day Julie documented her shopping and cooking experiences on a blog. At first she thought her stories were evaporating in cyberspace, but gradually she started receiving comments and realized people were actually reading what she wrote. Ultimately she gained national recognition, fulfilling her lifelong ambition to become a writer and becoming the subject of a movie about herself and Julia Child.

Blogging has grown into a completely new way of sharing information, receiving information, having discussions, and doing business. Bloggers, often referred to as "citizen journalists," engage in multi-threaded online conversations. They share thoughts and ideas, foster personal relationships and communities, build personal and corporate credibility, and grab search-engine attention. With just a few clicks, every digital photo, PowerPoint presentation, email, government report, and more can be broadcast into the blogosphere.

Although blogs are part of the social-networking phenomenon, I'm breaking them into a separate chapter because there's a lot to share. Check out Chapter 1 to learn more about social media and social networking.

Big businesses are blogging

Boeing, Kodak, Monster, Delta, General Motors, Dell, Adobe, Ford, and other big names are blogging to extend their reach and build stronger relationships with key target groups. Each year Technorati (an Internet search engine that searches through blogs) lists the 15 most popular corporate blogs, and businesses compete for a "Technorati ranking." Companies are turning to blogging as powerful tools to:

- Position themselves as experts and thought leaders.
- Build rapport between themselves and their customers.
- Provide instant access to company news.
- Augment brand awareness.
- Provide a workspace where members of internal teams can collaborate.
- Provide a gateway for readers to find information and resources.
- Establish a channel for recruiting.
- Publish an idea to see if it garners interest.
- Launch a trial balloon for a new idea or concept.
- Post details of a new product or service or changes in an existing one.
- Rank higher in the search engines.

 Every minute of every day your prospects are seeking answers to their questions online. Make sure they are able to find you.

Get started

Before you start blogging, here are a few things you need to do:

Create a URL. Create a URL (domain name) that represents your business, so people can find you during a search. A domain name is like your street address, so make it as easy as Main Street. For example, Canton Photography is more straightforward in a search than Canton Studios (which could be a photography studio, karate studio, production studio, or any other type of studio).

Choose a host. There are lots of hosting companies; some are free, others charge nominal fees. Two popular free sites are www.blogger.com and www.wordpress.com. To find others, Google "free blog sites." A free site is a good way to start, but consider a paid host as you go along for these reasons:

- You'll own your site and no third party can shut you down.
- You'll have more functionality.
- You'll have more credibility.

 If you have one of the free blogs, don't include it as part of your email signature block. I did for a while and realized that certain people weren't getting my messages. Their hosts viewed them as spam and blocked them.

Select a theme. Your theme is the template you select. Most of the hosting sites have a number of choices. But if you want something else, check out http://www.woothemes.com and purchase a theme for a small cost. Or you can hire a professional designer to create a theme.

Monologue or dialogue? Decide if your blog will be a monologue or a dialogue. Although some people and companies use monologue blogs as places to post articles, press releases, and more, there is great benefit in a dialogue. People enjoy reading what others have posted, whether or not they comment themselves.

Realize, however, that dialoguing comes with inherent risks. If you want to interact with your customers, expect to hear from those who are disgruntled. Respond to all comments. When you respond to a negative comment, thank the person for expressing his opinion and ask how you can make an improvement. Some people are cranks; others have good ideas.

 One downside to dialoguing is that everyone and his cousin will ask to connect with you on social networking sites.

Develop high-quality content

No matter how great your site looks, it's all about high-quality content. Create content that will make for a good discussion, provoke thought, or add value for your readers.

> ## Use a blog to facilitate team/project information sharing.
>
> Blogs (as well as wikis) are very strong communication tools for teams and projects, and they're supplanting corporate intranets. Blogs are being used at every level of savvy organizations for the following reasons:
> - To keep stakeholders in the loop.
> - To present an open communication platform in the spirit of collaboration and learning.
> - To transfer information as a viable alternative to meetings.
> - To become a vehicle for sharing problems and garnering solutions.
> - To serve as a history for lessons learned.

Understand what you want from your blog. It's appropriate to have several blogs for different reasons. If you do, keep each one separate.

Professional blog

- Do you want to improve customer relationships, enhance channel relationships, build brand awareness, induce a product trial, expand your market share, or boost your marketing return on investment?
- Do you want to increase awareness of charitable or civic activities?
- Do you want to brand yourself as the expert in a certain industry or genre?

Personal blog

- Do you want to dialogue about a special interest or passion?
- Have you traveled to a unique place that you think others might be interested in?
- Do you have an unusual hobby or collection?

Create a list of 20 topics that relate to your passion or business. Reference a television show or current event that relates to your topic. State three things they don't teach you in school that relate to your topic. Identify the top 10 mistakes people make. Write about a faux pas you made during a presentation or interaction with a customer. Share what you learned from the experience and what you would do differently the next time.

Once you've identified your topic, explode it. For example, if your passion or business is dog training, your topics could be *clicker dog training, puppy dog training, socialization dog training, housebreaking dog training.* Notice that the phrase "dog training" appears in every topic. This is to give you greater visibility in a search. Check out Google Wonder Wheel and learn to brainstorm on topics.

Certain host services give you the option of distributing your content at preapproved dates and times. You can create lots of content, submit it, and leave the sending to someone else.

Create a compelling opening paragraph. The first paragraph will determine if the reader keeps reading or loses interest. Write something compelling that's relevant to your topic. Ask a question, share an ancedote or quote, use an analogy, cite an interesting or shocking statistic.

Keep the content simple. Here are a few simple ways to make your content simple and engaging:

- Create text that's no longer than 500 words. (Consider breaking longer posts into two or three posts.)
- Chose a topic that's unique and will add value for your readers.
- Use simple language and avoid jargon.
- Use proper grammar, punctuation, and spelling.
- Introduce only one concept per post, and find creative ways to reinforce your key point.
- Create provocative titles. In their book *Made to Stick*, Chip and Dan Heath provide a contrast between two titles. The first is significantly more alluring and has an emotional hook.

    Provocative: Sun Exposure: How to Get Old Prematurely
    Dull: Sun Exposure: Precautions and Protection
- Use headings with lots of keywords to break down your text into identifiable chunks of information. In this way, readers can capture information at a glance.

- Add zing with capitalization, italics, underlining, but don't get too carried away. Too many font styles are difficult to read.

Add links. Adding links will increase readership, get you more visibility, and increase search engine optimization.

- Link to your website and social networking sites.
- Link to the blogs of corporations, professional associations, educational institutions, and nonprofits—when they apply to your topic.
- Make sure your links are credible and current. Many links have been around for years and people have already seen them or they're no longer relevant.
- Secure links that are indexed by Google.
- Avoid paid links such as those that say *Sponsored, Advertisements,* or *Partners.*
- Place your links within your content rather than as footnotes.

 To get the most value from your blog and social networking sites, link them together through RSS feeds. This will let you post to one site and populate the others. It's relatively easy to do. If you can't do it yourself, ask someone with some technical savvy.

Make your blog readable. Here are some hints for making your blog more readable:

- Use short sentences.
- Add headlines that give key information at a glance.
- Limit blocks of text to no more than eight lines.
- Use bulleted and numbered lists.
- Leave one line space above and below your lists.
- Allow for plenty of white space.

Create a schedule and stick to it. Have you ever visited a company's website and checked out its news stories and press releases only to find that the latest posting is six months old? If so, you probably asked yourself, Hasn't anything newsworthy happened since then? Or you may have asked, Who's minding the store? Keeping your blog current should be a key part of your marketing strategy. Post at regular intervals—every day, every week, or every month. Stick to a schedule so your followers can anticipate your new posts.

Keep in mind that the major search engines assign higher rankings to sites that update frequently. When you post to a blog several times a week, the search engines will reward your effort with improved search engine rankings.

 If you want a break from blogging, will be unavailable for a period of time, or want to share another point of view, recruit a guest blogger. If you don't know anyone personally, check out http://www.bloggerlinkup .com.

Hello, world. Here I am!

A blog isn't the answer to growing your business; it's merely one more tool in your marketing toolbox and *you must tend to it.* Here are some tips for writing a blog that reflects your purpose and your company's personality:

Check out the competition. Look at the websites and blogs of your competitors. Whether you're a small-business owner or you work at a large company, it's important to know what the competition is doing.

Be consistent with the frequency. It's worth repeating that once you establish a time frame for writing your blog, you should be consistent. The people following you will expect to read your blog every day at 9 AM, every week on Monday, or in whatever pattern you establish. If you disappoint them, they'll stop coming back.

Involve your customers or clients. Ask customers to send pictures of their products and showcase them. Include stories and conversations with your customers (both with written permission). Include current events relating to the industry or other hot topics of interest.

Don't expect immediate success. You must give before you get. Julie Powell (mentioned in the opening paragraph of this chapter) waited many months for just one comment, but she ultimately skyrocketed to fame. That doesn't mean you will also, but you do need to be patient. Many people claim that if you publish one blog each week, you will start to see activity in three to six months. If you don't, rethink the blog's value, its content, and how you are approaching it.

 Avoid the mistakes of novices. People who start blogging often make the mistakes of not including a contact page, search box, or archives. Their blogs may have difficult navigation, invisible links, and too many ads.

Make money from your blog

Although many blogs are posted by people who just want to get their names out there, you can also make money from blogging. This is no different from making money in a conventional business. It takes lots of time and hard work. Here are some ways to get recognition so you can make money.

Use CPM ads. To make money on blogs that have in excess of 5,000 readers, consider CPM (cost per thousand) ads where you pay for every 1,000 impressions of your ad. Popular CPM ad networks include Technorati Media, ValueClick, Tribal Fusion, and Casale Media, to name a few.

Get direct advertisers and sponsors. Once your blog becomes known (and there's no magical number to let you know you've gotten there), create an "Advertise with us" page. To get started, check who's advertising on the blogs of people or companies in your niche, search Google for keywords related to your blog, or contact advertising networks such as www.BuySellAds.com or SponsoredReviews.com.

Use affiliate marketing. Affiliate marketing is a system of revenue sharing between online advertisers, merchants, publishers, salespeople, and the like whereby compensation is based on sales, clicks, the amount of traffic generated, or whatever you arrange. Make a list of all the online products and services websites you already use. If they have an affiliate program, write honest reviews about the products or services. In order to be successful you must own your website, provide quality content, and offer incentives.

 To see lots of articles on what people are saying about infinity marketing, check out Twitter updates at http://www.affiliate1on1.com.

Harness the power of email marketing. Having a list of people who've opted in is one of the best forms of marketing. Start building your list from current and former clients, friends, colleagues, and anyone else you want to market to. Although some services are free, it may be wise to steer away from them because of potential spam problems. The most popular email marketing service is Constant Contact. Others are iContact and AWeber.

Remember your blogging manners

Always be mindful that a blog is someone's Internet home, so be respectful and honest. People who aren't lose credibility in the blogging community.

Do's

- When posting to a blog for the first time, introduce yourself. Include your name, location, blog, and URL. Say what drew you to the blog and what you like (or don't like) about the content.
- Ask the blog host if he has time to chat.
- Get to the point without being too wordy.

- Provide something of value.
- You may be posting to a blog in another time zone or another country, so be aware of language differences and time sensitivities.
- If you disagree with the blogger, tactfully say why and propose a solution or different point of view.
- Be courteous and use respectable language.
- Post on topic and make sure your comments reflect the appropriate tone.
- Allow breathing room for the blog host to respond.
- End by thanking the blog host for his time.

You can also become a professional blog writer. Blogs are quickly replacing the mainstream news, and many bloggers are paid to write and report the news.

Join blogging conversations, but limit your input to topics you're passionate about. I gave input on a question about PowerPoint presentations. Within one week I received more than 100 emails with counter-responses. Needless to say, I didn't read many of them. They became *noise*.

Taboos
- Getting personal when you don't know someone well.
- Bashing a product or service. If you're using the blog to offer comments, make the comments constructive.
- Being a spoiler and divulging information such as the ending to a hot new book or movie.
- Expecting the blog host to be there waiting for your comments.

Responding to other blogs can be just as important as posting original material. Focus your conversation on the writer of the blog while keeping the rest of the audience in mind.

You don't have time to blog?

You may think that your day is busy and you don't have time to read and respond to blogs. Blogging doesn't have to be time-consuming unless you allow it to be. If you can spare 15 to 20 minutes a day you can blog. For example, think of all the waiting you do. With today's technology you can blog from anywhere. In the airport while waiting for a plane. At the bus or train station. During a meal if you're eating alone. And anyplace else where you have some down time. Even during a boring webinar.

How companies benefit from blogs

Fewer and fewer people listen to sanitized, static advertising/marketing messages. Blogs are absolutely one of the best low-cost, interactive advertising/marketing tools for any business today. Blogs can brand your company as knowledgeable and authentic and help to create a loyal community. Here's a sampling of ways in which companies in a variety of industries are using blogs for business:

Software. MathWorks, the leading global provider of software for technical computing and model-based design, publishes both internal and external blogs. MathWorks web community manager Ned Gulley explains that employees are free to write about whatever they want on the internal blogs. Although most people discuss work-related topics, some discuss outside interests and semi-personal issues. The external blogs are used to enhance the brand, provide access to information, and engage customers in conversations—many of whom they wouldn't otherwise hear from.

What's unique about the external blogs at MathWorks is that active developers within the company write them. These are people with sharp technical skills and professional insight who are passionate, articulate, and have valuable information to share. Topics can range from object-oriented programming, to tables made easy, to computing the colored area on a curved surface, to writing to STL files, to anything else they may want to discuss. These bloggers appreciate the opportunity to have conversations with like-minded people in their own voices, as opposed to publishing in a journal where the information is static and their voices would be heavily edited. Bloggers must have good writing skills, hold to a disciplined schedule of posting once a week, and respond to all comments.

Information Technology (IT). Corporations are often slow to change. Merging a website and blog is a difficult concept for marketing managers to sell to management. However, smaller companies are leading the charge. Emily Greenwood, President of EKG Networking (an IT consulting company), wanted to communicate more often with customers to offer them tips and tricks. In that way customers could focus on their businesses, not on their technology. At first Emily thought of producing a newsletter and having members of her company contribute articles. But that never happened. Her next thought was to blog, because blogs can be short, interactive, generated faster, and they provide a historical archive.

Wanting to provide a comprehensive landing spot for customers,

Emily decided to abandon her static website and combine her website and blog, using social media to drive traffic to the site. One way Emily has proactively kept up with (or ahead of) her clients' needs is with poll questions such as "Are you going to upgrade to [latest operating system] within the next year? Do you have people who work virtually? Are you going to invest in new technology next year?" Merging the website and blog has helped EKG Networking to educate customers by providing on-going resources, and it's growing the business.

Entrepreneurs. I have a blog for my business that is hosted by one of the free blog services. My blog is an archive for articles I've written about communication. People find my articles by searching on Google, through a link on my website, via my email business-writing tips, or by word of mouth. Because of my blog, my workshops, my networks, and my books, people view me as an expert. My blog has generated more marketing and workshop business because it's one more way for people to find me.

Email marketing solutions. Martin Lieberman, Constant Contact's managing editor, says that Constant Contact uses blogs as platforms to demonstrate the company's expertise in email marketing, online surveys, and event marketing best practices, as well as other areas of interest to small businesses and organizations. Constant Contact uses blogs as a megaphone to broadcast the company's perspective on issues and topics that are relevant to small business audiences.

Blogs allow Constant Contact to communicate in a timely fashion and in a way that complements their ongoing newsletter strategy. Not only can the company participate in discussions happening in the marketplace, it can also lead discussions by sharing its perspective on hot topics that were brought up in a newsletter or on another site. Hopefully, the unique voice it shares on the blogs will allow the company to further differentiate itself in the marketplace.

Supermarket chain. Roche Bros. (also known as Sudbury Farms), a Massachusetts supermarket chain, posts a blog via Facebook. Human Resources Assistant Bobby DiMarino shares the following:

The blog has helped us make a better name for our organization. I have heard customers mention how helpful the blog has been, because no matter what questions they have, they can post them and receive a response within 24 hours. The blog has also helped with our marketing. I have noticed that more merchandisers are using blogs to promote many of their products. Blogging is not just about pushing products. It's about strengthening the relationship between our organization, our stores, and our customers. Here are just some of the special things our blog does:

- Helps to bring relief to disaster areas. For example, we used our blog to raise money for the Haitian Relief Fund after the 2010 earthquake.
- Informs people about recalls and other public health issues.
- Aids in healthier eating and living through a program called Full Yield.

Work is the curse of the drinking classes.
—Oscar Wilde, Irish-born writer

Chapter 3

Get Ready, Get Set, Get a Job

In this chapter

- *Get yourself started in the participation age*
- *Make a good online impression*
- *Hop aboard the social networking bandwagon*
- *Refresh your resume*
- *Hone your cover letter*
- *Prepare for the interview(s)*
- *Send thank-you letters*

In days of yore . . . job hunters would pour through the classified ads in the newspapers, especially on Sunday mornings, hoping to catch a glimpse of something for which they might remotely qualify.

Wanted: Lion Tamer

No experience needed. Must be able to use a whip, run fast, and love cats. No medical coverage or life insurance. (The premiums would kill us.)

If interested, call Leo Lyons at 800.555.LYON

Perhaps the above classified ad wouldn't have been your dream job, but most ads appealed to someone somewhere. Job hunters would put their resumes and cover letters in an envelope, pop them in the mail, and wait for the phone to ring. Eventually they found jobs that closely, or remotely, matched what they were looking for.

Today, newspapers are slowly disappearing, and job hunters have to be more resourceful. They may learn of openings through colleagues, recruiters, friends, and family, but online resources, such as social networks, job sites, blogs, and YouTube, are becoming more and more important.

Get yourself started in the participation age

We've gone from the industrial age to the information age to the participation age. Here are a few simple tips to help you participate:

Create a professional-sounding email address and IM ID. Keep it simple, and consider using your name. For example, an email address such as brianhotlips3@aol.com isn't hot and won't get you any responses. (Actually it may, but not the kind you're hoping for.) A more appropriate address would be brian.keith@aol.com.

Check out local employment sites. For example, search Google for "local job sites, boston, ma" and a plethora of listings pop up.

Join job sites. Some popular sites are monster.com, flipdog.com, careerbuilder.com, and indeed.com. There are also government sites and industry-specific sites. Look online for organizations and publications related to your industry.

Join a job/resume bank. These sites are intended to help you find employment. Many provide links to other resources and have helpful information on career assessment, job search techniques, resume preparation, and related topics. Check out http://counsel.southern.edu/main/sub/banks.htm for a host of job and resume banks.

 If you're currently working and post on these sites, you run the risk of your current employer learning that you're job hunting. Or you may be surprised to find your own job listed.

Participate in professional organizations. These organizations will help you stay current with industry news and developments. You'll meet leaders in your field and make professional connections. If you're not working, this will help you to stay in the game. The websites of these organizations often share job postings as well.

Enter the world of social networking. If you don't have a social networking presence, you appear archaic, and you may not be what recruiters and hiring managers are looking for in today's environment. (Check out Chapter 1, "Build the Buzz with Social Networking and Social Media.")

Sign on to LinkedIn, Twitter, and Facebook. Those are the three primary sites where it's all happening. (Learn more about these sites to enhance your job search later in this chapter.)

 Be very careful what you post on your social networking sites. A picture of you dancing on the table at a party won't land you the job you want. Remember that others can take your picture and post it. Check regularly, and pick your friends and associates carefully.

Start a blog. Consider starting a blog related to your career interests. Blog about industry trends, news, and related topics. People will start to find you and view you as an expert. (Be careful that you don't post anything you wouldn't want a recruiter or hiring manager to read.) You can learn more about blogging in Chapter 2, "I Blog, Therefore, I Am."

Make sure you have a clean credit report. Check your credit report to learn what a potential employer may see. Some potential employers check the credit histories of job applicants. A blemished report may eliminate you from the running. (Congress is considering blocking employers from access to most credit-report data, but as of this writing, your credit report is fair game.)

Volunteer. If you aren't working and have free time, now is a great opportunity to volunteer in your community. Serve on a board, help in the schools, organize a neighborhood recycling program, or design marketing pieces for a charity. Along the way you may meet someone who can help you get a job. Even if you don't, at least you're not sitting at home waiting for the phone to ring.

Make a good online impression

It's worth repeating that you need to be mindful of what you put on the Internet. Recruiters and employers are looking. Many employers have found content on social networking sites that caused them to disqualify candidates they were considering, including content about drinking or drugs, offensive comments about someone's gender or ethnicity, complaints about a company or coworkers, lies about qualifications, links to porn sites, inappropriate photos, and classified company information. Sloppy writing, the use of emoticons, and text language (such as BTW for "by the way") don't bode well either. Here are a few ways to manage your personal brand so you maintain a professional image:

Ditch the digital dirt. Remove any content on any site you think would speak negatively of you. Check Google Alerts and TweetBeep.com alerts to see what other people have posted about you.

Start your own professional group. With Ning.com you can start your own professional group. If you are in a niche market or have a unique profession, starting a group will help to create a sense of community and eliminate some of the isolation you may feel.

Follow the leaders. Participate in the online conversations of thought leaders in your industry to learn what's happening. Learn where the jobs are. Learn where your industry is headed. Share your insights and experiences.

Don't gripe. Keep your content positive. Everyone likes a winner.

 Consider posting an online video, if appropriate. For example, if you're a corporate trainer, post a video of yourself in front of an audience. If you deliver keynote speeches, post a video of yourself speaking at an event.

 If you're applying for a government job that requires high-level clearance, the Patriot Act allows investigators to view your online profiles even if they aren't accessible to the general public.

Hop aboard the social networking bandwagon

When you're looking for a job, you're a salesperson—you're selling yourself. When you're looking to fill a job, you're a salesperson—you're selling your company. This chapter focuses on LinkedIn, Twitter, and Facebook—the most relevant networking sites to businesspeople. You can learn more about these three sites in the general sense in Chapter 1, "Build the Buzz with Social Networking and Social Media."

LinkedIn

If you're not already on LinkedIn, you're missing out on lots of opportunities for finding a job. LinkedIn is the most popular professional site that lets you connect to people you know and the social networks of people they know. You can exchange private emails, ask for introductions to third parties through your connections, post messages to networking groups, and examine job listings, which are typically posted directly by the hiring coordinators at firms and companies. Here's how to use LinkedIn to help your job search:

Do a company search. If you're interested in a specific company, search on that company and you may find people there who know someone you know.

Invite people you know to connect with you. This builds your site, exponentially extends your search, and connects you with people you may have lost track of.

Find job postings. Employers often post jobs on their sites. These are generally high-quality, professional jobs.

Use the email feature. People who are laid off often send an email to their LinkedIn connections asking for help. This is a great way to get the word out and let your colleagues know you're on the hunt.

Post a blog link on your profile. Let everyone you're connected with see your blog. Use the blog to share anything that might be of interest to your professional network.

Incorporate a Twitter link. This will pull in conversations from Twitter so you can see what your connections are tweeting about.

Post recommendations. Ask former bosses, peers, subordinates, vendors, clients, and other professionals you know to write recommendations. This will give recruiters and potential employers a first-hand look at what others think and say about you. Recommendations are "instant" references.

Participate in Q&A discussions. If you want to be perceived as a thought leader, participate in question-and-answer discussions. If a recruiter or prospective employer is part of the "conversation," you become someone they may want to contact.

Here are a few tips to enhance your LinkedIn profile:
- Copy and paste from your resume as appropriate.
- Add a professional-looking photo.
- Include past job experience and your education.
- Add recommendations.

Don't be afraid to say you're looking for a job, unless you're currently employed.

Twitter

Twitter is the new microblog on the social media block. Every communication—even your profile—is limited to 140 characters. Twitter is popular with younger generations because they think in sound bites, not paragraphs. When you use Twitter you demonstrate your technical savvy and draw attention to recruiters and people in your industry who may want to hire you. Once you're following a few people, you're ready to start tweeting yourself. You can tweet from your website, phone, or handheld. Twitter can help you to:

Stay abreast of what's happening around you. Twitter is an easy way to keep up on the latest information, news, and current state of your industry. For example, major legal publications, law firms, legal blogs, and newspapers post on Twitter. And many organizations are starting to list jobs on Twitter.

Engage in basic networking. One of the strengths of Twitter is that you can connect to people you don't know. This extends your network beyond anything you can imagine.

Look for recruiters in your industry and follow them. Many recruiters post jobs on Twitter. Follow those who recruit in your field.

Find job postings. Many companies have a corporate presence on Twitter. Search by the company name to find them. Here are some other places to search:

- http://www.twitjobsearch.com. TwitJobSearch searches Twitter for jobs that match the keywords that you enter.
- http://jobshouts.com. JobShouts is a free resource for both employers and job seekers. Employers can post their jobs for free; the positions are then automatically "tweeted" to users on Twitter.
- http://www.jobangels.org. JobAngels began as a Twitter account and attracted more than 1,000 followers in its first two weeks.
- http://socialmediajobwire.com. Social Media Job Wire helps you "find a job you don't hate in blogging, Social Media, IT, development, design and startups."

 When setting up your Twitter account, use your own name. That will make it easier for people to find you.

The following is reprinted with permission from Cathy's Clean Slate, the blog of Cathy Browne, "a tech-savvy PR gal who's seen the public relations profession evolve from typewriters and Liquid Paper to email and social media."

Twitter as Job Search Tool? Absolutely!

I've been looking for a PR job for many months, first in Silicon Valley, where I had lived for several years, and now in Vancouver, where I came after my visitor visa had expired. It's been hard, and the current downturn has made it even more challenging. At first, I relied on craigslist, LinkedIn, and Facebook. I even paid a hefty monthly fee to a well-known organization to give me "exclusive" access to choice positions.

Twitter wasn't part of my search strategy—but it is now. One single tweet changed that for me in December.

I had been using Twitter to connect and engage people in conversation, but I had never really brought up my situation. Then, on a particularly tough day, I announced that I was on the verge of losing everything and would have to leave the US.

The response was immediate—and overwhelming. Since then, I've had the opportunity to tell my story through guest blogs, media interviews, speaking engagements, and Internet radio shows. Several people offered to circulate my resume to friends and colleagues. To this day, folks I've never met and probably will never meet write me to see how I'm doing, feed me leads, give me encouragement, and tell me things will get better. And happily, I'm talking with some promising companies with neat technology who are in the process of getting funding. I have hope.

If you are job hunting, or know someone who is, here are a few tips based on my experience on Twitter:

- **Build up your network**—follow people you respect, and follow the people who respect them. Use tools like Twellow.com to find like-minded people who may be helpful resources. And follow job sources such as @JobAngels, @SocialMediaJob, @MicroJobs, and more.

- **Take a good look at your skills,** and make sure that your Twitter bio reflects them. Be direct. My bio says I am job hunting in the first line!

- **Make sure you have a twesume**—what you do in 140 characters—and tweet it on a regular basis. (No spamming, though . . .)
- **Let your followers know you are looking,** and if there are certain contacts or companies you'd like an introduction to. This is no time to hang back. If no one knows, no one can help you.
- **Keep your followers posted on how the search is going.** We can all relate to your frustration, and cheer you on when things look promising.
- **Share information.** If you find a great new tool, or if you know of opportunities that aren't a fit for you, tell the world. Someone will benefit. Twitter is all about helping each other.
- **Talk about your job search** in your blog or ask bloggers you follow if they accept guest posts, so you can provide your own insights on social media and job searches. Post the link on Twitter.
- **And never give up.** I'm not.

Facebook

Although Facebook started as a social networking site for connecting with friends and family, it's now becoming popular in the professional arena (even though the people you connect with are called *friends*). Here's how Facebook can help you in your job search:

Consider setting up two Facebook accounts. Use one for professional contacts only and one for family and friends.

Keep your professional profile clean. Although you may be tempted to post cute and cool photos and comments, don't do so on your professional profile. Keep it clean and on-brand.

Renew old acquaintances. You can join affiliate and alumni groups for your college, past jobs, and current job. You can search for and join groups for your elementary school or high school, old neighbors, clubs, and more. You never know who (directly or indirectly) knows someone who's looking for your skill set.

Conduct a Google search. You can conduct a Google search using Facebook and "career search" or "job hunting." You'll find career articles, resume design tools, and job postings.

Create Facebook ads. A colleague told me she posted a Facebook ad and received nearly 700 clicks, 50 emails, and 10 Facebook messages in response. Out of this, she received several interviews and a job offer, which she accepted.

Use Facebook apps. An increasing number of companies are using Facebook as a recruiting tool. The employment website Jobster, for example, has launched a Facebook app with several hundred partner employers.

Attach your business cards. Scan your business card and attach it to your messages.

 If you're concerned about employers (or others) seeing your information on Facebook, change your Facebook privacy settings so only the people you allow can view your profile.

 Job-search karma says that if you want to get, you first must give. Give without expecting to receive. Volunteer your expertise. Send articles that may be of interest. Connect people with other people. What you do for others, tomorrow they may do for you.

Don't forget traditional face-to-face networking.

Although social networking is all the rage—and a wonderful way to network beyond your geographic community—don't ignore the traditional networking opportunities. Recruiters and hiring managers often want a *safe hire*—someone whose name was passed along by a friend, relative or colleague. Network at conferences, conventions, trade shows, chambers of commerce, professional associations, PTA meetings, community service groups, and more. Networking also takes place in (and at) gyms, airplanes, banks, sporting events, golf courses, supermarkets, doggie parks, doctors' offices, restaurants, sushi bars, cocktail parties, nightclubs, or just about anywhere you find people.

Refresh your resume

The basic content of a resume hasn't changed much over the years. However, today many companies ask you to submit your resume electronically, and they have databases to scan them. Electronic resumes are about content, not appearance. The nice formatting that makes your resume look good on paper also makes it unscannable.

Prepare a resume suitable for scanning. Here are some tips for preparing a scannable resume that can be read across different platforms:

- Use a sans serif font such as Courier, Ariel, or Helvetica in 12 point.
- Avoid shading, borders, graphics, boxes, bullets, underlining, and italics. Replace boxes with a stream of hyphens, bullets with asterisks, and underlining and italics with boldface.
- Use the space bar instead of the tab key to indent.
- Save your resume as a text file (filename.txt).

Type your name and contact information. Type only your name on the top line and your address, phone number, and email below. Otherwise you'll confuse the scanner. Your heading may look like this:

Mark Lawrence
204 Main Street, Monsey, NY 10952 • 845.543.2234 • mark@aol.com

Use the heading *Career Highlights*, not *Objectives*. *Objectives* was the usual opening heading years ago. However, meaningless vanilla phrases such as *To use my education and marketing experience in a dynamic work environment* are boring and don't add value to your resume. Instead, start with the heading *Career Highlights* or *Professional Highlights*. List three to five relevant career highlights at the top of the page, following your heading. (Odd numbers seem to work better than even numbers.) Quantify them with dollar amounts, numbers, and percentages when you can. Here's an example:

Career Highlights

* Performed time studies that helped better optimize cycle time, improve ergonomics and machine throughput. The increased efficiency allowed company to shut down a reactor and realize a $200,000 annual savings in water, electricity, and maintenance/parts costs.

* Helped company to save more than $100,000 annually by becoming first to implement a reclaimed test monitor program in my area.

* Voted "Employee of the Month" for saving $3M account using SQC, DOE, TQM techniques, and customer interface which led to a $7M account from the same customer for a new part.

For online submissions, include the heading *Keywords*. Put *Keywords* below *Career Highlights*. Computers will search for industry terms, buzzwords, jargon, trade terms, and the like. Keep your keywords job-specific. Don't include overused generalities such as *team player, good communication skills, strong organizational skills,* or *go-to person.* Here's how a keywords heading may read:

Keywords: Semiconductor, process engineer, thin films, PVD, PECCVD, etching, silicon, applications, vacuum, solder bumping, flip chip.

The following are a few tips to help you get noticed:
- Use keywords throughout your resume. The more times they appear (within reason, of course), the more likely it is that your resume will pop up.
- Use keywords for a twesume (a 140-character resume you post on Twitter) that you send to a few key people only. You do this by typing @[username] [space] [keywords].
- If you're seeking mid-level management, use phrases containing the words *Manager* or *Director,* such as *Director of Finance, Finance Director, Finance Manager, Manager of Finance,* etc.
- Review job postings in your industry to see what skills hiring managers are looking for. Incorporate these words into your resume and you have a greater chance of being noticed.
- If you're fluent or conversant in a foreign language (especially a widely spoken language such as Mandarin Chinese), be sure to note it. That's a real plus in this global workplace.

Know what to omit. Here are a few hints as to what to leave off your resume:

- **Your photo.** Unless you're applying for a modeling job, don't include your photo.

- **Trite phrases.** Phrases such as *I'm reliable, I have a good personality,* or *I have good worth ethics* are worthless. After all, who would say they're unreliable, have a lousy personality, or have poor worth ethics?

- **"References upon request."** No one will check your references until they meet you and consider you a viable candidate. Therefore, it's understood that you'll furnish references upon request.

- **Hobbies.** Include hobbies only if they're relevant to the position or you're a recent college graduate with limited work experience.

- **Personal information.** Don't mention your height, weight, age, date of birth, place of birth, marital status, gender, race or ethnicity, health, social security number, or religious or political affiliations.

- **Lies.** Background checks will fail you.

- **Salary information.** Save that for the interview unless the posting requires it.

- **Reason for leaving a job.** Save that for the interview as well.

The following are guaranteed to sink your employment chances:
- Typographical errors.
- No highlights or summary at the beginning.
- Focusing on responsibilities rather than on results.
- Too many big words.

Open your completed resume in editing software such as Notepad or WordPad to see that it's free of graphic elements. Then send it to yourself and someone you trust to see how it transmits.

Hone your cover letter

A cover letter (also known as an application letter) should be part of your arsenal because you must send one with each resume—paper or electronic. Although you can reuse a lot of the same wording from one letter to another, when you customize the letter, you have a much higher chance of getting a positive response. Use your cover letter to your advantage; it's the first thing a potential employer will see.

Begin your email cover letter with any job numbers and titles that describe the job or jobs for which you're applying. Then proceed as you would with any other letter.

Take the time to plan. Your well-written cover letter can launch an interview and determine the course of your career. It takes a lot of thought and planning to write a dynamite cover letter, but the time you invest is well worth the effort. Following are some helpful hints:

- Direct your letter to an individual by name and title whenever possible. There are many resources to help you find this information. The Internet or the company's receptionist are good places to start.
- Keep the letter short—generally three paragraphs.
- Select the highlights and qualifications from your resume that best

"sell you." Don't reiterate all the information in your resume, just the key points.

- Make the letter results-oriented. For example, say how you helped other companies.
- Emphasize the contribution you can make to the company.
- Mention that your resume is enclosed or attached.

Compose three compelling paragraphs. Prepare three compelling paragraphs that will whet the reader's appetite.

Opening paragraph:

Keep it interesting and identify your source.

- My broad experience in <field> is an excellent match for the needs you describe in <publication or website> on <date>.

- <Profession, such as pediatric nursing> is my first love. That's why <person> has informed me that you'll soon be needing a <job title>. Please consider this as my letter of application.

Middle paragraph:

Elaborate on your qualifications and explain how they can serve the company. Try to point out how you can do a better job for the company because of lessons you learned at previous jobs or in school (if you're a recent graduate).

- My background includes 16 years of experience in manufacturing and engineering. I am experienced in the construction of production machinery and plant engineering requirements. Former supervisors have praised me for my ability to direct and motivate others and meet very tight deadlines.

- For five years I was the Manager of Marketing Communications at Sterling Corporation. I managed a $3.6 million budget, against which I saved $760,000 in one year. My responsibilities included a broad range of assignments for international audiences, including sales and customer training, newsletters, product brochures, advertising, news releases, user documentation, and video productions.

Closing paragraph:

Request an interview, and include a telephone number where you can be reached. It's not necessary to repeat your phone number if it appears on your letterhead.

- I would welcome the opportunity to meet with you so that you can evaluate the creative contributions I can make to <company name>. You can reach me at <phone number> any afternoon at two o'clock.

- I'll call you next week to set up a time when we can discuss these opportunities further.

 When you can, cut and paste your cover letter and resume into the body of your email. Many recruiters and hiring managers don't open attachments for fear of viruses, or they simply don't want to be bothered. When a recruiter or hiring mananger is swamped with hundreds of applications, merely opening a Word file can seem like too much work.

Prepare for the interview(s)

The interviewer has already seen your resume and read your cover letter, so the company has decided you have the right qualifications. The purpose of the interview is to determine if you and the company are well matched. Do you have the right personality to fit into the culture? Do you conduct yourself professionally? Can you perform well under pressure? Do you show a genuine interest in the company? Why should the company invest in you? Remember, just as the interviewer is assessing you, you are assessing her and the company. The following are the types of interviews you may face—everything from plain vanilla to rocky road.

 It may put you somewhat at ease to know that the interview is often as stressful for the interviewer as it is for you. To make the interview go smoothly, anticipate what questions you may be asked and what questions you may ask. My book *Speaking Your Way to Success* has an entire chapter on interviewing and contains a plethora of such questions.

 Before any interview, *turn off your cell phone.*

Telephone interview. The phone interview is used to screen candidates prior to bringing them in for a personal interview. Prepare for a phone interview as if you were meeting face-to-face. Make sure you're in a quiet place without background noise. Keep in front of you a cheat sheet that lists experiences relevant to the position, education and special training, core competencies, and questions you want to ask.

One-to-one. This is the standard interview where the interviewer and candidate sit across from each other trying to decide if this is the right fit. Although you should be prepared for standard questions, there are no standard responses. Make your responses clear and relevant to the question and the situation. Listen carefully, pause briefly before answering, get directly to the point, be truthful, and don't open yourself to areas of questioning that could present difficulties for you. Consider closing with questions such as the following:

- "I am very interested in this position. Are there any concerns you'd like me to address before I leave?"

- "What about my qualifications makes me the right candidate?" (Although you may think this is bold, it forces the interviewer to recap your strengths. That's a positive way to end the interview.)

Virtual interview. A virtual interview can be done anywhere in the world and is less costly than flying a candidate to an office to meet face-to-face. If this interview goes well, ultimately the company will want to meet with you personally. Prepare for the virtual interview as you would for any other. At the basic level, all you need is a microphone, camera, and compatible software (such as Skype). At a more sophisticated level, the interview can be conducted via telepresence, where you appear at a local

Cisco TelePresence System 1100: Recruiting center. *Courtesy of Cisco Systems*

location. Following is a photo of a telepresence interview. (Learn more about telepresence and how companies are using it for virtual meetings in Chapter 8, "Virtual Meetings: From Sleep-Inducing to Sizzling.")

Panel interview. In a panel interview, two or more people (a panel) interview you at the same time. The panel interview lets the interviewers see how you react to different types of people while under pressure. You will be evaluated on your interpersonal skills, qualifications, and your ability to think on your feet. At the outset of the interview, ask each person for a business card and place each card in front of you in the order of seating. This will let you personalize the interview by using people's names. Make eye contact with the person asking or answering the question.

Audition interview. Audition interviews may be required for certain jobs, such as classroom instructor, computer programmer, mechanic, musician, or actor, when the employer wants to see you in action before making a decision. You will be asked to demonstrate your abilities in person or in some cases send a video.

Behavioral interview. The behavioral interview is typically reserved for people applying for high-level positions. Be prepared to discuss one or two difficult situations from past employment, the tasks you needed to perform (or supervise), the actions you and your team took, and the results. Interviewers are looking to determine your problem-solving skills and techniques, adaptability, conflict resolution, ability for multitasking, and how you behave in difficult or stressful situations.

Mealtime interview. This type of interview is to determine your demeanor in a social setting. Although a mealtime interview may seem less formal than an interview conducted in the office, it's just as critical. Brush up on your table manners, don't order alcohol (even if the interviewer does), and order food that isn't messy to eat. Expect the interviewer to pick up the tab.

Informational interview. Informational interviews are underutilized by job seekers. They're low-stress and help you to gain knowledge about a company or industry. Although you're not asking for a job, you never know when the person you meet with will have an opening or know of one. People are more than happy to share information about themselves, their jobs, and their companies. This is a great way for recent college graduates to learn about their chosen field.

Send thank-you letters

You must write a thank-you letter after each job interview. Send one to every person who interviewed you, keeping the essentials the same but briefly personalizing each one. Since fewer than 10 percent of all people interviewed send thank-you letters, sending one will make you stand out from the crowd. Here are some suggestions:

- Compose a handwritten, typewritten, or email letter.
- Keep it very brief.
- Express your appreciation for the time the interviewer spent with you.
- Mention something you said during the interview that resonated with the interviewer.
- Relate something you didn't get a chance to tell the interviewer.
- Address any unresolved points or questions you feel you didn't answer fully.
- Reemphasize your strong desire to work for the company and your enthusiasm for taking the next step.
- Proofread the letter very carefully.
- Send it within 24 hours.

Part Two

Creating Harmony

IN TODAY'S GLOBAL MARKETPLACE, most companies employ a diverse workforce of men and women from multiple generations belonging to many ethnic, religious, and cultural groups. Diversity in the workplace adds a special richness, but it also brings distinct challenges. In order to improve employee satisfaction, productivity, retention, and the bottom line, employers must fully embrace the benefits that diversity brings.

> Age is not important unless you're a cheese [or wine].
> —Helen Hayes, American actress

Chapter 4

Bridging the Multigenerational Divide

In this chapter

- *Embrace the differences*
- *Apply the golden rules*
- *Remember what's common to all generations*
- *Recruit*
- *Interview*
- *Start onboarding*
- *Reward and motivate*
- *Be sensitive to reporting structures*
- *Establish a plan for succession*

Have you ever heard people of the older generations say that hard work is its own reward? They espoused that people should work for the satisfaction of a job well done. They lived through tough economic times and saw their parents unemployed, many standing on bread lines. People of the older generations are patriotic, fiscally conservative, hard-working, conventional, duty bound, rule bound, loyal, conscientious, respectful of authority, and may be at the same company for a lifetime.

Younger generations are often amazed at the way older generations view the world. The younger generations became accustomed to seeing businesses merge, downsize, and go bankrupt. They don't trust the permanence of their jobs. They build parallel careers and see their skills as portable so they can move on when the time is right.

 As I did research for this chapter, I noticed that many discussions focus on how the older generations need to understand the younger generations. That's very shortsighted. It's important for all generations to learn from each other. Each has much to offer.

Embrace the differences

The workplace has become the new melting pot. For the first time ever, four generations of diverse workers can be found chatting near the water cooler or sitting around the conference-room table. The differences between generations are more pronounced than ever before, due to the historical events they've experienced, the new products they've seen introduced, the types of entertainment they've grown up with, the technology they use, and more. Notice the following changes through the generations:

Traditionalists (born between 1927 and 1945) saw the introduction of aerosol cans, atomic bombs, ballpoint pens, bubblegum, car radios, commercial airlines, electric razors, fluorescent light bulbs, FM radios, freeze-dried foods, gasoline-powered lawn mowers, guided missiles, helicopters, instant photography, Laundromats, LEGOs, parking meters, penicillin, photocopying, polyethylene, Scotch tape, stereophonic sound recording, supermarkets, Teflon, and tape recorders.

They like to hear *We respect your experience, We value your perseverance and will reward it,* and *It's valuable for everyone to hear from you what has and hasn't worked in the past.*

Baby boomers (born between 1946 and 1964) saw the introduction of airbags, air conditioning, ATMs, Barbie dolls, bar codes, credit cards, fiber optics, holography, integrated circuits, lasers, light-emitting diodes (LEDs), liquid crystal displays (LCDs), McDonald's, the pill, the polio vaccine, televisions, satellite communications, thermonuclear (hydrogen) bombs, transistors, and Tupperware.

They like to hear *You're key to our success, You're valued here, We need you,* and *You're making a unique and important contribution.*

Generation X (born between 1965 and 1980) saw the introduction of cable TV, cell phones, digital wristwatches, email, fax machines, genetic engineering, handheld computers, the Internet, in vitro fertilization, personal computers, microwave ovens, pagers, Post-it notes, rollerblades, satellite TV, VCRs, and video games.

They like to hear *Try it your way, We have the latest technology,* and *We're not very bureaucratic.*

Generation Y (born between 1981 and 2000) saw the introduction of camcorders, CDs, cell phones, the global positioning system (GPS) for cars, iPod digital music players, DVDs, Google, instant messaging (IM),

LinkedIn, Twitter, Facebook, personal digital assistants (PDAs), the Internet, the World Wide Web, laptop computers, smartphones, texting, virtual reality, avatars, and YouTube.

They like to hear *You'll be working with intelligent and creative people, You and your colleagues can help turn this company around,* and *You can make a real contribution.*

 When we think about the differences between our grandparents, parents, ourselves, our children, and our grandchildren, we can only wonder what life will be like when Generation Z (or whatever we'll call them) enters the workforce.

Apply the golden rules

Regardless of when you were born and where you are on the continuum of these generations, apply these four golden rules to create a positive and all-inclusive environment:

1. **Focus on your commonalities rather than your differences.** All workers (regardless of their generation) want to succeed and feel valued, to enjoy what they're doing, to point in the same direction for the greater good.

2. **Don't attach labels to people.** Labels are harmful and disrespectful. Everyone has something of value to offer, even though they may have different approaches.

3. **Show understanding, respect, and dignity to everyone.** Understanding, respect, and dignity are the most important attributes—regardless of the generation. Never make a person feel he's too young to be of value or too old to fit in.

4. **Never make assumptions.** One size doesn't fit all. For example, go to YouTube and type in "Feed Me Bubbe." You'll see a 21st-century phenomenon—an 83-year-old bubbe (the Yiddish word for *grandmother*)—starring in an online kosher cooking show produced by her grandson. She's received rave reviews from fans of all ages from as far away as China and Africa. Bubbe has a blog and a website, and is on Facebook and Twitter.

Remember what's common to all generations

The companies that thrive (not merely survive) are the ones harnessing the potential of today's rich and diverse multigenerational workforce. Many older workers have said that the younger generation doesn't share the same worth ethic. That doesn't mean, however, that they're not hard-working. The younger generation must balance competing demands. While they may leave work early to attend a child's soccer game, they'll work late into the evening to get their work done.

Younger workers are driving change in the workplace, and what's important to them is now becoming important to older workers as well. Rather than look for differences, focus on the commonalities and needs, and you'll begin to build bridges. Every worker needs:

- Trust and respect
- A challenging and collaborative work environment
- The opportunity to learn and grow
- Dynamic technology
- A sense of social responsibility
- Volunteer opportunities
- A choice of career paths
- Satisfying and rewarding work
- Recognition and appreciation
- A work-life balance.

The needs of traditionalists have changed over the years. They see that things are done differently now that younger people have entered the workforce. Traditionalists may want to continue working past retirement and may be interested in working a four-day week or working from home on some days to ease the commute. Or they may want a flexible schedule to take care of their grandchildren or to take self-enrichment courses.

Boomers also need flexibility because a work-life balance has always been critical. They want to attend their children's sporting events and school plays. Older boomers, sometimes referred to as "the sandwich generation," are often caretakers for older parents and may need time to take parents to doctor's appointments. They also want to spend more time with their families.

Gen Xers are willing to work hard but they want to decide when they work and where they work. Flexible scheduling is one of the smartest benefits you can offer them.

Gen Yers think that freedom and mobility are more important than salary. They may want to telecommute or work in certain parts of the country or world, and they want employers who are flexible enough to accommodate them.

Recruit

Corporate America has always relied on the infusion of young, talented, entry-level people to balance its ranks of valuable employees and managers. Today this tradition is complicated by changes in employment practices and recruiting practices. While many traditionalists and baby boomers once relied on word of mouth, search firms, or the newspaper as the main vehicles for job searching, younger generations rely on online social networks, online job sites, members-only postings for trade associations, and even sites for classified ads such as craigslist. Companies need to adapt their recruitment strategies accordingly, as well as their interview questions.

Put a diverse team in place. This means diverse ages, genders, ethnicities, and skill sets. You must have the right people in place and be ready to shift when the need shifts. For example, if you need someone who's willing to travel on a moment's notice, do you have that person? If customers need help Saturday and Sunday, do you have staff members willing to work weekends at the last minute? Rather than creating a conflict by asking people to do something they're uncomfortable with, select the right mix of people. Members of the older generation are typically more willing to travel and put in the extra time. And if you only have one person of the older generation in the mix, you can't expect him to constantly travel or put in overtime.

Add to the mix that lifestyle and social changes have dramatically affected the motivations, needs, and desires of workers over the past three decades. Younger people crave stimulation, have an unrelenting desire to learn leading-edge technology, want to keep options open, and value a balanced lifestyle. They also consider experience more important than salary.

Interview

The older generations are used to old-style, formal interviews. They wear a suit and tie to the interview and expect to answer more questions than they ask. They wouldn't bring up salary or benefits on the first interview because they wouldn't want the interviewer to think their values weren't in the right place.

The younger generations are able to ask the tough questions from the get-go. They want to know about the technology, what their title will be, where they'll be working, whether they can work at home, and reasons they should join the company. Here are some commonly asked questions from both sides of the desk:

Questions interviewers may ask:
- Describe what an outstanding job would be.
- Describe your ideal work-life balance.
- What qualities do you think are necessary for this position?
- Where do you see yourself five years from now?
- When you have a dilemma, how do you approach it?
- How do you spend your free time?
- After I hire you, what steps will you take to advance from this position?
- Do you believe the concept of "paying your dues" is archaic?

Questions interviewees may ask:
- What benefits do you offer?
- Will I be able to travel outside the country for this position?
- How diverse is your company?
- Can I work from home?
- How high-tech are you?
- Will I advance within the next six months?

- Can I bring my dog to work?
- Can I wear flip-flops?
- Why? Why? Why?

Questions interviewees ask change with economic conditions. During difficult employment periods, for example, candidates won't be very interested in whether they can wear flip-flops or bring their dog to work. They'll be happy to get a job offer. And that goes for candidates of all generations.

Check out Chapter 3, "Get Ready, Get Set, Get a Job" to see how social networking plays into searching for jobs and finding the right people to fill them.

Start onboarding

Onboarding is today's term for acquiring, accommodating, and orienting new hires to your organization. Onboarding programs are like employee Welcome Wagons. Years ago orientations were limited to showing new hires where to find their desks, the bathrooms, the lunchroom, and the supply closets. The adage of older workers, "I learned the hard way—so can you" doesn't fly anymore. Today it's about teaching new hires the ropes so they can hit the ground running.

> ## Leverage appropriate communication methods.
>
> No generation has the best way, the right way, or the only way. Be flexible. A best practice in today's multigenerational workplace is to factor in generational communication preferences. (Check out Chapter 13, "What's the Best Communication Method?")
>
> - Older workers respond well to phone calls, face-to-face meetings, letters, and memos.
> - Younger workers prefer instant messaging and texting.
> - Both use email, which is a common denominator, although many people in the younger generation feel that email is passé.

Older workers

Companies today are looking to attract older workers because of their lifelong expertise and talent. What do they need? (No, not hearing aids.)

- Knowing you value their expertise.
- To be able to contribute to the big picture, because they want to put their stamp on something.
- Training opportunities that include any necessary technical instruction.

Younger workers

Younger workers bring energy, a quest to learn, and a sense of speed. After all, these are the generations of ATM machines, microwave ovens, texting, and everything quick. They are probably familiar with onboarding processes (unless they're right out of school), because they change jobs nearly as often as they change their socks.

- Discuss the technology. Innovation is important to them.
- Deliver information in small chunks because they think in snippets, not speeches.
- Use sound bites, not paragraphs, to break training modules into 15-minute increments. (This works well for any generation.)
- Give them hands-on training so they have an idea of what it's like to work at your company.
- Have answers ready because they question everything and want access to information.

Training isn't limited to an instructor standing up in front of a classroom. It can be blended, just in time (JIT), delivered via webinar, video, podcast, and more. Today's training is more accessible. People can learn at their own pace, anywhere, anytime. Check out Chapter 7, "Virtual Learning: From Enervating to Empowering."

Reward and motivate

When it comes to rewards and perks, there isn't a one-size-fits-all approach for every generation. To keep valued employees, you must be flexible enough to do what's right for each generation and each employee. Find out what people want—it isn't always money. Perhaps someone wants an office with a window, an extra day off, the ability to leave early on certain days, or flexible insurance plans.

In order for your company to be successful, you must understand the value of each generation. Let's take a look at what some companies are doing to keep employees motivated and productive. Some of these ideas cost money, others don't. Remember, it's often the little things that mean the most.

Perks for the older generations

- **Recognition.** The older generations want recognition. This doesn't have to be money. For example, a plaque for their wall can make them feel as if they've won an Emmy.

- **Retirement and financial planning.** Older employees need to start planning for retirement and making good investments. Assistance can include financial and legal advice, volunteer opportunities, new social contacts, and part-time options.

- **Reimbursement for membership in professional organizations.** This contributes to their professional growth and makes them feel valued.

- **Mentoring programs.** People from older generations enjoy mentoring their younger coworkers. Mentoring programs acknowledge the wisdom that older workers have acquired, and they give younger workers a chance to learn from people with years of experience.

My colleague is a partner in an accounting firm that provides some wonderful perks for families during the crunch time of tax season:
- Meals for families one night a week at the office when the CPAs can't get home to share dinner with their families.
- Pizza for lunch when employees work on weekends.
- Dry cleaning pick-up and delivery service.
- A massage therapist who comes to the office two afternoons a week to give 15-minute massages.

Perks for the younger generations

- **Flexibility.** The younger generations typically shun rigid work schedules. If they come in late it doesn't necessarily mean they're lazy or irresponsible. Many young employees work late nights and weekends. They also want to be able to work from home at times.

- **A participatory environment.** Younger workers want to participate in meaningful projects, work in teams, have flexible schedules, report to managers they relate to, and take part in decision-making as it relates to them and their assignments. They were probably raised by parents who valued communication and allowed the whole family to contribute to decisions, from where to go on vacation to what cereal to buy. Trained from an early age, young employees bring decision-making ability to the workforce.

- **Gadgets.** The younger generations crave the latest gadgets. Give them the tools they need, including a laptop or notebook, handheld computer, and connectivity to the mother ship. This will allow them to work from home, put in more hours, and create the work-life balance that is an important component in their lives.

Perks for all generations

- **Fringe benefits, cafeteria style.** These can be as simple as flexible insurance plans. For example, if a working spouse covers your employee, give the employee a cash benefit in lieu of insurance. Provide flexible start and end times so people don't have to sit in rush-hour traffic, can take loves ones to doctor's appointments, and pick up their kids from school.

- **Counseling.** Offer professional help for financing a car or buying a home, paying off student loans, debt reduction, caring for a sick family member, depression, drug or alcohol addiction, and life changes such as divorce or the death of a loved one.

- **Courier services.** These services can pick up and deliver parcels and run certain errands. Imagine the time it saves employees when they don't have to sit in heavy traffic and the extra time they can spend working when they don't have to leave early to run errands.

- **Ongoing training.** This will help employees feel valued and enable them to attain the skills to advance in the company. Yes, the skills you provide are portable, and employees may take them elsewhere. But there are no assurances in life.

- **Company events.** The best places for people to get to know each other and form bonded relationships are outside the usual work environment. Consider organizing lunch-time pizza, a picnic, a party, or other event that is compatible with the culture and interests of all coworkers.

 How do you handle fairness? By tying rewards to job performance. Reward salespeople who generate a certain dollar amount in revenue, teams that finish projects on time and on budget, or people who submit good ideas that save the company money.

When you give positive feedback, put it in writing. This lets the recipient read the feedback over and over, each time feeling the glow. When you give constructive or negative feedback, give it verbally. It's important to provide the recipient an opportunity to discuss the situation.

Be sensitive to reporting structures

Companies are experiencing breakdowns in communication between managers and subordinates. These breakdowns go right to the bottom line as hidden costs in the form of missed opportunities, delayed results, and high turnover. Remember the age-old adage, "If you want respect, you must give respect."

Younger generations reporting to older generations

Members of the older generations must leave their egos at the door and not expect the younger generations to feel compelled to conform to their styles and preferences. The following do's and taboos will help you to create the followership you need to be an effective leader:

Do's

- Take the time to explain the business logic behind requests that might be challenged when compliance isn't a choice.
- Encourage collaboration. The younger generation takes teamwork seriously and works well in groups.
- Treat younger workers as peers and colleagues, not subordinates and interns. Involve them in decision-making processes.
- View questions as opportunities to revisit the appropriateness of how you're doing things.
- Encourage younger workers to communicate openly. Learn their motivations. Understand what they like about the workplace and what they'd like to change. Find out what matters to them.
- Make your language, tone, and body language reflect your intentions.
- Provide challenging work opportunities.
- When delegating, delegate both the assignments and the freedom to determine how to achieve the outcome.
- Offer increasing responsibility as a reward for accomplishment.

- Acknowledge a job well done.
- Spend time getting to know the people you lead as individuals and learn their capabilities.
- Provide ongoing training and learning opportunities.
- Maintain a focus on the work, but be personable.
- Mentor and collaborate on plans for career development.
- Have a sense of humor.
- Talk the talk and walk the walk!

Taboos

- Being close-minded. Even though something has worked well in the past, welcome new ideas and let the younger generations be the contributors they see themselves to be.
- Looking at the world through your own lens. Allow for flexibility.
- Using words such as *Read my lips . . . Just do what I'm asking . . . Make it easy, just do it my way . . . I don't care how it's done somewhere else, this is how we do it here . . . I've been down this road before, this is the way we need to do it . . . Do what I'm telling you and stop questioning.* Words or expressions such as these marginalize younger workers.
- Engaging in a monologue instead of a dialogue.
- Talking down to or bullying people.
- Encouraging unethical, immoral, dishonest, or illegal behavior.

 Somewhere towards the end of your career, you'll be the older worker and need to be open to what the younger folks bring to the table.

Understand a different perspective. People from younger generations bring a different perspective. For example, if a younger person finishes his work at 3:00, he may want to leave early to attend his child's school performance. If that creates tension, ask yourself:

- What values are in conflict?
- What's the need to have this person remain until 5:00 on that day?
- Are these repeated requests that deviate from the norm?
- What other types of allowances and concessions can be made?

- What's the impact of saying *yes* and saying *no*?
- If I do this for him, will others expect the same treatment?

The caveat, of course, is to have sufficient staff and a good generational mix that will allow you to be flexible and still satisfy any coverage requirements.

Benefit from a team-approach mindset. The younger generation grew up with strong team bonding. They learned that when everyone does their best, everyone is rewarded. In school sports, for example, everyone got a trophy for (at least) participating. In the big leagues, known as the business world, only the winners get the trophies. This is a major paradigm shift. It helps to understand it.

 Check out Chapter 12, "Go, Team!"

Older generations reporting to younger generations

Many older workers are electing to take life a little easier or step out of management or leadership roles to spend their remaining working years as individual contributors. If you're one of these people, you may report to a younger manager who's less experienced than you. Remember, it's what you've done in the past that allows you to make a valuable contribution.

If you feel your expertise is being challenged, what's your first emotion? What's your reaction? In your new role, you need to craft and define the framework for your responsibilities and how you choose to work going forward.

- Get clarity on the purpose of your role. Why does it exist?
- Create relationships with younger managers that work for you and for them.
- Get clarity on the boundaries of your role and honor those boundaries.
- Anticipate that the majority of your communication won't be face to face.

Check your ego at the door. If you're in a situation where your needs and values aren't aligned with the rewards and you opt not to adapt, you may be a misfit (to put it bluntly). If you can adapt, remember that you're selling your time for money. If you can't adapt, the situation will drain your energy and everyone's around you—both at home and at the office.

Before this happens, leave of your own accord. Don't worry about not being employable. You will find a more suitable opportunity.

Continue learning. Every moment represents a choice on how you act and behave. Don't become obsolete. If you want to be taken seriously, shift and adapt. Learn the latest technologies and methods. Although you may not grasp things relating to technology as easily as younger people, you can learn by being shown. Ask your manager about taking courses, getting a technical mentor, and anything else that will help you continue to grow. As a young manager, do you feel you'd rather put your training dollars into your younger workers? If so, remember this: Younger workers may move on as soon as the next opportunity comes along. Older workers tend to remain loyal.

 I read with great interest an article called "How to Train the Aging Brain" in the Education Life section of *The New York Times* (December 12, 2009). (My brain is aging fast enough. I don't want it to get any older than it has to be.) Author Barbara Strauch discussed the importance of continuous learning and mental challenges to keep brain connections in good condition and to continue to build brain pathways.

Is the traditional employer/employee relationship in peril?

As employers seek new ways to curtail costs and make the employment relationship more flexible, they have increasingly relied on *contingent workers*. These are temporary workers, such as freelancers and consultants, who get no benefits and are paid by the hour or by the project. According to the US Government Accounting Office, in the early part of the 21st century nearly one-third of the workforce consisted of contingent workers. And forecasters predict this number will rise dramatically. Many younger people today see their resumes as a combination of contingent jobs, with engagements often happening simultaneously.

Many contingent workers, especially those who work from home offices, complain about the solitary nature of their jobs. As the contingent workforce grows, so does the number of new clubs, guilds, and unions that provide various levels of socialization and benefits. Social networks are also filling the void for many contingent workers.

Establish a plan for succession

Succession planning determines how the management of a company will be passed down from one person or generation to the next. Lines of succession are nothing new. They date back to the earliest Chinese dynasties and continue today with the monarchies in European and other countries.

For a long time people thought of succession planning as applying to family-owned businesses only. With traditionalists and baby boomers retiring in record numbers, however, succession planning should be a proactive part of every company's strategic plan. Effective succession planning ensures that competent people are ready and available to move into key positions when the current generation of managers leaves the company.

Even if your company has younger managers at the helm, these people can leave for other opportunities, die, get kidnapped by aliens, or leave for a host of other reasons. Without proper planning, employees can take the breadth and depth of the company with them when they go. The company risks losing key expertise and business knowledge, damaging client relationships, and interrupting the flow of business. Without a viable plan, you will waste time, effort, and resources recruiting and training replacements.

Privately owned and corporate businesses

All business leaders should prepare themselves and their successors as part of a contingency plan. It isn't merely about replacing the top-level executives. The plan should cascade down to whatever levels the company deems appropriate to ensure a seamless transition. Here's what good succession planning will do for your company:

- Give you a cadre of well-trained people, alignment of future needs with the appropriate resources, defined career paths, and more strategic recruitment.

- Supply an ongoing stream of managers who are constantly reviewing, questioning, and distilling policies and procedures.

- Earn the company a reputation for being an exciting and challenging place to work. This will help you attract and retain the best and the brightest employees.

- Empower your workforce and retain good employees.

Succession planning takes time and money, so be sure you have a commitment from the big guns at the top. Engage your top performers early in the process so it doesn't appear to be a clandestine activity going on behind closed doors. Let your top performers know what's in their future so they remain loyal to your company.

 If your successor will come from inside your company, take the time to teach him the ropes so you're ready to move up when the time is right. If the person succeeding you will be a first-time manager, provide him with the management and technical training he'll need to be successful.

What keeps companies from succession planning? Many don't have an internal program in place, and the time and resources to develop one present obstacles. The day-to-day running of any business can overpower the most well-intended planners. Traditionalists are staying healthier, living longer, and working longer, and boomers are either postponing retirement or moving into new careers. Neither group wants to feel as if they're training successors so they can hand over the reigns and be pushed out the door.

Family-owned businesses

If you own and manage a family business, deciding who will succeed you when you step down is paramount to the continued success of your business. You must decide to whom ownership and management will be transferred, how they will be transferred, or if you should sell.

Get your family involved. Remember that ownership and management aren't the same thing. You may have a family member who wants to be the owner but doesn't want to manage, a family member who wants to own and manage, a family member who wants to own and manage but isn't qualified. Realizing that everyone may not be entitled to an equal share, how do you divvy things up? Involving everyone in the planning is the best way to keep peace and harmony now and after you're gone.

Get outside help and start early. Five to ten years in advance of your anticipated departure isn't too early. Involve your attorney, accountant, and financial planner. Additionally, consider engaging a succession planning company that can facilitate the process and work with your family as well as with the succession issues. There's also software available if you have an uncomplicated process and want to plan the succession yourself.

Train your successor(s). This is like any apprenticeship. Your successor must learn all aspects of the business, from the bottom up. The earlier your successor starts, the better prepared he'll be to jump in when the time is right.

 Despite your best efforts, conflicts may arise that you're unable to resolve. If the people involved are valuable to the organization, bring in a professional to offer guidance. This can be someone from Learning and Development, Human Resources, or an outside consultant. Seeking help will let the people involved know they're important and you take their concerns seriously.

We all have differences. Men of different ancestries, men of different tongues, men of different colors, men of different environments, men of different geographies, do not see everything alike. Even in our own country we do not see everything alike. If we did, we would all want the same wife—and that would be a problem, wouldn't it?

—Lyndon B. Johnson, 36th president
of the United States

Chapter 5

Synergy Across Cultures

In this chapter

- *In their own words*
- *Lessons learned*
- *Benefits of a cross-cultural workforce*
- *Communication tips*
- *Different gestures*
- *Traveling abroad*
- *Large-scale faux pas*
- *Helpful hints*

Immigration is what the United States is all about. Except for Native Americans, most of us can trace our ancestors back to other parts of the world. As the population changes, so does the American workforce. Let's celebrate these differences. It would be a very dull world if we were all alike. Each group contributes new threads to the tapestry of our national culture, in languages, food, religion, values, priorities, learning styles, clothing, body language, gender roles, family structure, and more.

In their own words

A lot has been written about cross-cultural environments from the viewpoint of Americans. I wonder, however, how often natural-born Americans step back to appreciate the challenges, frustrations, emotions, and often amusing experiences immigrants have faced (and continue to face) as they try to assimilate. Following are the unique experiences of people I talked with who came to work and live in the United States. Enjoy their stories for the depths they bring and the lessons we can learn. (These stories are in their own words; I just made a few grammatical changes.)

Jurgen (from Germany)

I was working for an American company with offices in Germany and spent three years in the American facility. I received a warm welcome, with no exception. Colleagues were very helpful, and conversations about technical matters were perfect. I did have a few challenges:

- The word *problem* is a no-no. There's just a *challenge*. The word *problem* seems to be restricted to life-threatening conditions only.

- If a customer had a technical problem (I stick to that term), I was told the problem was *contained*. I still do not understand what that means. Either the problem is solved or not.

- Project meetings always had a large attendance, 20 to 50 people, but only a few contributed. Most just sat there.

- What I hated most was the arrogance that German company top managers displayed. After their visits to the US, I needed a long time to reestablish the good relationships I had before. (That same situation applied to US top managers when they visited our German location.)

- I had a problem with working in a cubicle with no natural light. In Germany it is a law that every permanent office working place has daylight access.

- Women's lib gave me some experiences. At one time I opened a door and a woman was walking behind me, so I held the door open for her. She rudely yelled at me, "I can open the door myself." So I just slammed the door in her face.

Robin (from Germany)

When I came to this country from Germany I was looked at as a "Nazi." My first challenge was and still is to meet as many Americans as possible to talk about my country, to let them know that not all Germans are/were Nazis. We are all human beings. *And in each country there are good and bad people.* I met a lot of Jewish people who did not like me at the beginning and became good friends of mine after long talks and disagreements. I have a few memories of Jewish families I became friendly with through strange circumstances, and they learned to have a better understanding of us Germans.

My second challenge was this: Most Americans have always been aware of Germans being good mechanics, keeping good records, and making sure everything is accurate. When I came to this country I was shocked when I read letters and other documents written by Americans and saw numerous mistakes in their writings. In Germany we were taught grammar until it came out of our ears. We disliked our English teacher because he was very strict, but after coming to the States, I thanked him a thousand times for making sure we would always spell, talk, and write correctly.

My third challenge (if you want to call it that) was to learn how to smoke and chew gum at the same time. There was a lady in my department who was always chewing gum and smoking at the same time. I thought it absolutely fascinating the way she made noise and blew bubbles at the same time with a cigarette in her mouth. I succeeded after a while, and it drove my family crazy. But I was very proud of myself. This was my way of becoming "more of an American."

Ari (from Israel)

I grew up in Israel in an orthodox Jewish family. I went to an all-boys school and after my bar mitzvah [for religious reasons] I wasn't allowed to have any physical contact with females, except for my mother, sisters, bubbe [grandmother], and later my wife and daughters. That meant no hugging, kissing, or even shaking hands. When I moved to the United States, I started my own consulting company. I dressed in regular street clothes but still wore my yarmulke [skullcap]. I found it uncomfortable to shake the hands of women because of my religious upbringing. I do shake women's hands to be polite, but it's uncomfortable for me.

Suzie (from Taiwan)

I'd like to share my challenges with you when I came to America. I'm from Taiwan. The challenges I have faced are as follows:

English → I learned English from my Taiwanese English teacher, so the pronunciation was way off from standard. I spent so much time to correct it and am still trying.

Religion → Here the churches are about Jesus. Mine are Confucian and Taoist temples.

Background → I was taught the more humble you are the better you are. Here you have to express yourself (speak out), otherwise people won't understand you or respect you.

Culture → I've learned to accept gay marriage, living together, and having kids without marriage.

Dress → Showing your body here is very wild. I've been taught the more you cover it the safer you will be.

Brigitte (from France)

I joined a large corporation at my first job here in the US and there were already a significant number of expats in the workforce from many countries. I found it to be a very cosmopolitan atmosphere, and I fit right in.

April (from China)

My Chinese name is Chunlin, and I adopted the American name April. Chunlin means "forest in the spring," and my parents wanted me to be lively, just like the trees that bloom in the springtime. When I lived in China I got my degree in English language and culture and I taught English there. So I was very well prepared to live in the US. I did find some cultural differences and was prepared for most of them.

- People here talk very fast and it took me a while to get used to that.

- In China it's commonplace to ask people personal questions about their families, their children, and their income. It shows that you care about them. In the US information like that is very private.

- People here are much more direct. In China we wouldn't disagree with you to your face because we wouldn't want to make you feel bad. So we try to show disagreement through body language and in other discreet ways.

Jianyao (from China)

Unlike most of the Chinese who come to this country as college or graduate students, I had many years of working experience in China. This was extremely beneficial towards my smooth transit into the different cultural environment. Actually I feel very comfortable with the working and social surroundings, particularly in the New York metropolitan area where amazingly you can meet all kinds of different people. *My understanding of human nature is that all people, no matter what race, color, where they grew up, what language they speak, do essentially share many more similarities in their deep heart than the differences shown on their outside surface.*

Am I saying there are no differences at all? Not really. There is something you may call cultural differences. For instance, Americans usually offer compliments on what you have done well. The Chinese don't, because there is always room for improvement. So do not jump up and down when your boss tells you "you did good job." He may just mean it is not too bad. In contrast, if someone Chinese said that you can do a much better job then don't be upset.

Another apparent difference is how people address others. Here in the States, everyone uses everyone's first name even if you are the president of the company, a respected professor, or a grandpa. You don't want to do this in China unless you're talking to a sibling or a friend of the same or a younger generation. Otherwise people will think you are rude and disrespectful. To the older generation or to people in higher positions, you better say their title first, then their last name, for example, Uncle Chen, Aunt Lee, or Manager Chou.

Aman (from India)

Having grown up in India, I came to the US with a very strong English accent and English lingo. I tried very hard to lose the accent and the lingo because I wanted to blend in. But I realized I wouldn't blend in, because I look different. I wear a turban. People at work were very welcoming, but I noticed that people in my neighborhood didn't talk to me—maybe because I am different.

My life in the US was good until 9/11 when I became the victim of a hate crime. The perps saw my turban and mistook me for a Muslim. As they victimized me, they shouted "Go back to Osama bin Laden." As a result, I'm now part of an organization based out of New York called Sikh Coalition. This is a nonprofit organization born in the aftermath of the bigotry, violence, and discrimination against New York City's Sikh population following the terrorist attacks of 9/11. We go to schools to help children understand Sikh traditions, such as why we never cut our hair and why we wear turbans. The goal of the organization is to teach understanding and tolerance.

Robert (from Russia)

People (from the former Soviet Union) who I am familiar with face challenges in language barriers along with "small talk" and professional jargon (slang). In my office, they tolerate my English skills, and I'm trying hard to improve. When I present an article for publication in a professional journal, the editor-in-chief assigns a dedicated editor to work with me closely.

Simon (from England)

Going out for "a pie and a pint" at lunchtime is somewhat of a tradition during the working day in England. Across the nation, many white- and blue-collar workers find themselves in the local pub at lunchtime downing a pint of their favorite beer. I'm sure there are some who follow one pint with a second or even a third, no doubt to help them slide through the afternoon with ease, though hopefully not literally! When I joined the ranks of Corporate America in San Francisco at the launch of my professional life here, I was welcomed with friendliness and helpfulness as I started to navigate my way around the different work culture to the one I was familiar with in London, England.

So, on my first day at work in the US, after my boss took me out for my "welcome lunch" along with my new work colleagues, I was promptly called into her office for a "chat." She told me, in no uncertain terms, that drinking alcohol during the workday would not be tolerated, and that the beer that I had ordered at lunch would, under normal circumstances, not be acceptable! Oh boy, that put away those work afternoons sliding by with ease, and I wondered what other little cultural work gems I was to discover.

As it turns out, I have never been pulled up on such a cultural nuance again, but working in Corporate America has shown some other more painful differences to those I was used to in dear old England.

The most challenging one that I still struggle with on occasion is that of the "work-life balance." The thought of having 2 weeks of vacation a year to reinvigorate and rejuvenate oneself after the stresses and strains of 50 weeks of work, seems a tall order. In my native England, and even across the rest of the (European) continent, where 6 weeks of vacation is typical, this thought would make people break out in a sweat. It would likely incite some to civil unrest.

The issue gets compounded as those 40 hours of work a week, for which one is contracted and paid, routinely end up being closer to 60 hours or more, spilling over into evenings and weekends. I have often been asked to work late or finish some work up over the weekend to meet a timeline, with no consideration given to other plans I might have. After numerous times missing a theatre performance, being late for a friend's birthday dinner, or disappointing myself or someone else as I allowed work to dictate my personal time, I realized I had to set my own boundaries. This hasn't always been easy, as one can often be perceived as not being a "team player," and with the knowledge that it's far easier to be fired in the US than in the UK, I have seen the softening of my own boundaries.

There is a reason why the US is one of the wealthiest countries in the world! Americans spend much of their time at work being productive. Even when they are not there, they are often talking about it, and when they are not talking about, they are thinking about it. I am almost always asked, within a minute or two of meeting someone new, what I do for a living. This extends to social settings also, and trying to use British humour to make light of this invariably falls flat. Satire is often misunderstood by Americans. Warning: Do not use satire in the workplace!

Fortunately I enjoy my work so I don't mind answering those questions sometimes. I do wonder how easy it ends up being for those of us working in the US to genuinely turn off from our heavily defined work roles, and turn our attentions to the many other rich facets of American life. Now I *know* it's possible with that wonderful American "can-do" attitude that puts many other countries' work culture to shame.

Muhammad (from Iran)

I came to the US from Iran to attend a university. After I got my PhD I got a job at a biotech company and got along well with all my colleagues. Then 9/11 hit. A few people started making comments in front of me about those [blank, blank] Muslims, and they made other comments that made me feel uncomfortable. Things quieted down after a few months, but every time there's an international terrorist incident, I notice people looking doubtfully at me. I came here with my family and we all became American citizens. I don't know why people don't trust my loyalty to this country. I love America.

Nalini (from India)

My biggest challenges were the American accent and colloquialisms. Although I knew English, I was unfamiliar with most phrases commonly used in a work setting including something as simple as "wrapping up a meeting." Even if I knew the phrases, they meant different things to me. I also noticed that people would ask questions that did not sound like questions to me. I often did not realize I was expected to respond until people looked at me. I frequently asked people to repeat things they said just to understand the accent but did not have the nerve to ask people to explain colloquialisms. After hearing them a few times, I interpreted what they meant by the context. I also thought people spoke a lot, not always related to the topic of discussion. I sometimes struggled with trying to figure out if the speaker was saying something important. My communication issues made me feel intimidated, and I didn't socialize or talk to anyone much, other than on work issues. I think people thought I was unfriendly, but I'm not.

Also, *time* was a problem at first. In India, maybe because the roads are so crowded, getting places on time isn't easy and isn't important. Instead of saying when we'll arrive, we say when we'll leave. I had to train myself to be places on time because that's important here.

Keiko (from Japan)

I came to the US to work for a pharmaceutical company that my Japanese company purchased. Everyone was very nice to me. A lot of the US managers made many trips to Japan, and I'm always glad to be able to help them understand Japanese customs and traditions.

Marita (from Sweden)

I was in for a few shocks when I came from Sweden to work in the US as a graphic designer. My first job was at a small advertising firm that had a small in-house staff and a lot of "on-the-road" salespeople. The owners were very unprofessional, immature, and downright mean to people (very stressful place to work). The two owners would brag about how they had reduced someone to tears or how they had turned down job applications because they weren't Caucasian or weren't good-looking enough. I found that if you looked good and didn't oppose anything, then you were less likely to be harassed or fired. Good work ethics were not valued at all—this was something I had a very hard time understanding, I still don't understand it, and I didn't stay there very long.

I interviewed at a publishing company and was told that I could "work with the other women and it would be less technical." That didn't sit too well with me. I did take the job though, because it came the closest to my job in Sweden, but even there I felt that it was a little sexist (starting with my job interview).

The overall biggest difference I notice in the US would be the sense of teamwork, or rather, lack of teamwork. It doesn't seem like the employees work together as a team. It's more like what can I do to get ahead instead of what can we do together as a team to make our product and services better. *I definitely felt less valued as an individual at any of these jobs than I ever felt at any of my jobs in Sweden.*

Akram (from Pakistan)

When I arrived here I had a very hard time finding a job. I had a bachelor's degree in chemistry from Pakistan, and every company I contacted wouldn't accept my degree. I went to college for four years in the United States and got a degree in chemical engineering. After that I got a job quickly. I had no problem fitting into the workforce. I got an entry-level job with low pay, but over the years I worked my way up to a nice job.

John (from Darfur)

I'm one of the "Lost Boys of the Sudan." I saw my mother and sisters raped and killed and my brothers and father killed. I was wounded and still walk with a bad limp. They thought I was dead or they would have killed me too. I came to America after I lived in a camp in Darfur for several years, and I changed my name to John. A charity brought me here and found me a place to live with three other boys from my country. After all the horrors we went through, we were shunned by the black community. We didn't fit in because we were too black.

The people from the charity were very nice. They helped me get into community college, and I work in a grocery store stocking shelves to help pay for my food and clothes. The people there treat me pretty well. Many white people have invited me to their homes for Thanksgiving and Christmas, and I like that. When I finish my education, I want to move back to Darfur to help the people who are still there. Maybe I'll even find some living relatives.

Tony (from Johannesburg)

I came to the US from South Africa when I was in my twenties and made an easy transition. That happened for two reasons. English was my first language. Also, students are educated to know that because of ongoing political strife in South Africa, they'll be leaving the country when they graduate. So I came to the US, had a family, and became an American citizen.

It wasn't until my children were in their teens that I learned I wasn't "an American." My son came home from school one day and announced, "Dad, I'm going to teach you how to be an American. First, you can't put your cars in the garage. The garage has to be full of junk. Second, you can be so innocent about us. We smoke and drink, so don't think we're innocent. American fathers already know that about their kids." Then when my son went off to college and my wife and I visited him, he said, "American fathers always empty their pockets before they leave." So is that what it takes to be an American, I wondered?

Claudio (from Brazil)

I'm trying hard to learn better English and take classes after work. The people I work with know I'm taking English classes, and one person always corrects my English. I get embarrassed, but I guess she's just trying to be helpful.

In my country we stand close together when we speak. In the US I found out that people like what I learned is called "more personal space." That worked for me because I work with someone who smells of garlic. Now I have a good reason to stand far away from her. Maybe I give her too much personal space, but that's OK.

Lessons learned

The United States has always drawn its strength and greatness from diversity, so let's learn from the challenges and experiences of others. Although the stories told by the people I interviewed are a brief sampling, they contain many lessons we all can learn from as we strive to make others feel welcome.

Check stereotypes at the door. When we're faced with uncertainty, our defenses seek to create some order or system from what we observe— that's stereotyping. Many stereotypes have been passed on by our families; others we've created ourselves. Stereotypes are destructive because they lead to invalid conclusions and rob people of their individuality. Always remember, you're communicating with a person, not a stereotype.

Never correct people's English unless they ask you to. People whose English is a second language are trying to speak correctly, and you make them feel uncomfortable by correcting them. If they say something offensive because of a problem with translation, mention it privately. Otherwise, offer corrections only if the person has asked. (Even people whose English is a primary language make mistakes.)

Allow for cultural differences. People from different cultures often have challenges in terms of language, etiquette, business practices, and behavior. While these differences must be respected, a company has an obligation to manage communication so that everyone can work together productively and cohesively.

Learn about gestures and other body language. Learn all you can about honoring personal space, gestures, cultural norms, eye contact, facial expressions, hand gestures, and the like. There's more about gestures later in this chapter.

Don't judge books by their covers. People may act certain ways because of cultural differences or experiences. For example, although some people may naturally be shy and reserved, others may just feel out of place or intimidated. Seek them out. Get to know them. Be inclusive.

Be kind to everyone. You don't know what troubles people have had in the past or continue to have in the present. Be kind and respectful to everyone you meet.

Avoid humor and jokes. People in many Western cultures try to build immediate rapport through humor, but this is not universally appropriate. Many cultures don't appreciate humor and jokes and may see laughter in business as a sign of disrespect.

Many great communicators have been embarrassed by botched attempts at humor. In August 1984 while running for reelection President Ronald Reagan was testing the microphone before his weekly address on National Public Radio. He joked, "My fellow Americans, I'm pleased to tell you today that I've signed legislation that will outlaw Russia forever. We begin bombing in five minutes." Although he was not on the air, the soundtrack was leaked to the press. The international community didn't appreciate the joke.

Sequence your message strategically. People from different cultures encode and decode messages differently. This increases the chances of being misunderstood. Recognizing this, think of a logical order in which to present information.

Be attuned to timing. People in the US are concerned with schedules and the consequences of arriving late and missing deadlines. People from other cultures are more blasé about time.

 And let's not forget the lesson learned from Simon (from England). Every American company should give its employees a six-week vacation.

Benefits of a cross-cultural workforce

Some Americans have an elitist attitude and believe that everyone in the world should speak English and do things as we do them here. To truly build international relationships, we gain a tremendous advantage by interacting with people who speak a variety of foreign languages and are knowledgeable in those cultures. Diversity—from multigenerational to multicultural—can make companies more productive and profitable. Here's how:

Gain new insights. People from other cultures often view issues differently. Because there's rarely only one way of doing something, getting varying input can be a tremendous advantage in working towards a common solution.

Develop new approaches. American businesses have long held that "time is money" and "getting to the bottom line" is paramount. Many

---

Other differences that must be recognized

- **Making decisions.** Decision-making styles vary across cultures. In the US, we tend to make quick decisions but implement them slowly. In many other countries, decisions take more time but implementation is fast.

- **Sharing information.** In the US, we tend to share information—sometimes too much and too often. In many other countries people parcel out information on an as-needed basis.

- **Participating.** In cultures where hierarchy is king, subordinates tend to wait until senior managers have spoken. They don't contradict senior managers or they risk disharmony. In other cultures, people enjoy lively give-and-take debates and jump in when appropriate.

other countries contend that time is for building relationships. They believe it's critical to get to know each other before doing business. What difference do you think that approach would make in your business?

Communication Tips

If you think back to when you were learning a foreign language, you may have found it very frustrating when trying to converse with a native speaker. You stumbled over your words as you tried to "think" in that language, and the other person spoke too quickly for you to understand. The following are tips for speaking and listening with people for whom English isn't a primary language:

Speaking

- **Speak slowly and enunciate clearly.** Speaking slowly and enunciating clearly may make you easier to understand. This holds true for speaking in different parts of the US as well. Many years ago I was facilitating a workshop in the South and could see early on that people's eyes were glazing over. I realized I was speaking at my rapid New York pace and had to slow way down. Once I did, the workshop was awesome.

- **Don't shout.** Many people speaking to foreigners think that shouting will make their message clearer. It doesn't; it only makes it louder.

- **Use silence correctly.** In some cultures silence before a response is a sign of thoughtfulness; in other cultures it's a sign of hostility. Learn what's appropriate for the people you interact with.

- **Avoid slang.** Although you should avoid slang in any business situation, foreigners will have an especially difficult time understanding slang, idioms, jargon, and the like. For example, some American expressions, such as "Get out of here!" or "No way!" can lead to misunderstandings and hurt feelings.

- **Be clear with questions.** Avoid questions that start or end with "isn't it?" or "aren't you?" Questions like that don't exist in many other languages and can be confusing to people whose English is a second language. For example, if you say "You're coming, aren't you?" the person may not know whether to answer yes or no. If

Prepare your website and blog for international audiences.

Here are a few tips to bring the world to your website and blog in a welcoming way:

- **Make sure your website or blog will load in 10 seconds.** Only a small portion of the world's population has access to broadband, and people "click out" if downloading takes longer than that.
- **Select your colors carefully.** Your color selections must speak to an international audience. (In the US, for example, white symbolizes purity; in many Asian countries it symbolizes death.) Black text on a white background is the easiest combination to read and is universally acceptable.
- **Be careful with sounds.** Different cultures will react differently to sounds. If you need music or sound, give people an easy way to turn the sound off.
- **Include your international calling code.** This will make it easier for worldwide customers to call you. (Add it to your letterhead and business cards as well.)
- **Be aware of regional distinctions.** If you do e-commerce and have fields for people to populate . . .
  - Remember that Zip Codes exist only in the US.
  - Include a field for the province or other regional distinctions.
  - Provide shipping carriers that handle overseas shipments.
  - Include a currency converter so people know what they're spending in their local currency.
- **Be attuned to numbers.**
  - Other countries use the metric system. Consider including a converter.
  - Most countries use a 24-hour clock.
  - Date formats vary. The US uses mm/dd/yy. Other parts of the world use yy/mm/dd or yy/dd/mm.
- **Optimize for international language search engines.** Find a good web developer who can help you accomplish this.

you end a meeting with "Is this a good place to stop, or should we continue?" the two questions asked together may be difficult to understand.

- **Summarize what you heard.** To make sure you understood the message, rephrase it as simply as possible.

Listening

- **Listen without interrupting.** Americans are often regarded as being too talkative. People from other cultures may view too much talking as disrespectful. Be an attentive listener.

- **Be patient.** When someone is trying to put an idea into words, listen patiently because it may take her longer than it would take you.

- **Ask for something to be repeated.** If someone repeats something and you still don't understand it, ask if she could phrase it differently.

- **Don't be offended.** When someone says something you may take the wrong way, realize it may not have been meant like that.

 Establish one spoken language in a company. It's impolite for a few people to have a conversation that others don't understand, even if it's around the water cooler.

Different gestures

Very few gestures are universally understood and interpreted. What's acceptable in the US may be rude, offensive, or obscene in other cultures. Here are a few gestures to be aware of:

Respecting personal space

- Generally, Germans, Chinese, and Japanese appreciate more personal space than Americans, and Americans prefer more personal space than Latin Americans, Italians, French, and Middle Easterners.
- Americans, Canadians, and Europeans often like a field of about 18 inches. If you get too close, they'll feel that you're "in their face" and may try to back away.
- People living in densely populated environments tend to require less personal space.

Shaking hands

- The French like a soft, quick handshake.
- The Japanese keep the arm fully extended and often bow.
- Middle Easteners place their free hand on the forearm of the other person.
- Orthodox Jewish men will not shake the hand of a woman.

Giving the thumbs-up

- In the US and Europe, the thumbs-up means something good.
- It's considered rude in many Asian and Islamic countries and a sign of displeasure in Spain.

Putting your hand up to indicate "stop"

- In some Asian countries this means you are requesting permission to speak.

Placing your hands on your hips

- In the US and Europe, placing the hands on the hips conveys an open and confident posture.
- In many Asian countries, it's considered arrogant.

Beckoning with your index finger

- In the US, this means "come here."
- In the Middle East, the Far East, Portugal, Spain, Latin America, Japan, Indonesia, Vietnam, and Hong Kong, it's insulting or even obscene.

Keeping your hands in your pockets

- In Finland, Sweden, France, Belgium, Indonesia, and Japan, this would be considered impolite in a business meeting.

Smiling

- Although smiling is universally understood as a pleasant gesture, in parts of Asia people smile when they're confused, angry, or embarrassed.

Forming a circle with your fingers

- In the US this means "okay."
- In Japan it means "money."
- In France it means "worthless" or "zero."
- In Brazil and Germany, it's obscene.

Making the V sign

- This is a sign of victory in the US.
- In Europe, when your palm faces away from you, the V sign means "victory," but when your palm faces toward you, it means "shove it."

Showing the soles of your shoes

- Americans often cross their legs and let the soles of their shoes show. (Be sure your soles don't have holes.)
- In Thailand, Japan, France, the Middle East, and Near East this is a sign of disrespect because you're exposing the lowest and dirtiest part of your body.

Passing an item with one hand

- In the US, that's the custom.
- In Japan it's considered rude to pass an item with one hand; two hands are the custom.
- In many Middle Eastern and Far Eastern countries you pass with your right hand only; your left hand is considered unclean.

Nodding your head up and down

- In the US this is a gesture for "yes."
- In Bulgaria and Greece it's a gesture for "no."

Bowing*

- Many Asian cultures bow in addition to or instead of shaking hands. The Japanese bow with their hands at their sides, and the depth of the bow reflects the level of respect being shown.
- Cambodians bow with their hands in front of their chests.
- Thais bow with their palms together and fingers outstretched.

*Bowing protocol is in dispute even at the highest ranks. On a visit to Saudi Arabia, President Obama bowed down to the Saudi king. On a visit to Japan, he bowed down to the emperor. Critics said the president should stand tall when representing the US overseas; otherwise he appears deferential. Others came to Obama's defense, saying his greetings expressed goodwill between nations that respect each other.

Traveling abroad

When you leave the United States you're an ambassador. The image you create will affect how people you meet will view all Americans. Following are a few ways to make your visit more pleasant and create a positive image:

Consider appropriate topics of conversation. It's appropriate to discuss art, sports, the weather, and other topics that don't have historical, political, or sensitive implications. Don't ask business acquaintances about their families unless you know them well. Don't discuss money or the cost of living.

Different cultures have different customs around who addresses whom, who has the right or duty to speak first, and the proper way to conclude a conversation.

Learn about the host country. Think about the beauty or accomplishments of your host country so you can comment on them. Become familiar with dress codes. Be aware of current events and be sympathetic to problems. Understand religious taboos.

Be attuned to and respectful of holidays. If someone from another country planned to visit you for business and requested a meeting on December 25, you'd probably think of her as naive. After all, she didn't bother to learn that December 25 is a national holiday and businesses are closed. When you visit another country, don't be naive. Learn about the holidays.

Learn some of the language. Take an adult education course, tune into radio stations, listen to CDs. You're not expected to be fluent, but aim to be conversational. At least know a few key terms such as *thank-you, hello, goodbye, good morning, good evening, I'm sorry, I don't understand, just a moment, chairman, president, vice president,* and *director.*

Mind your table manners. It's critical to display proper table manners.

Following are a few things to keep in mind:

- Europeans hold their forks with the tines down, and they don't switch their knives and forks after cutting. If you want to eat like a European, hold your fork in your left hand and your knife in your right to cut your food. Still holding your knife in your right hand, use it to push your food to the back of your fork. (Lefties, do the opposite.)

- In many Asian countries, people eat with chopsticks. Although you can request a fork and spoon in most restaurants, your hosts will appreciate your effort to use chopsticks. (You won't need a knife because food is generally cut into small pieces.)

 Outside the US tips are often included in the bill. In some countries tipping isn't expected and may even be insulting. Check before you go.

Bring plenty of business cards. If you travel a lot to a particular country, have your name, company, and address printed on the reverse side in the language of the host country. If you travel to that country infrequently, hand-write your name, company, and address on the reverse side in the native language. Offer the card with the native-language side showing.

Take appropriate gifts. When bringing a gift is appropriate, learn what is and isn't acceptable. For example, you wouldn't give liquor to a strictly observant Muslim. The following are reasonably safe for any country:
- Classical, jazz, or folk music
- Coffee-table book from your state or region
- Crystal, china, or porcelain
- Local handicraft or nonperishable food item
- Pen-and-pencil set with refills
- Something that reflects your colleague's special interest or hobby.

A word of caution . . . When you're in another country and venture out to see the area, exercise reasonable precautions, just as you would in the US. Stick to well-trafficked and well-lit areas. (Ask the hotel staff to advise you.) If you carry a shoulder bag, place it diagonally across your body. Secure a clutch under your arm. And carry your handbag so it faces inward, away from the road.

 When I travel to a foreign country, I always take something from the hotel that has its name and address. I've gotten lost a few times and wasn't well versed in the language. Each time I was able to show a cab driver a matchbook or stationery from my hotel and was brought "home."

Large-Scale Faux Pas

Even people who should know better create human international follies. You could fill a book with them, but here are just a few:

- In 2009 Secretary of State Hillary Clinton presented Russian Foreign Minister Sergei Lavrov with a mock "reset" button inscribed with the word *peregruzka* to symbolize the resetting of the Russian-American relationship. Mr. Lavrov pointed out that *peregruzka* means "overcharged," not "reset." Despite the embarrassment, they smiled and pressed the button together in front of the cameras.

- In 1995 Bill Richardson, a member of the House Intelligence Committee, innocently crossed his legs during a meeting with Saddam Hussein. The sole of his shoe was exposed, and Hussein left the room. In the Arab world, showing the soles of one's shoes to someone is a sign of contempt.

- A map released in Microsoft's Windows 95 did not show all of the disputed Kashmir territory as part of India. The Indian government took offense, and Microsoft had to quickly remove 200,000 copies of Windows 95 from the shelves.

- In the 1960s Pepsi-Cola ran a "Come alive with Pepsi" campaign. It was Pepsi's battle cry as the company expanded its markets. The slogan was mistranslated in Taiwanese as "Pepsi brings your ancestors back from the grave."

- When Chevrolet introduced the Nova, the company failed to realize that in Spanish *No va* means "Doesn't go." Is it any wonder the Nova sold poorly in Spanish-speaking countries?

- When touring Australia in 1992, President George H. W. Bush gave the V-for-victory sign to the crowd from his limousine. He later learned that in Australia, the V sign means "Up yours, mate."

 I had two of my own miscommunications:

Before my trip to China, I took a course in conversational Mandarin. (Communicating in Mandarin is heavily dependent on verbal intonations.) I stepped into an elevator with a Chinese man. He looked at me as if to ask, "What floor?" I answered in Mandarin, intending to say, "Seventh floor, please." He started to chuckle and told me in English that I had just invited him to my room.

When I was in Japan, I wanted to get a Japanese massage. The hotel didn't allow women in the massage area, so I called for a massage in my room. At the appointed time there was a knock on my door. I opened the door dressed in a short robe. A startled man looked quizzically at me. To make a long story short, when I phoned the desk to schedule a massage, the desk clerk misunderstood me and thought I wanted to send a message. So he sent a messenger to my room. Trying to communicate in English with someone who barely spoke the language could have gotten me into trouble.

Helpful hints

Following are some helpful hints for a successful trip:

Confirm all reservations in advance. Verify all airline, hotel, car rental, and other reservations one or two days before your departure. And make sure to pack your tickets and all confirmation numbers.

Call your credit card companies. Decide which cards to take on your trip and let the companies know the places you'll be traveling. Otherwise, for your protection they may cancel your card on the spot when you try to use it.

Contact your mobile phone provider. Standard mobile phones typically don't extend to other countries. Find out about purchasing an international cell phone for emergency use or having your phone temporarily configured for foreign service.

Prepare a well-thought-out itinerary. Make the best possible use of your time, keeping in mind your goals and relative priorities. Don't try to overload your schedule and rush from one meeting to another. If possible, build in an extra day after you arrive to deal with jet lag.

Get local currency. Exchange some US dollars for local currency before you leave the US or at the airport. This will get you started with cabs and anything you may need immediately. Respect the country you are in. Avoid rude-American comments such as "This is just like Monopoly money."

Check your overseas medical insurance coverage. Ask your medical insurance company if your policy applies overseas, and if it covers emergency expenses such as medical evacuation. If it does not, consider supplemental insurance.

Know where to get medical assistance. Before you leave, contact the International Society of Travel Medicine Clinic Directory to locate healthcare professionals in the area you'll be staying.

Have a current passport and visa (if needed). Make sure you have a signed, valid passport, and a visa, if required. Fill in the emergency information page of your passport. Leave copies of your itinerary, passport data page, and visas with family or friends, so you can get critical information if you lose or misplace these valuable documents.

Use emergency contact information. Consular personnel at US embassies and consulates abroad and in the US are available 24 hours a day, 7 days a week, to provide emergency assistance to US citizens. Contact information appears on the Bureau of Consular Affairs website at http://travel.state.gov. You can also contact the Office of Overseas Citizen Services in the State Department's Bureau of Consular Affairs for assistance with emergencies at 1-888-407-4747 if calling from the US or Canada, or at 202-501-4444 if calling from overseas.

 It's very fitting to end this chapter with an unedited story written by a very special woman. It warmed my heart, and I hope it will warm yours as well.

From India to America — with love

by Simerpreet Kaur

"I really, really want to go to the US. Can you take me?" This was a question that my maternal uncle who lives in New York always heard every time he came to visit me in India. "I'll pack you in my luggage and take you one day," he always said with a laugh.

May 19, 2002, was a day like any other when I went to the temple. I did not realize this day would become a turning point in my life; this day will remain a beautiful memory today and for the rest of my life. I met my husband for the first time. I got engaged to this stranger who I had never seen and not known anything about . . . except for his zodiac sign and musical interests. All I saw for the rest of the week were people running around to make arrangements, trips to the boutique for dresses, and the list of exotic dishes to be put on the menu. Exactly one week later, May 27, 2002, I was Mrs. Amandeep Singh.

I guess my destiny was not done with so much excitement. Twenty days later I was flying 11,000 miles away from the place that I had called home for 21 years to a place that I will be calling home at least for the next few years. On June 15, 2002, I was in the United States, an unknown land, amongst unknown people and above all with a person almost unknown to me. Nevertheless, I was excited to explore this new world! A world where cherries are the size of lemons and lemons are the size of oranges when compared to ones we get in India. A world where people say hello to anyone they meet as opposed to people in India who say hello to only those they know. A world where the culture was so exhilaratingly different from India that it took quite a breather for me to be able to adapt to it.

For the first few days I was enthralled. Everything seemed nice and beautiful. Slowly, as life came into a daily routine and reality started kicking in, I seemed to be feeling more lost than at home. Who cleans the house? Who washes the car? Who waters the plants? Who picks up the trash and, most importantly, who does the dishes? Back home in India, it was a custom to have a maid who did the dishes, a sweeper who mopped the floor, a driver who drove you to school or work and cleaned the car, and a gardener who made sure that the lawn was mowed and plants were watered. These were a few of the numerous questions I was asking myself. I had no clue which one to ask first of my husband. When I did, to my surprise (or rather, to my horror!!) his reply was "We do." For a moment, the word *We* didn't make sense to me at all. Did he mean *Us* by *We*? Nah!! He was just joking or teasing me.

All day long I was contemplating this thought and it was probably written all over my face when he came back from work that evening. "Don't worry . . . we'll be able to manage everything together," he said. The more he used plurals such as *We, Us* and *together* . . . the more I dreaded being here. How in the world could I touch the trash can and mop the floor? This was meant for the household help! What in the world was I thinking?? Is this what they call American life? I guess it was, and now I had to deal with it. I told myself I could either sulk all day, pretend to be rich and spoiled and make my life miserable, or I could get on with it and start doing the dishes before the pile reached the kitchen cabinets. Well . . . as wise as I was (since I won't be getting a maid anyway), I chose the latter. We cleaned the house, mopped the floor, and took out the trash, and before we knew it, I was a pro in household work!

As life moved on (and as I was already an expert at doing chores), I wanted to explore further. I was desperately looking to use my skills better when opportunity knocked on my door. A friend of ours had opened up a new store and the person he hired had to leave due to an emergency so he needed some help. "I would love to help!" was my immediate response. Excitement was back in my life, but along with all of this excitement came the overwhelming fear of the unknown. I didn't know how to talk to people. I hadn't had a chance to actually interact with anyone besides my husband's friends. Nevertheless, now that I was used to a variety of challenges, I accepted this one too. The first few days, I felt shy and withdrawn. To my pleasant surprise, it was the same friendliness and casual nature of the people here, which I had first found so different from the reserved and formal nature of Indians, that made me overcome all of my inhibitions.

As the days passed, I became more and more confident in being out and working my way through the daily hassles of life. I now had something more to look forward to every morning as I woke up. I was independent, optimistic, and self-assured, and before I knew it, I was working at a company that was the perfect environment to prove that I could do much more. A place that gave me the opportunity to show my skills and become the positive person I have come to be. Last but not least, it introduced me to people who make me feel that I'm not away from the home that I left four years back.

Four short years have passed. Or maybe four long years that taught me so much about life. I can surely say that I have come a long way. A long, good, bad, depressing, enlightening, encouraging way. Believe it or not, I'm glad I did. I'm glad I did not give up, and whether I live in the US or go back to India, I will always give credit to these precious years of my life; correction, OUR life! I have finally fallen in love with the plurals too :-)

Buy old masters. They fetch a better price than old mistresses.

—William Maxwell Aitken, British newspaper publisher

Chapter 6

Martians and Venusians

In this chapter

- *Fact or myth?*
- *Don't walk on thin ice*
- *Clothing communicates a message*
- *Use gender-neutral terms*
- *Avoid sexual harassment*
- *Challenges of working moms*
- *Socializing (dating) outside the office*

We learn gender influences early in life. Boys are made of "snips and snails and puppy-dog tails." Girls are made of "sugar and spice and everything nice." Since the beginning of time, men and women have had clearly defined roles and responsibilities in the workplace and in the home. Men brought home the bacon; women cooked it. Everyone knew what was expected of them based on tradition and perceived strengths and abilities.

During World War II, while men were off serving their country, women became predominant in the workforce. When the war ended, women went home and started rethinking their roles. In the 1960s, women began entering the workforce in record numbers and a new era was ushered in. All of a sudden, all the old rules went out the window.

Although women have made great strides in the workplace, statistics continue to show that very few have broken the notorious glass ceiling. A study of women business leaders by the University of California, Davis, found the following:

- Women hold 9.4 percent of the 3,283 board seats in the 400 largest public companies in California, up from 8.8 percent in 2006.
- Almost half—47 percent—of the companies have no women directors and more than a third—34.3 percent—have only one.
- Women hold 11.6 percent of the companies' 2,878 top executive offices, down slightly from 11.7 percent in 2006.
- Half—49.8 percent—of the companies have no women in executive offices and less than a quarter—21.9 percent—have two or more.
- Only 3 percent of the companies have a woman serving as CEO.

Fact or myth?

Every race, culture, civilization, and society shares two commonalities: men and women. Each gender often acts out old scripts. The user manual for men teaches them not to ask for directions. (Perhaps that's why Moses roamed the desert for 40 years.) The user manual for women teaches them not to change flat tires. (Maybe that's why we have the American Automobile Association [AAA]).

Studies continue to show that men and women are different in the way their brains are wired. Experiments by Dr. Matthias Riepe, a neurologist at the University of Ulm in Germany, found differences in the way men and women process information about the spaces around them. One difference involves the hippocampus, a banana-shaped structure on each side of the brain that plays an important role in memory and navigation. Both sexes used the right hippocampus to negotiate space. However, only the men also used the left hippocampus. By contrast, the women also used the right prefrontal cortex, whereas the men did not. What does this mean? Essentially, that women relate better to landmarks and to directions such as "Turn left at the bank on the corner and make a right after the pharmacy." Men relate to geometry, such as the kind you find on a road map. These differences don't imply that either gender is superior or inferior. It implies that each is specialized.

Be aware of different styles of communication.

Men and women need to be aware of each other's communication styles in order to avoid misunderstandings. All styles are necessary to deal with the complexity and diversity of today's workplace. When you recognize and appreciate the differences, you can capitalize on them to create harmony in the workplace and home. According to many studies, here's some of what makes us different. These are tendencies, not absolutes.

Women	Men
Women soften their demands and use phrases such as *If you don't mind* or *don't you think?*	Men are direct with their requests.
Women ask questions to show interest in another person and to cultivate a relationship.	Men ask questions primarily to gather information.
Women are relationship-oriented.	Men are task-oriented.
Women often hold conversations that are labyrinthine.	Men tell the facts and move on.
Women process aloud.	Men process internally.
Women talk in-depth about the context of disputes and the nature of their relationship with the other person.	Men use a rational, linear, and legalistic approach.
Women become quieter during a conflict and try to find ways to keep the relationship intact.	Men become louder and more competitive.
Women hold grudges.	Men let it go and move on.
Women solve problems by focusing on what works for the group and talking through issues. They don't need to take credit for the solution.	Men see problem-solving as an opportunity to demonstrate their competence and the strength of their resolve.
Women consider the connections between problems. They may have difficulty separating problems from their personal experiences.	Men tend to focus on one problem at a time and can easily separate themselves from their problems.

Vive la différence. Although there's a lot of speculation about the impact of nature versus nurture, there are more similarities between the genders than there are differences. Both men and women can be active, adventurous, and swashbuckling, as well as quiet, cautious, and reserved. Much of what makes us human is the same.

Don't walk on thin ice

First and foremost, don't always feel as though you're walking on ice that's thinner than filament. Do what's respectful and what comes naturally and comfortably.

Guidelines for men

Here are the answers to some questions men typically ask:

- **Walking.** When you walk down the street with a woman, walk on the curb side. If you're in a dangerous neighborhood, walk on the side of the buildings.

- **Elevators.** When entering an elevator, go first and hold the door open for the women. When exiting, let the person closest to the door go first.

- **Coats.** Offer to hang up a woman's coat.

- **Dinner checks.** If a woman invited you to a meal, let her pay the check if she offers. If you invited her, pay the check yourself. It's appropriate to split the check if it makes you both more comfortable.

- **Conversations.** Never exclude a woman—or a man—from a conversation. Avoid cussing and foul language.

- **Terminology.** A female isn't a *chick, girl,* or *dame.* She's a woman. (So never refer to "the girl who works in the mailroom.")

Guidelines for women

Here are the answers to some questions women typically ask:

- **Doors.** Open your own doors and hold the door open for others who follow you in. If a man holds a door open for you, be gracious and thank him.

- **Foul language.** Don't participate in off-color jokes or use foul language just to fit in with men.

- **Femininity.** Professionalism and success have nothing to do with femininity. If you wear a feminine dress or a striped pantsuit and a tie, you're still a woman. Always look and act the part of a professional and don't expect any special treatment because of your gender.

- **Compliments.** Many compliments are meant sincerely, and you should take them as such. For example, if you dress conservatively and suddenly come to work in a flowery dress, chances are someone will notice and comment. If a male coworker says you look especially nice, he probably means it as a compliment. Just thank him.

- **Anger.** When women become angry, they can sound shrill. When you want to get your point across, moderate your voice and speak directly and firmly.

 Women shouldn't get hung up on words in the English language that appear sexist. For example, many contain the word *man* such as *woman, manhole, manpower,* and others. During the early years of the women's movement it was suggested that we use *personhole* rather than *manhole.* This is political correctness run amuck.

Clothing communicates a message

Look around at what people in the workplace are wearing and check with Human Resources for official guidelines. No dress code can cover all contingencies, so use good judgment. Here are some suggestions:

Guidelines for men and women

- Never wear clothing that's wrinkled, stained, tattered, torn, sloppy, or too tight.
- If you aspire to get a promotion, mimic how your superiors dress.
- When traveling for business, wear appropriate clothing. For example, if you're staying at a hotel with a pool women shouldn't wear bikinis and men shouldn't wear Speedos.
- Always be discreet. There's a big difference between casual dress, dress-down Fridays, and oh-my-gosh.
- Spend your money wisely and buy clothes that complement what you already own.
- Although trendy clothes create a buzz, they're usually not appropriate for business.
- Don't be swayed by what people wear on television; it often doesn't translate to real life.

Guidelines for men

- **Suits.** Although suits aren't worn as often as they once were, you should have at least one in black, navy blue, or gray. Pinstripes are fine as long as they're understated and professional. Your jacket should fit well and not restrict movement or strain at the buttons. Single-breasted suits are always fashionable; double-breasted suits go in and out of fashion.

- **Shirts.** Long-sleeve shirts are dressier and more appropriate for the office than short-sleeve shirts. It looks more professional to roll up the sleeves on a long-sleeve shirt than to wear a short-sleeve shirt. Stick to traditional solids and stripes.

- **Ties.** In conservative industries, men still wear ties. It never hurts to overdress slightly. If you're going to a function and are unsure of the dress, wear a tie. You can always remove it.

- **Belts.** Belts are required unless you wear suspenders or braces. Keep the buckle simple and match your belt to your shoes.

- **Socks.** Wear dark socks that match your pants. They should be long enough so you don't display your hairy legs when your legs are crossed.

- **Grooming.** If you have facial hair, make sure it's well groomed. Cut your fingernails to a reasonable length and make sure they're clean. (As obvious as the latter may be, it's surprising how many men have dirty fingernails.)

Guidelines for women

- **Fabrics.** Consider materials such as silk, cotton, acrylic, nylon, cashmere, wool, linen, twill, khaki, and corduroy. Avoid velvets, satins, and chiffons.

- **Skirts and dresses.** Don't wear skorts, sundresses, spaghetti straps, gym clothes, or T-shirts to work. The length of your skirt or dress should be long enough so when you sit down you don't expose too much of your thigh. If you're wearing a skirt or dress with a slit, make sure the slit is no higher than the back of your knee.

- **Pants.** Wear solid, conservative colors or muted stripes. Pants should be tailored and not too tight or too flowing.

- **Jackets.** Consider a conservative jacket or blazer as a way to get respect and show power.

- **Shoes.** Wear shoes that are comfortable and appropriate for your outfit. Avoid very high heels, flashy athletic shoes, thongs, flip-flops, slippers, and any shoe with an open toe. If you wear boots because of rain or snow, change to shoes when you arrive at the office.

- **Undergarments.** Bras and panties should support your figure and not be on display. That means your panty line shouldn't show through your pants and your bra straps shouldn't be visible.

- **Scents.** Avoid perfume and heavily scented soap, hair spray, or hair gel. Many people have allergies.

- **Accessories.** Scarves, belts, and simple jewelry add a nice flair to any outfit. Don't, however, wear bangle bracelets, dangly earrings, or other jewelry that makes noise or is distracting. Save the bling for after hours.

- **Hats.** Hats and head coverings aren't appropriate for an office unless you wear them for religious or cultural reasons.

- **Grooming.** Wear makeup that looks natural, and remember that less is more. Avoid extremes in nail polish. That means no garish colors or snappy decals.

 Check out the *Encyclopedia of Associations* for information on organizations you may consider joining and supporting. Involvement in a group can be a springboard to your own career development. And consider playing golf. A lot of business is conducted on the golf course.

Use gender-neutral terms

One way to show respect for both sexes is to use gender-neutral terms, such as the ones that follow:

Instead of ...	Use ...
clergyman	member of the clergy
fireman	firefighter
insurance man	insurance agent
layman	nonprofessional
mailman, postman	mail carrier
newsman	reporter
policeman, policewoman	police officer
repairman	service technician
spokesman	spokesperson
steward, stewardess	flight attendant
stock boy	stock clerk
waiter, waitress	server
weatherman	meteorologist
workman	worker

Avoid sexual harassment

Sexual harassment occurs when unwelcome, sexually oriented words or actions create an abusive or hostile work environment or interfere with an employee's ability to perform his job. Both men and women can be victims of sexual harassment. Although male-filed claims used to be rare, they have grown steadily since 1998 when the Supreme Court ruled that men are protected from harassment at work under the Civil Rights Act of 1964.

Even a poorly chosen joke or off-the-cuff remark intended to be funny can raise issues. Employees who commit sexual harassment may be subject to severe disciplinary action, including the notorious pink slip or a lawsuit. Sexual harassment may include any of the following:

- Threatening someone with termination, demotion, or intimidation for refusing sexual advances
- Commenting on a person's physical attributes
- Telling racy jokes
- Using demeaning or inappropriate terms and nicknames
- Discussing sexual activities
- Ostracizing someone on the basis of gender
- Using crude or offensive language
- Touching someone unnecessarily or inappropriately
- Using suggestive gestures

- Gawking
- Displaying sexually suggestive objects, pictures, posters, or other visual materials.

If you're the victim of sexual harassment and the offense is minor, try handling it yourself. Tactfully tell the person you're offended. If the offender refuses to take the hint, bring the situation to the attention of your supervisor. If the offender is your supervisor, take the issue to a higher level. If all else fails, talk to someone in Human Resources. (If the offense is serious, however, go directly to your supervisor or HR.)

 Don't look for innuendoes in everything you hear. Some things are said innocently and without malice.

Challenges of working moms

As more and more families have dual incomes, spouses and partners are sharing more of the household responsibilities. In most cases, however, women still assume the lion's share of caring for the home and the children. Working women (and men who are single parents) face a multitude of challenges and have incredible demands on their time, energy, and resources. In addition to handling a job, they must do laundry, shop, clean the house, help kids with homework and take them to their activities, and hopefully find a little time for themselves. Yes, you can be a working mom and successful professional. Talk it over with your spouse or partner. Be direct. Lower your standards. Negotiate. Be flexible. Following are some of the ways in which women can conquer the challenge:

Get a good night's sleep. Aim for seven to eight hours of sleep each night so your body can restore itself. It's harder to deal with emotional and physical stress when we don't get enough sleep.

Examine the flow of your day. Keep a log to track the flow of your day. Learn where the bottlenecks are. For example, do you spend time looking for your keys or glasses each morning? If so, pay attention to your habits and make sure you always put things in the same place.

De-stress your mornings. The evening before, arrange everything you need for the morning for yourself and your children. This means your clothes and the children's clothes, backpacks, lunches, and anything else that can cause time delays. Follow the same routine each day so you and your children know what to expect.

- Get up before your children to sit quietly and have a cup of coffee.
- Get showered and dressed before they wake up.
- Let your children do as much themselves as they're capable of doing. This may include brushing their hair and teeth, pouring their own cereal, and putting their dishes in the sink.

Organize errands. Organize and prioritize errands to minimize your running-around time. Plan a route that takes you past the supermarket, post office, dry cleaner, bank, and any other places you need to stop. If you don't accomplish everything on one trip, most of your errands can probably wait until your next trip.

Find a family-friendly workplace. More and more companies are making accommodations for work-life balance. Some companies offer job sharing, flextime, onsite child care, maternity leave for moms and dads, chill-out zones for watching TV or relaxing, parent-and-child exercise classes, and much more.

Don't try to do it all. Don't try to be supermom. You'll cheat yourself and your family.

- If you have a spouse or partner, discuss sharing domestic chores. As your salary contributes to the household income, this is only fair.
- If you can afford to, hire someone to clean the house, do the laundry, and help with the cooking.
- Arrange for a neighbor or friend to help out with the children. You can reciprocate in some way.

Leave your work at the office. Even though we live in a 24/7 society, there's no reason to be connected constantly. You deserve quality time with your family and they deserve quality time with you. Leave tensions at the office and don't vent your frustrations on your innocent family.

Spend quality time with your family. Your family needs to realize that while your work is important, they're more important. There's an old saying, "No man [or woman] ever went to the grave wishing he had spent more time at the office." Make the time you spend with your family quality time. Eat dinner together and talk about what each of you did during the day. Ask what made them happy, frustrated, or angry. Encourage them to talk about their feelings.

Create quiet time. Scarcity of time can make you forget you're an important person. Take at least 10 to 15 minutes each day to have quite time. Not only do you deserve it, it will keep you emotionally and physically healthier. Turn off the phone. Play relaxing music. Exercise. Meditate. Read. Take a bath. Get a massage.

Socializing (dating) outside the office

People spend more time at the office than anywhere else, so it's a natural place for single people to meet. Without the opportunity for employees to develop office romances, Bill Gates might still be a lonely bachelor. He met his future wife, Melinda French, when she worked at Microsoft. Unless your office has a policy about not dating coworkers, there's nothing wrong with single people meeting, dating, falling in love, and marrying. Be aware, however, of the pros and cons.

Pros

A poll conducted by the Society for Human Resource Management (SHRM) revealed that 55 percent of the people involved in office romances eventually marry. You already know what the other person is like, so there are fewer surprises. You have an understanding of each other's work schedules, so there should be no surprises about having to work late or travel often. If you're discreet, you don't let your personal relationship interfere with your professional responsibilities, you don't flirt at work, you don't send romantic emails, and you don't come back from a long lunch looking disheveled, an office romance may be right for you.

 The longer you can keep your relationship away from the wagging tongues of coworkers, the better it will be for the growth and healthy development of the relationship.

Cons

Studies also show that 58 percent of executives view office romances as unprofessional, and 38 percent feel they end in disaster. Many more believe that they wreak havoc on morale and may lead to sexual harassment lawsuits. Also, too much togetherness can spell disaster. If the relationship sours, it can be awkward and may result in one of you being asked to leave the group or the company.

Here are a few comments from couples who've had successful office romances that led to marriage:

- Make sure you're not violating company policy.
- Don't get involved unless you intend to be in the relationship for the long haul.
- Many of our coworkers knew we were attracted to each other before we did. That was a shock.
- Don't mix business and pleasure during working hours, and that includes lunchtime. Begin your date when the workday is over.
- Office romances are no different from romances between people who live in small, remote villages. It's likely that they'll date each other because they see each other regularly. If a romance doesn't work out, they still have to coexist.
- Keep the relationship as discreet as you can for as long as you can. That means staying out of the office closet and off the conference table.

Part Three

Virtually Speaking

TODAY'S VIRTUAL EVENTS have become multifaceted and highly interactive. Technologies have advanced to the point where virtual events look and feel amazingly like their live counterparts. Those hosting virtual events have an economical way to accommodate large numbers of attendees. Those who participate can learn, attend meetings, and tour trade shows right from their desks. Predictions are that the term *virtual events* will be replaced with the broader term *collaboration applications* as industry and technology change, morph, and adapt to market needs.

If you give a man a fish, he will eat once; if you teach
him how to fish, he will eat for the rest of his life.
—Chinese proverb

Chapter 7

Virtual Learning: From Enervating to Empowering

In this chapter

- *Learning and development trends*
- *Asking the right questions*
- *Storyboarding*
- *Blended learning*
- *Videos*
- *Virtual classrooms and webinars*
- *Virtual coaching*
- *Podcasting*
- *Just-in-Time Training (JITT)*
- *Measuring success*

The increased demand for learning new skills and competencies more quickly, combined with drastically reduced travel budgets, is forcing more organizations to seek out virtual learning and development (L&D) solutions to replace or supplement traditional stand-up classroom instruction. Fortunately, the advent of technologies has made it easier to implement distance-learning solutions. When designed thoughtfully, virtual learning programs can be at least as effective as classroom instruction. When they're not, participants are likely to tune out and miss important learning opportunities.

Learning and development trends

Today's workplace is ushering in a new way of thinking. During the early part of this century the focus was on compliance-driven learning. Now companies are broadening their thinking because of the need to develop human capital effectively and efficiently. They understand that the current workplace is all about interaction. The following are some of the trends we're seeing now and can expect to continue:

Instructor-led in the classroom. Despite the evolving trend towards the virtual classroom, a survey from the *Chief Learning Officer* Business Intelligence Board released in 2010 reports that "forty-one percent of learning executives indicated they continue to use classroom training." Many companies still favor classroom training because it provides for the building of relationships that are an inherent part of the workplace culture.

Virtual classroom. This type of learning will continue to expand as technology is becoming increasingly more sophisticated, allowing more interaction than ever before. Some virtual classrooms are instructor-led; others are self-contained. Virtual learning has become so widespread that schools are starting to offer MDE (Master of Distance Education and E-Learning) degrees.

Video. To make a low-end video, such as those on YouTube, all you need is a camera and some basic editing savvy. High-end videos are expensive, but the cost can be justified for certain types of training. You can make videos highly interactive by including pauses where learners need to interact or perform certain tasks.

Social networks and social learning. Social networks are creeping into companies and many have embraced Twitter within their own organizations. Others have created homegrown internal social networks. In addition to instant messages (IM) and chats, social networks offer ways for people to get information and answers to questions quickly.

3-D. The gaming industry has popularized 3-D avatars, and greater use of 3-D for training isn't far behind. With computers and projectors, learners can engage 3-D technology to see places and things in a real-life context.

Podcasts. With the prevalence of MP3 players, podcasts are gaining a strong foothold in the training arena. When implemented properly, podcast training can be very effective. Be on the lookout for video podcasts, often referred to as vodcasts.

Simulations and virtual labs. These are used mostly in technical and scientific learning. You can make a quick simulation, drop it into the learning challenge, and participants experience a simulated lab.

Suitcase programs. A curriculum is created and delivered by local trainers to offices around the globe. Sometimes one or two facilitators travel with the program. Some suitcase programs incorporate video and videoconferencing.

Expertise location. This refers to a group of techniques whereby subject matter experts (SMEs) within a company are called upon to share their special knowledge and skills.

Mentoring. Mentoring programs are adding a lot of zest to L&D as companies are onboarding new hires, bridging the multigenerational and cross-cultural divides, transitioning people into management roles, and spearheading succession planning.

Mobile. Mobile technology (also called m-learning) is still evolving for training purposes. Presently, what may work well on one mobile phone may not work well on another. However, that's rapidly changing.

Informal training. It's long been known that people learn best where they spend the most time. Informal training occurs when learning is integrated into everyday interactions. It can involve (but isn't limited to) mentoring, guest speakers, ad hoc training sessions by staff members, books, and other reference materials.

 Cloud computing is a trend worth watching. A cloud is a wireless network that offers coordinated Internet service. Cloud providers deliver applications online that are accessed from a web browser. Cloud users can "rent" computing services as needed, and they don't have to pay for overhead, data centers, or other resources they aren't using. When demand increases they pay for more services; when demand decreases they pay for fewer. Even companies with robust revenue streams are focusing on cost efficiencies.

According to Eric Bloom, President of Manager Mechanics, "Cloud computing allows companies to implement new software technologies very quickly. For example, if the training department of a large corporation wants to provide online training classes to its employees worldwide, it can simply contract with a training firm that provides the needed classes via the web. Then, once the contract is signed and the user login IDs are created, the training is ready for use."

Asking the right questions

Learning is all about acquiring new knowledge, behaviors, skills, values, preferences, and understanding. Virtual learning can be highly successful when the content and facilitator are engaging, there's interaction, and the learner is taught transferable skills.

Design a program from the learners' perspectives. In order to design a program for maximum results, it's best (when possible) to interview the person who requested the training, the person responsible for the outcome, and the learners themselves. (Preparation is similar to designing a program for face-to-face training, with the added considerations of technology and logistics.) Start by exploring the five basic questions as they relate to your learners: *Who? What? When? Where? Why? How?*

The following are generic questions, many of which you can use as a starting point. Most of the questions can be answered by the people you interview. The rest you will answer yourself based on your findings.

Who ...

- Are my primary learners? (managers, peers, subordinates, clients, customers, potential customers, or others)
- Are my secondary learners? (percentage for each group, if available)
- May have had their arms twisted to register?

What ...

- Are the demographics?
- Is their level of understanding?
- Preconceived ideas may they have?
- Barriers are there to understanding?
- Acronyms, jargon, or abbreviations will they need explained?
- Keeps them up at night?
- Materials do I have that will address these concerns?
- Props, slides, or handouts should I prepare?
- Stories can I share that will add value?
- Questions will people need answered?
- Type of equipment will they have?
- Do I want them to do, think, or feel?

- Is the best delivery medium?
- Parts of the goal can be fully achieved through training?
- Remaining issues need to be addressed to meet the overall goal?

When . . .

- Is the best time to deliver the session?
- Should I send prework (if applicable)?

Where . . .

- Can learners get more information?
- Will the learning take place?

Why . . .

- Are they attending?
- Am I qualified to deliver the training?

How . . .

- May they resist?
- Will I engage everyone?
- Can learners apply this information?
- Can I best reach them?
- Can I encourage learners to interact with each other?
- Can I enhance the learning experience?

Remember that people learn in different ways.

The old expression "different strokes for different folks" certainly applies to learning. People must learn in their own styles and at their own pace, or the best training will wash over them like rain washes over a nylon tent. Here are some different learning styles:

Visual: Pictures, images, and spatial understanding.

Aural: Sound and music.

Verbal: Spoken and written words.

Kinesthetic: Body language and doing.

Logical: Logic, process, step-by-step instruction, reasoning, and systems.

Social: Interaction with other people or groups.

Solitary: Self-study or working alone.

For example, academic, scientific, and technical people tend to be logical. They relate to processes, steps, reasoning, and systems. People with backgrounds in business and law are verbal and answer-oriented. They respond to the spoken and written word—but the information needs to be delivered quickly. Creative people are visual.

With all the learning options available today, it's easier than ever to tailor training programs to meet your needs. If you don't have the benefit of knowing your audience, *mix it up* so there's something for everyone.

- Will the company or learners measure the return on investment (ROI) or the return on expectations (ROE) for the short and long term? (Learn more about ROI and ROE later in this chapter.)

Identify the questions your learners will want answered. Now make a list of questions you think your learners will want you to address in the presentation, or questions they may ask you themselves. These questions will be specific, not generic. For example, they may ask:

- **Who** can I call for more information?
- **What** preexisting knowledge or training do I need to be successful?
- **When** will this be available?
- **Where** is [name of item] located?
- **Why** are you recommending this approach?
- **How** will we measure success?

Engage the senses. When delivering training, hone in on what people see, hear, think, taste, and/or feel. For example, you may say "I was at a company picnic yesterday and can still smell the charred steak beaded with hot, red juices as it sizzled atop the smoky, hot grill."

 Some studies maintain that we remember 10 percent of what we read, 20 percent of what we hear, 30 percent of what we see, 50 percent of what we hear and see, 70 percent of what we say, and 90 percent of what we say and do. Follow up to see if the skills taught were retained and used.

Storyboarding

Storyboarding is where it all begins. A training program without a storyboard is like a cart without a horse. A storyboard consists of a sequence of panels depicting what to *tell* and what to *show*. It's used to outline scripts, ads, presentations, and training.

Your training session, like all stories, will have a beginning, middle, and ending, in logical sequence. Perhaps the beginning can highlight the reason for the training. In the following example, notice how the presenter used a story to turn a *blah* opening into an *a-ha* opening for a training session on safety:

Blah: "It is the basic policy of JSC [Johnson Space Center] to take all practical steps to avoid loss of life, personnel injury or illness, property loss or damage, or environmental loss or damage."

A-ha: "One hypergel technician didn't follow requirements. By leaving the tool untethered, he burned himself and caused two employees to spill a caustic battery electrolyte on their hands. That technician could have been you."

Preparing a storyboard

When you create a storyboard, you prepare to connect with your learners, see the continuity of your message, identify gaps, discover if you told too much or too little, and identify how to supplement the words for greater understanding and retention. Here's how to set up the panels:

1. Using your word processing software, create two columns.
2. Populate the left column, "Tell," with highlights of the information you'll convey—not your full text, just keywords and thoughts.

3. Populate the right column, "Show," with descriptions of the visuals or activities you'll use to support your points. (Learn more about options to show in Step 2 on pages 127–128.)

Remove the Power from PowerPoints.

In their book *Speaking Skills for Business Careers,* Dennis and Paula Becker state: "Your audience attends [joins] your presentation to get information from you. You are not a human aid. You do not aid the visuals. The visuals are there to aid you." This is true whether your presentation is live or virtual.

Don't default to PowerPoints because you think that's what people expect. They may expect a PowerPoint presentation because that's what they've grown accustomed to, but it may not be what they need to learn the task at hand. Here are two cases in point from storyboarding workshops I've presented to clients. Each person who attends is asked to bring in a presentation to prepare or (if nothing new is on the immediate horizon) one she has completed.

High-tech company: An in-house trainer was tasked with training a group of colleagues on the use of new software the company had just purchased. She brought in a thick printout of the PowerPoint presentation she intended to present, and I thought, "Ouch!" She had laboriously captured screenshots of all the screens and pasted them into slides. I asked her why she wasn't planning to demo the software in real time. She thought for a moment and said, "PowerPoints are part of the corporate culture here, so I've always done training that way." By the end of the workshop she had *eliminated all her PowerPoints* and created a dynamic storyboard of talking points to accompany a live software demonstration. She sent me an email after the presentation to let me know it was very successful.

Large hospital: A department head was going to demonstrate to a group of doctors a new piece of equipment the hospital had purchased. His plan was to prepare a PowerPoint presentation. I asked him why he wasn't planning to bring the doctors into the room where the equipment "lives" and *show* them. Once again, he mentioned that PowerPoints are widely used at the hospital, so he immediately went into PowerPoint mode. He ultimately prepared a storyboard of talking points and delivered the presentation with the machine being his only prop.

✓ Later in this chapter you'll learn how to design PowerPoints when they are needed to enhance your words.

Step 1: Start by populating the "Tell" column. Refer to the questions you outlined to help determine what to include. The following is the beginning of the storyboard for a virtual email workshop.

Title: Emails that Mean Business™

Tell	Show
(Easy-listening music with slide while people are joining the virtual classroom.)	
• Good morning (afternoon) . . . • Thanks for joining . . .	
Opening: Email is a serious business communications tool and you should treat it with the same respect as any other document you write. • Mention etiquette of ordering spaghetti at a business dinner.	
Poll: What's your biggest pet peeve about email? • Give directions for filling out poll.	
Do's First, change the subject line when replying to a message. Discuss why subject lines can be a problem.	
And so forth . . .	

Step 2: Populate the "Show" column to add dimension to your words. You can show PowerPoint slides to support some of your text, but think of other options as well. Consider audio, video, handouts (sent in advance), individual or group activities, polls, chats, Q&A, a whiteboard, brainstorming, and anything else that may be appropriate. Mix up what you'll show to make your presentation interactive and engaging.

Title: Emails that Mean Business™

Tell	Show
(Easy-listening music with slide while people are joining the virtual classroom.)	Slide: On behalf of [company], Sheryl Lindsell-Roberts welcomes you to Emails that Mean Business!™ Please stand by for a few moments while the other groups join us.
• Good morning (afternoon) . . . • Thanks for joining . . .	Graphic
Opening: Email is a serious business communications tool and you should treat it with the same respect as any other document you write. • Mention etiquette of ordering spaghetti at a business dinner.	Slide: Email is a serious business communications tool and you should treat it with the same respect as any other document you write.
Poll: What's your biggest pet peeve about email? • Give directions for filling out poll.	Area for completing poll
Do's First, change the subject line when replying to a message. Discuss why subject lines can be a problem.	Show email message with following subject line: Confirming our mtg. on May 2 @ 9 AM.
And so forth . . .	

Preparing Effective PowerPoints

When you determine that PowerPoints will add value to what you'll tell, make them engaging and visual. For a virtual classroom, prepare more slides rather than fewer (the opposite of preparing for a live presentation). Change your slides every 30–60 seconds. Participants tend to stay more engaged if they feel they may miss something by multitasking. Here are some tips for creating engaging slides:

Guidelines for word slides
- Include one topic per slide.
- Put the "takeaway" in the title of each slide.
- Use uppercase and lowercase, never all caps (even for the headline).
- Limit each visual to 5–7 lines of text.

- Use bulleted or numbered lists that are left-justified. (Remember that bullets kill; don't overuse them.)
- Use a 24-point font for headlines and an 18-point font for text.
- Consider a sans serif font (such as Arial) for the headlines and a serif font (such as Times Roman) for the text.
- Use italics sparingly, if at all.
- Use black text on a light-colored background for the best readability.

 I can't emphasize enough the importance of proofreading carefully. If people notice an error, they'll be proofreading your slides and listening for mistakes throughout the rest of your presentation rather than garnering information from you. If someone does notice an error and mentions it in front of the group, say "Thanks. I'm going to change that right now." Go into edit mode and make the change on the spot. We all make mistakes. It's how graciously we correct them that separates the professionals from the amateurs.

Guidelines for graphic slides

- Place graphics in a similar location on each slide.
- When a picture or graphic can tell the story, exclude text.
- Use graphics to create visual evidence.
- Limit data to what's absolutely necessary.
- Label axes, data lines, and charts for easy understanding.
- Create a legend when you need to explain a graphic.
- Use an array of colors to emphasize certain information (for example, to differentiate between percentages on a pie chart).
- Keep lines, boxes, borders, and white space consistent.

 Use pie charts to show parts of a whole, line charts to show trends or the change of one or more variables over time, bar charts to show comparisons between categories, scatter plots to display relationships between variables, and flow charts to show steps in processes.

Guidelines for animation

- Use animation only when it will enhance your message; otherwise it becomes distracting and annoying.
- Stick to one animation mode throughout.
- Use animation to present changes over time (such as in a morphing project), to demonstrate how elements interact with each other, to show the basics of how a product works, to provide entertainment value, or to add bullet points to a slide as you discuss them.

Copyright laws apply to online as well as hard copy. If you incorporate copyrighted materials (text or graphics), be sure to get written permission. If you can't get permission, find text, graphics, and animation that are copyright cleared or are covered by a Creative Commons license. (Creative Commons is a nonprofit organization that offers copyright protection for creative works.)

Preparing a script

A script is an option when your learners can't see you and you feel more comfortable with all the words in front of you. You prepare a script in much the same way as you prepare a storyboard, except you put down every word. Notice how the example on page 131 relates to the panels in the completed storyboard on page 128.

The value of prework

The following is what I sent as a prework package in preparation for a virtual class on email to learners who would be attending simultaneously from three locations. This prework package engaged the learners, created interest, got them to a certain level of readiness, and helped me to establish a connection directly with them. I called the package "Getting Started."

- **My bio.** Learners don't want to spend the first several minutes of their learning experience listening to a sales pitch from the facilitator. Let them get to know you and build credibility in advance.
- **The agenda.** It's important for people to have a roadmap before they attend. They can decide to opt out of a session if it doesn't suit their needs, making room for others.
- **Case study.** I teamed people in groups of two or three and asked them to discuss the case study before the workshop, then answer a few questions.
- **Article.** I asked them to read an article I wrote titled "Handheld Computers and the Changing Face of Email" that we'd reference during the workshop. (You can find the article on page 254.)
- **Workbook.** This is for activities during various parts of the workshop. People aren't wired to sit in front of their computers staring at a screen. They're wired to use their fingers. Rather than having them use their fingers to multitask (check email and such), a workbook helps them use their fingers to stay on task. Learn more about workbooks later in this chapter.

Note: There's more about prework in a general sense later in this chapter.

Practice your script repeatedly so you sound spontaneous and unrehearsed. (Meryl Streep can get away with delivering her lines very naturally. You'll probably need to work at it.)

Title: Emails that Mean Business™

Tell	Show
(Easy-listening music with slide while people are joining the virtual classroom.)	Slide On behalf of [company], Sheryl Lindsell-Roberts welcomes you to Emails that Mean Business!™ Please stand by for a few moments while a few more people join us.
Good morning [or afternoon], and thank you for joining us for this very interactive program, Emails that Mean Business!	Graphic
Opening It's important to remember that email is a serious business communications tool and you should treat it with the same respect as any other document you write. So think about it—email etiquette is just as important as dining etiquette. You wouldn't go out to dinner with a client you're trying to impress and order a big plate of spaghetti for fear of slobbering the sauce all over your shirt. So don't send emails that are the equivalent of slobbering. [Pause]	Slide Email is a serious business communications tool and you should treat it with the same respect as any other document you write.
Poll Let me start by asking, What's your biggest pet peeve about email? Type your answer in the [describe what they're seeing on the screen]. [Then give tally.] We'll be discussing all of these issues as we go through the do's and taboos of email.	Area for completing poll

Do's	Show email message with following subject line
Let's talk about some of the email etiquette do's. First, change the subject line when replying to a message. Why is this important? Here's a perfect example: A client left me a phone message asking me to confirm a meeting for the following day. I sent an email that said in the subject line "Confirming our mtg tomorrow @ 9AM." Several weeks later the same person sent me an email with the same subject line. I looked at the subject line and was confused. I checked my calendar, and we didn't have anything scheduled for the following day. I called my client and said, "I don't have anything on my calendar for tomorrow. Your email message is confirming a 9 AM meeting." She'd just clicked on the old email to write the new message to me, which had nothing to do with a meeting. Always change the subject line when replying to someone's message.	Subject: Confirming our mtg. tomorrow @ 9 AM
And so forth . . .	

 I strongly recommend a book titled *Resonate* by Nancy Duarte. It discusses how to present visual stories that transform audiences.

Blended learning

The hottest buzzword in business training, blended learning is simply designing and blending the best methodologies to meet the learning objective. One of the simplest examples is the blending of electronic content with a live instructor. Many companies, for example, are using the blended learning approach to roll out comprehensive customer relation management (CRM) or enterprise resource planning (ERP) programs. Participants join an initial conference call or videoconference, attend a series of meetings, then take online courses. This culminates with a follow-up meeting and evaluation prior to the rollout.

Think proactively and strategically.

Learning modalities should be driven by the learners' needs and learning styles. Rather than just bringing in an instructor because someone suggested a great person or offering a program because several people asked for it, blended learning forces you to think more tactically.

- **Understand the problem that has created the need for training.** Are you sure this is a problem that will be solved by training? Or would a series of meetings or some other form of communication be more appropriate?

- **Identify your business goals.** Are you introducing a new product and designing training on how to use it?

- **Who is your audience?** How much do they already know? What are the demographics? What kind of learning style best supports the learning? Can you assemble everyone in one place? Are they motivated or are their arms being twisted?

- **What's the distinctiveness of the content?** Will the content be outdated before too long? What equipment can people access?

- **How will you measure success?** Determine how you will know if the program was a success. Will you provide evaluations, give tests, hold a competition? (Check out "The Kirkpatrick Model" on pages 155–156.)

 One of the biggest obstacles to success in virtual learning may be the limitations of your learners' equipment. In many places (including areas of the rural US as well as abroad) people don't have the latest technology or high-speed Internet access. Find out as much as you can about your learners' environments before designing any training.

 I was doing a three-hour stand-up training workshop for a company and blended one person in on the phone via a little speaker on the conference-room table. To include her as much as possible I did the following, which worked well:

- Sent her all the materials in advance. This included prework, handouts, and the few PowerPoint slides.
- Asked for her photo in advance and placed it on an A-frame placard on the table in front of the speaker so everyone could see her.
- When I showed a slide, mentioned the slide number so she could follow along.
- Included her in all conversations by asking her questions and asking questions for her.
- When we had breakout groups, included her in the group that was closest to the speaker.

At the conclusion of the workshop (she was still awake), I asked her how productive it was for her given that she couldn't see what was going on. She felt that it went quite well and she got a lot out of the session. (Not as much, of course, as those who attended, but it was better than missing the session altogether.)

Videos

Videos for learning aren't new, but now we have more technology, such as webcams, cell phones, video cameras, and Internet TV, to facilitate their effectiveness. Videos—through color, motion, and sound—help learners to retain more than they would just by reading a how-to manual. Video training is convenient, reasonably affordable, portable, and (done well) interactive and informative. You can give the learner a high-quality and realistic re-creation of the environment in which she'll perform certain tasks. Instructional videos are an excellent training tool for demonstrating everything from how to assemble machinery, to how to onboard new hires, to how to safely use an electric drill.

Questions to ask beforehand

Before you decide a video is the right medium, ask yourself the following questions:

- How many people will view the video?
- Is the content stable or subject to ongoing change?
- What resources are in place at offices or plants for viewing?
- How much time and money is the organization willing to invest in video training?
- Is the work environment conducive to video training?

 Your medium must be appropriate for the intended environment. Several years ago I was working with a manufacturing company. The people on the shop floor received a training video on a CD illustrating how to operate a specific piece of equipment. The problem was that this type of shop floor typically didn't have computers in the area. The lesson here is to learn what medium is most appropriate for the situation and in what environment it will be used. You need to merge both elements to be successful.

Categories of video productions

There are basically three categories of video productions. They vary in equipment, time, cost, and results.

- **Basic video:** This can be a do-it-yourself production where all you need is a camera and proper lighting.

- **Enhanced video:** For this you need someone with a camera, basic editing skills, and the ability to incorporate text, slides, video footage, photographs, visual effects (such as transitions), and the like.

- **Professional-quality video:** This involves a professional crew to create a high-quality video with all the bells and whistles including lighting, directing, camera angles, talent, and more.

Writing the script

Check out the storyboarding section of this chapter and prepare a word-for-word script. During the entire video, create a continuous and smooth flow where learning pours in. Put the emphasis on the *show*, not on the *tell*. A video where someone stands in front of the camera speaking isn't effective. Here are a few ways to engage learners:

- **Use humor.** Videos, including those with serious content, can drive points home with humor.

- **Use a conversational style.** Even though many people will view your video, direct the narration as if you're speaking to one person.

- **Use *you, your,* and *we.*** This will establish a personalized experience for each learner.

- **Allow for plenty of pauses.** Use pauses for emphasis to give the learners a moment to digest the information.

- **Write transitions into the narration.** For example, "Now let's take a look at . . ." This will add continuity to your message and carry the viewer from one event to the next.

- **Incorporate a call to action at the end.** Stress exactly want you want the learner to do.

Read your copy aloud. This narration will be heard, not read, so it must be appealing to the ear and easy to read. For example, if you trip over any words, change the text.

 If you need someone with a professional-sounding voice to narrate the script, check out www.voices.com. For royalty-free music, check out www.audiojungle.net.

Stages of a video presentation

Welcome to the world of videos and multimedia. When you prepare a video, you must capture the audience's interest, hold their attention, and share meaningful information. Your understanding of the process will help you to communicate your message clearly and effectively, contain costs, and use resources effectively.

There are three basic stages of a video presentation: preproduction or design, production, and postproduction.

Stages	Steps
Preproduction or design This is the most critical part of the process—the work of the script writer that goes on behind the scenes. Approximately 75 percent of the total effort goes into preproduction. If every step of this stage is handled diligently and everyone does her homework, there should be a minimum number of changes after the video has been produced.	1. Prepare a schedule. 2. Gather the information. 3. Start the script. 4. Gather/create visuals. 5. Get the script approved. 6. Locate a narrator (if applicable). 7. Rehearse (if appropriate). 8. Finalize script.
Production This is where a good production crew will make the difference between a home-quality video and a professional-quality video.	1. Start field recording. 2. Assemble lights, cameras, recorders, microphones, monitors, etc. 3. Record and edit narration (if applicable). 4. Edit in studio.

Postproduction

On with the show. Remember, edits and re-shoots at this point are time-consuming and costly.

1. Preview the video.
2. Make necessary edits.
3. Review edits (if applicable).
4. Copy or post.

 Shorter is better. Three 10-minute segments make more of an impact than a 30-minute video. People have short attention spans.

YouTube video

To fully realize the viral marketing impact of YouTube, remember the Scottish singing sensation Susan Boyle who made her debut on *Britain's Got Talent*. Her YouTube video was seen around the world and skyrocketed her to instant fame. Here's how to get your video noticed:

What you need to do first

- **Set up an account.** You can set up a free account by going to www.youtube .com.
- **Get a good camera and microphone.** You don't need a high-end camera; a good-quality camera for around $150 will work well. Use a separate microphone for better sound quality.

Designing the video

- **Have a plan.** Know what you want to accomplish. Identify your target audience including the demographics.
- **Write a storyboard or script.** Just as professional performers use storyboards or scripts, you also need one. (See the storyboarding and script section earlier in this chapter.)
- **Provide valuable information.** Provide valuable information so people can learn something, such as tips or best practices.
- **Let the viewers know how to contact you.** End your video with your web address, email, or whatever is appropriate so viewers can follow up.

Shooting and editing

- **Remember your brand.** Use colors that match or complement your company logo and/or website.
- **Include honest and realistic headlines.** Use headlines that tell your story without exaggerating. For example, don't claim to be No. 1 in your field if nobody really knows you. This will cost you your reputation.
- **Act and think like your audience.** Put yourself in your audience's seat. What would whet your appetite? What would encourage you to want to learn more?

- **Close with contact information.** End with a screen letting your audience know what they should do and where they can get more information.

After the lights go out

- **Learn about video editing.** Unless you have your video shot by a professional, you will need to edit it. You can search for tutorials on the web. If necessary, hire a professional—it's worth the cost, because an amateurish video is worthless.
- **Limit your video to three minutes or less.** This isn't a feature film; it's a quick peek. If you need more time, post another video.
- **Make your video search-friendly.** Use tags and descriptions that are friendly. If you're not familiar with how to do this, contact a web person or someone who is technically savvy.
- **Market it.** Once your YouTube has gone live, market it, market it, market it! Send the link to everyone you know. Post the link on your social networking sites. Market to online message boards. Have your video appear on your website and blog.

 Understand what you can do yourself and where you need professional help.

Virtual classrooms and webinars

Many people use the terms *virtual classrooms* and *webinars* interchangeably, but there is a subtle difference. A webinar is primarily for sharing ideas and is typically driven by PowerPoints and a faceless person jabbering in the background—somewhat like the Wizard of Oz behind the curtain. A virtual classroom is for the express purpose of learning and changing performance. It's facilitated by a trainer who may use slides, whiteboards, chats, prework, mid-session work, and post-work to facilitate the learning experience either synchronously or asynchronously (see definitions that follow). In this chapter, I'll be referring to virtual classrooms, although much of the information applies to webinars as well.

Selecting web collaboration tools

Virtual classrooms can be wonderful learning tools when the content and facilitator are engaging, there's interaction, and the learner is taught transferable skills. When deciding on the tools that are right for you, remember that you may want to use the same tools for conducting virtual meetings. Consider the dynamics, learning objectives, and outcomes in determining which of the following elements may be important:

- **Video.** Is it important for people to see you and each other or would that be distracting?

- **Polling.** These capabilities can be a little sophomoric, but they're a good way to change the energy of a group. They can be useful to get a group consensus or to narrow down topics for discussions.

- **Voice.** During a virtual classroom, is it important for people to have voice capabilities, or would keyboarding capabilities be adequate? (For meetings, voice is needed.)

- **Anonymity.** Keyboarding capabilities may be important for companies that are hierarchical, where everyone defers to the highest-level managers. Keyboarding is also important for people whose English is a second language. They may feel more comfortable keyboarding than speaking.

Understanding the difference between synchronous and asynchronous

Synchronous communication requires all learners to be engaged at the same time. This can be through face-to-face communication, chatrooms, instant messaging, the telephone, video and web conferencing, or classroom training. Synchronous communication is appropriate when:

- Real-time interaction is critical.
- Participants need to share ideas concurrently.
- There's a need to adjust the level of information depending on the way participants respond to the material.
- A live session will ensure that learning is complete.

Asynchronous communication can be self-paced and all learners don't need to be engaged at the same time. It can involve letters, emails, blogs, forums, and parts of the virtual classroom experience (such as prework, mid-session work, and post-work). Asynchronous communication is appropriate when:

- You need to accommodate different learning styles.
- Participants can benefit from learning in small chunks.
- Learning takes place in different locations.
- Material needs to be available just-in-time (on demand).

Your virtual classes will be most productive if they are 60 minutes or less, with 90 minutes being the absolute limit. If there is more than one session, provide asynchronous activities for learners to complete between classes to facilitate additional learning.

- **A simple login process.** If your virtual classroom is intended for people who are participating voluntarily, a simple login process may be important. If they're participating as part of their job requirements, it's not critical.

- **Pricing.** Pricing is all over the place and may be by the minute, hour, quarter, or year. Although the pricing must fit your budget, don't forsake valuable features for a lower price. You get what you pay for.

Here are a few tips for selecting tools:
- If you're preparing a virtual classroom for a specific company, find out if the company has a license for web collaborating tools. That will save you the expense.
- If you're purchasing tools, check with the IT group to be sure they're in sync with your selection so there are no bandwidth or security issues.

Selecting a facilitator

Whether you're selecting a facilitator or you're a self-appointed facilitator, certain characteristics are critical. The following checklist appeared in *Infoline*, a publication of the American Society for Training and Development (ASTD).

Choose an Online Training Facilitator who:

☐ **Shows enthusiasm for becoming an online facilitator.** Facilitators must want to be online. If not, they will never be comfortable there.

☐ **Has a history as an accomplished onsite facilitator.** An outstanding track record as a classroom facilitator should be a basic requirement for an online facilitator.

☐ **Is capable of directing learning or relinquishing control as needed.** The online facilitator must have both of these somewhat opposite abilities.

☐ **Practices learner-centered instruction.** If the individual likes being the oracle in front of the classroom, chances are he or she will not make it online.

☐ **Exhibits flexibility.** This trait is important in learning the technology of synchronous Web-based training and in continuing on when that technology fails.

☐ **Is adaptable.** E-learning facilitation is not a place for loners. A good program uses a team approach, and the facilitator needs to be comfortable as part of a team that doesn't always do things his or her way.

☐ **Has a good sense of humor.** A dry e-learning presentation seldom brings learners back to their computers for another round. This also is an important characteristic when technology failures occur.

☐ **Listens.** When the facilitator can't see the learners this becomes the most important skill.

☐ **Is willing to learn about new technologies.** The technology is your classroom in online learning and not being comfortable with learning about it—much less using it—will make for a much less effective facilitator.

☐ **Provides effective, timely feedback.** Facilitators who don't do this are one of the learner's top barriers to success in e-learning.

☐ **Can facilitate interactive learning.** Just having interaction designed into a program doesn't make it happen. The facilitator must be expert at making the interactions happen, and dealing with the chaos that sometimes results.

☐ **Will practice using the equipment and rehearsing delivery.** If an individual is too busy or too experienced to feel the need for plenty of practice and rehearsal, then they will probably fail as a synchronous Web-based training facilitator.

☐ **Makes the learners feel that they are part of a team.** Synchronous Web-based training, when designed well, is often a team process. The facilitator sets this environment.

- Send an advance email that includes a thank-you for registering, the topic, start and end times, URL or dial-in number, name of facilitator, and system requirements. If the virtual classroom event is in the afternoon, resend the notice that morning. If it's in the morning, resend it the afternoon before.
- It's ideal to have two computers in the room. The facilitator can look at one screen and the moderator can look at what the learners are seeing. If there's a problem, the facilitator will know immediately.

Be an engaged and engaging facilitator.

If you're sitting and staring at a screen, it may be hard to become engaged and be engaging. Here are a few suggestions:

- View the list of learners beforehand so you become familiar with them.
- Email or use the web tools to communicate with everyone prior to the session.
- If the group is small, call everyone before the session.
- Get photos of the learners and create a visual of each person sitting around a conference table. This will make them appear more real. If your technology allows, let them see each other sitting around the table.
- Use people's names throughout the session.
- Stand up during the session to add vitality to your voice.
- If you're delivering a PowerPoint presentation and you're the only presenter, put a few pictures of people you know on the desk near the screen and pretend you're talking to them.
- Keep a pen and paper handy to jot down observations or actions.
- Sit in a comfortable chair and have water on hand to keep your throat moist.

Understanding the roles of the moderator (producer) and facilitator

If possible, try to arrange for the moderator and facilitator to be two separate people because they serve two different functions. It's difficult for one person to do it all, and it's reassuring to have someone watching your back.

Moderator

- Send out invitations.
- Open the session by introducing the facilitator, the program, and the learning objectives.
- Review the housekeeping issues such as where to find all the nooks and crannies, whether to send questions throughout or hold them until the end, and anything else learners need to know.
- Gather questions that come in through the chat function; edit them for spelling, punctuation, and grammar (if they'll be posted); prioritize them, and give them to the facilitator at the appropriate time.
- Clear chat and polling pods.

- Refer to people (by name) randomly so they're more apt to pay attention and not get caught off guard.

- Provide constructive feedback to the facilitator such as *Talk louder, Flip to the next slide, Speed up or you'll run late,* or anything else that will be useful.

- Wrap up by thanking everyone for attending. Also mention any books or white papers to buy, links of interest, newsletters to subscribe to, and whether everyone will receive a PDF and/or audio version of the presentation.

Facilitator

- Send an introductory email before the program and include any prework needed.

- Deliver the goods.

- Maintain a high level of energy and let your personality show.

- Keep the virtual classroom focused.

- Advance slides, set up chats, and run polls.

- Share stories and anecdotes to illustrate key points.

- Sound spontaneous.

- Recover gracefully from mistakes.

 If you're new at facilitating virtual classroom sessions, join as many sessions as a participant as you can. You'll learn a great deal from other facilitators and discover what you like and don't like.

 When you're in front of people, you can enhance your presentation with eye contact and body language. When you facilitate a virtual classroom, you're in a void and must purposefully animate your voice and create deliberate pauses. Vary the pitch and tone; otherwise your voice will sound flat, causing learners to become drowsy.

Ways to engage learners

You should engage your learners in a variety of ways—before, during, and after the virtual classroom experience. Follow these steps:

1. Send them the initial invitation and registration form.

2. Follow immediately with a confirmation and login instructions.

3. Send two email reminders before the event—each with a different,

distinct subject line and message (teasers, perhaps).

4. Send another reminder just before the event. If it's in the morning, send the reminder with the login instructions the day before. If it's in the afternoon, send a reminder with the login instructions that same morning.

5. Send prework (as discussed below).

6. Interact during the presentation. (If you typically deliver live presentations, consider what you can transfer to the virtual classroom that will make it interactive.)

7. To maximize participation, use virtual breakout rooms. Divide learners into small groups and give them a structured assignment to be completed within a limited amount of time.

8. After the workshop, send a thank-you with access to the presentation's on-demand recording.

 When you send the thank-you, ask if your learners would like to subscribe to your newsletter, follow you on Twitter, or stay connected to you in some other way.

Send out prework. As mentioned earlier in this chapter, prework is a key ingredient for engaging people prior to the virtual classroom experience. Prework can shape the direction and content of the event and start the learning process before the learners even show up.

- **Ask for photos.** This will let you "see" everyone and let them "see" each other, helping to form connections. You can prepare a slide that shows everyone around a conference table (or tables if the group is large). This will lend itself to group discussions if that's part of your virtual classroom.

- **Solicit questions.** This prepares participants for meaningful conversations and can address any concerns and issues on their minds.

- **Send something to read or listen to.** This can be a white paper, website, link to a publication, case study, podcast, vodcast, questionnaire, personal reflection activities, or anything that will get learners prepared to jump in and be ready to go when the session starts.

- **Send a self-assessment survey.** Help them to understand where they are in the learning experience.

- **Pair learners up for brief phone conversations.** Even a 15-minute conversation about something you sent (the prereading, perhaps) will build in accountability.

- **Send a case study.** Pair up learners and help them get a head start. Include a case study with questions at the end asking the pairs how they would have handled the situation. Ask them to send you their answers by a certain date.

- **Send the slides.** This will enable learners to discuss them. A novel approach is to include a question on all or several slides to promote discussion through voice or chat during the virtual classroom.

- **Send a workbook.** See the next section for more about workbooks.

 You establish your "front-of-the-room" presence (your virtual personality) through the tone of the materials you send in advance. Use a conversational tone. In your bio, include what attracted you to this topic and which life events propelled you along the way. Weave in anecdotes, gentle humor, and whatever will help learners get to know you and look forward to learning from you.

Designate an activity where they'll use pen and paper. Have them draw something, make a list, create a chart, or complete another activity using pen and paper. At the end, ask learners to write down two or three things they learned that they, their team, or their company can apply immediately.

Incorporate interactivity. You must incorporate interactivity into your presentation so your learners stay engaged. Consider any or all of the following:

- Chats
- Colorful slides
- Brainstorming

- Polling
- Whiteboarding
- Surveys

- Streaming video
- Hard-copy workbook
- Questions and answers

Include a workbook. Remember the workbooks we had in school? Consider going back to the future, because workbooks are a great way to engage your learners. In advance of the virtual classroom experience, send workbooks in PDF format and ask participants to print out a hard copy. Leave lots of white space for notes.

During the session you can introduce a workbook activity by saying "I'm now going to give you two minutes [or other amount of time] to . . ." When time is up, divide students into teams and have them share their answers through the chat function or call on certain people to share their answers with the entire class. This helps to simulate face-to-face learning. After the workshop the participants have good reference materials in their own handwritten notes.

Following are workbook pages prepared by Dave Yakonich, Manager, Quality Systems Training, at Boston Scientific. They were prepared to introduce a project management process for launching company-wide HR programs. The virtual training is delivered in two parts to project team members to provide an overview of the process, tools, and governance.

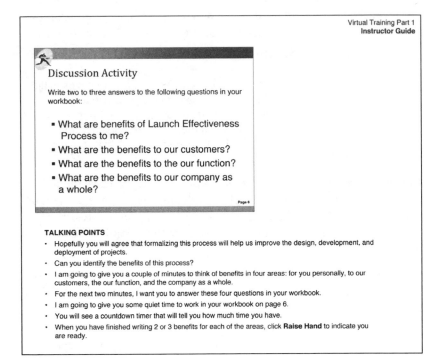

Virtual Training Part 1
Instructor Guide

Discussion Activity

Write two to three answers to the following questions in your workbook:

- What are benefits of Launch Effectiveness Process to me?
- What are the benefits to our customers?
- What are the benefits to the our function?
- What are the benefits to our company as a whole?

Page 6

TALKING POINTS

- Hopefully you will agree that formalizing this process will help us improve the design, development, and deployment of projects.
- Can you identify the benefits of this process?
- I am going to give you a couple of minutes to think of benefits in four areas: for you personally, to our customers, the our function, and the company as a whole.
- For the next two minutes, I want you to answer these four questions in your workbook.
- I am going to give you some quiet time to work in your workbook on page 6.
- You will see a countdown timer that will tell you how much time you have.
- When you have finished writing 2 or 3 benefits for each of the areas, click **Raise Hand** to indicate you are ready.

Prepare for the worst. A successful virtual classroom is dependent on technology such as the Internet provider, the phone provider, the web meeting tools, the host's computer, and other factors. Check everything beforehand. Despite your best planning, however, calamity may rear its ugly head. Try to anticipate what you would do in a variety of circumstances. For example, if there's a thunderstorm and you're worried about getting disconnected, mention that there's a storm in your area and what Plan B is should you lose contact.

146   PART THREE: VIRTUALLY SPEAKING

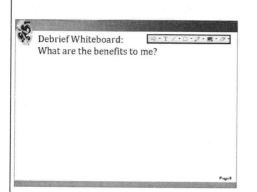

Debrief Whiteboard:
What are the benefits to me?

TECHNICAL NOTES
- This debrief will be done through participants providing their feedback through whiteboard.
- As people share the benefits, type the responses.
- *Debrief the benefits to them as* **L&D Producer** *documents on the whiteboard.*

Benefits Activity

Discussion Question (2 minutes)

Identify two to three answers for each the following questions in the space below:

What are benefits of Launch Effectiveness Process to me?

What are the benefits to our customers?

What are the benefits to the our function?

What are the benefits to our company as a whole?

One way to keep learners participating until the end is to let them know you'll be offering something for free at the end of the virtual classroom experience. It can be a book, white paper, coaching, or anything else they may find worthwhile.

Getting and using feedback

As a facilitator, you should always be looking for ways to improve your content and e-facilitation skills. Take all the comments to heart—the good, the bad, and the ugly. When you deliver the training the next time, understand what worked, what didn't work, what was in your control, and what was out of your control. Following is what an online evaluation form may look like:

Session Feedback Survey

Please let us know how well this session worked for you - including the asynchronous pre-work and the real-time webinar. Your feedback with help us with future sessions.

Save and Submit	Cancel

Level of Agreement

Session Content
Please select your level of agreement to the following statements about this webinar experience

1 The pre-work activities and materials provided ahead of time were valuable additions to the webinar. — Strongly Agree ▼ / Click here / Strongly Agree / Agree / Neutral / Disagree / Strongly Disagree

2 I picked up practical new ideas and techniques for preparing and running virtual meetings and webinars.

What was your key take-away?

3 The information provided/explored has

4 After participating in this webinar I see th virtual meeting/learning experiences.

Level of Agreement

Votes Received

Description	Value	
Click here	0	(0)
Strongly Agree	5	(13)
Agree	4	(6)
Neutral	3	(0)
Disagree	2	(0)
Strongly Disagree	1	(0)

Group Avg: 4.68 - Voters: 19 - Standard Deviation: 0.48

Session Process
Please select your level of agreement to the

5 The session provided a good balance b

6 I found myself fully participating througho

When/where did you start to lose attenti back?

7 The FacilitatePro software that we used today added significant value to this webinar experience. — Click here ▼

For more information about FacilitatePro click here or to contact Julia directly click here.

General Comments

8 Any further comments? Thank you for your participation and feedback.

Courtesy of FacilitatePro Web Meeting Software at www.Facilitate.com.

If your feedback is less than stellar, approach critical comments as a way to improve your technique or your materials. Be clear about what you'll change in the future.

Virtual coaching

Virtual coaching has made business/life coaching affordable, accessible, instant, and green.

Need a coach?

Do you spend too much time working in your business rather than on your business? Are you a workaholic? Do you have trouble committing to and meeting goals? Have you been thinking of starting a new business? Are you having trouble balancing your work and personal life? If you relate to any of these questions, consider engaging the services of a coach. When you engage a virtual coach, you

- **Keep the cost down.** Virtual coaching can be less costly than face-to-face coaching when you're working with a coach who's outside a reasonable driving distance or who must incur out-of-pocket travel expenses.

- **Get Just-in-Time (JIT) coaching.** When you need a quick coaching conversation, you can contact your virtual coach via phone, email, instant messaging, or text.

- **Gain worldwide access.** Have access to coaches in a multiplicity of industries and geographic areas.

Be a coach.

To learn the art of coaching, attend classes from your own home or office without being limited to any geographic location. The following organizations are a good place to start:

International Coaching Federation (http://coachfederation.org)
Certified Coaches Federation (http://certifiedcoachesfederation.com)
International Association of Coaching (http://certifiedcoach.org)
Certified Coaches Alliance (http://certifiedcoachesalliance.com)

Podcasting

Some people refer to a podcast as "radio on demand." Wikipedia defines a podcast as "a series of audio or video digital-media files which is distributed over the Internet by syndicated download, through Web feeds, to portable media players and personal computers." Podcasts are becoming widely used in business to expand marketing reach, increase sales and conversion rates, and open lines of communication with listeners. When you provide industry news, trends, and other information your listeners value, you create followship and become known as knowledgeable in your industry.

Consider if podcasting is appropriate for your target market. For example, podcasts work well for salespeople who consider the phone to be an ear appendage. A three- to five-minute podcast with quick sales tips and tricks is a great way to enhance time spent sitting in an airport or waiting for a meeting to start.

 Mention at the outset of the podcast that you'll be incorporating a few questions at the end and listeners will be asked to text in their answers. This promotes active listening.

 Don't make your topic too broad. For example, instead of podcasting on Chinese cuisine, focus on the better-known Cantonese delicacies. Creating your niche is a great way of developing a loyal audience.

Getting started

Decide if your podcast will be a daily, weekly, or monthly event. Target a specific audience and select a format that will be interesting to them. This can include interviews, guests, and industry experts. Here's what you'll need to get started:

- Computer
- Computer software that can capture digital audio or video and allow some basic editing
- Good quality microphone (built-in or external)
- A program that supports MP3 format
- Headphones (optional, but recommended)
- Digital video camera if your podcast is a vodcast (video podcast)
- A place on a file server to host your podcast.

You can prepare a podcast yourself or have one done professionally. The decision depends on your audience and your desired outcome.

A colleague recently prepared a podcast to be used as prework for a training session for managers. He knew it had to be of professional quality. His script included a "he said/she said" case study. By auditioning people from www.voices.com, he found a man and woman who made the presentation interesting and engaging. He added royalty-free bumper music from www.audiojungle.net. The result was a dynamic podcast that everyone listened to and raved about.

The devil is in the details

Start with 10 to 15 seconds of royalty-free or used-with-permission music. Then identify your podcast by name, date, episode, originator, host, speaker(s), and purpose. Here's more:

- **Make your material "snackable."** Deliver your podcast in short segments of less than 10 minutes each. (It can be slightly longer if you're interviewing a well-known person and the audience will find the information to be riveting.)

- **Generate an outline, not a script.** If you read from a script, you won't sound natural. Once you prepare the outline, practice, practice, practice.

- **Reduce noise.** It's obvious that you won't have a barking dog in the room with you when you're recording, but consider the noises coming from air conditioners, fans, computers, fluorescent lighting, and other internal and external sources. A colleague told me he puts a blanket over his head when holding his microphone to reduce the background noise he can't eliminate.

- **Test equipment before you begin.** Check sound quality and volume levels to make sure that the settings are correct.

- **Thank listeners for tuning in.** Let listeners know how they can get more information. You can refer them to a blog, wiki, website, book, or anything else that will add to your message.

Interviewing a guest

Consider offering listeners more than one speaker. Guests add variety and make the podcast more interesting. Keep in mind that there's something dynamic between a male and female speaker. When you're interviewing someone, prepare questions ahead of time and prep the guest.

- Research your guest so you can create a brief, yet stimulating, bio.
- Confirm pronunciation of the guest's name.

- Prepare open-ended questions in advance and give them to your guest in advance. If you can, do a dry run of Q&A.
- Let the guest do most of the talking.
- Let the guest know what time cues you'll provide if her answers are running long.
- Be sure to say thank-you at the end and provide a link to her site.

Marketing your podcast

Visibility is critical to building a listener base. To attract more listeners, integrate social media marketing with traditional marketing. Have an iTunes-friendly Really Simple Syndication (RSS) feed; send updates to your email base; create press releases; ask your listeners to spread the word; publish the podcast on your own network server or globally on a file transfer protocol (FTP) server that's used to exchange files over the Internet; and post it on your website and blog.

Just-in-Time Training (JITT)

Studies show that learners lose nearly 40 percent of the benefits of training after one month, and 90 percent after six months. JIT training (or JITT with the final *T* for *Training*) solves that problem. The rapid response capabilities of JITT let companies respond to changes in business conditions, new acquisitions, new technologies, and immediate needs.

JITT is often rolled out or launched immediately before employees need to perform certain functions or tasks—strengthening the affinity between learning and performance. It is autonomous and can be done at a person's own time and pace. Training programs can be purchased or homegrown. They can include testing, evaluating, and remediating.

Know when JITT is appropriate

JITT works well when companies need to train groups of employees in multiple areas on a fully automated basis. It can encompass job training, job aids, hints, tips, and reminders, as well as extensive programs. It's on demand, effective, targeted, and can be tailored to the learner's prior knowledge and experience. Learning can be interactive, incorporating videos, podcasts, PowerPoint presentations, worksheets, Q&A, chats, and more.

- Identify when you should implement JITT.
- Single out the tasks for which you'll need to train people.

- Divide tasks into cognitive and action steps.
- Determine the best method of delivery.
- Create job aids the trainee will use as a resource. They can include worksheets, flow charts, sequential steps, a graphic organizer, or a combination.
- Prepare evaluations and remediation.

JITT applications

Here are just a few:

- **New hires.** A new hire joins your company and must learn the policies, procedures, and compliance issues. Managers can assign lessons, have the test scores emailed, evaluate the new employee's score, and decide on the next steps.

- **Project teams.** You're assembling a project team that needs to learn a special software application. JITT can help them to be up and running quickly.

- **Managers.** You need immediate tips for dealing with a sexual harassment complaint or other pressing issue.

- **Emergency preparedness volunteers.** You want to give volunteers refresher information to triage people following a disaster.

- **Safety.** You need to coordinate a workplace-safety training program.

- **Lean manufacturing.** A client has placed a unique order and you need to teach operators how to "build the widgets."

- **Sales.** A salesperson is meeting with a potential client and needs last-minute sales tips and key product features.

Measuring success

Learning professionals are often challenged to justify training investments. A critical first step is to establish *up front* the expected benefits of the learning intervention in terms of return on investment (ROI) or return on expectations (ROE). So don't wave the banner and claim success just because everyone enjoyed the training and turned in a glowing smile sheet (evaluation).

ROI vs. ROE

Stakeholders have traditionally considered ROI to be the most important factor in determining success. But how do you measure ROI, especially for soft-skills training? On the Internet, you'll find dozens of formulas, but nobody is quite sure what the appropriate metrics are.

That's why more and more stakeholders are starting to measure ROE, which can ultimately support ROI. ROE can have an indirect (and sometimes intangible) impact on ROI, but the two are perceived differently. For example, one of my clients is training administrative assistants to prepare PowerPoint presentations for senior-level managers. It would be difficult to quantify in dollars the value of this training, but the company is expecting that it will save managers time and result in higher-quality slides. To measure ROE, ask yourself these questions:

- What do you expect employees to be able to do after the training that they couldn't before?

- What do you expect to be the overall impact of the training?

- Will this new skill save time or increase productivity? If so, to approximately what extent?

- Will this training help to close more business or retain more customers? If so, to approximately what extent?

- What would be the impact if you didn't achieve the desired behavior?

- Over what period of time can stakeholders anticipate seeing the payback they expect?
- Is there anecdotal evidence of changed attitudes, decreased absenteeism, improved motivation, and anything else that's expected?

 Equate ROE to a newly formed company that prepares a business plan to acquire funding. Potential funders have no assurances that the monetary projections are correct because many factors and risks come into play. However, the business plan sets expectations for projected revenue, growth, milestones, and more. The funders will invest on the faith of those expectations and the people running company.

The Kirkpatrick Model

The Kirkpatrick model, developed by business professor Don Kirkpatrick in 1959, is a standard for measuring the effectiveness of business training programs that is still being used today. The basic structure of Kirkpatrick's four-level model is shown below.

Throughout this section, let's assume that a company wants to perk up the quality of its customer-service department. One of its strategies is to prepare a virtual classroom to improve the telephone skills of its customer-service representatives. All the representatives will join the classroom as a group, which will be available for JITT as new members sign on.

Level 1: Reaction: Ask learners to fill out an evaluation form immediately following the session. Did they like it? Was the facilitator effective? Was the material relevant to their work? Cast the questions to get the most comprehensive answers.

Ask the following:

- Will what you learned improve your ability to deliver superior customer service? If so, by what percentage? *This gives a quantifiable expectation that can be measured against original goals.*
- What three things did you learn that you can apply immediately? *This gives immediate feedback.*

As opposed to:

- Can you apply what you learned to improve the customer service you provide? *This question requires a yes or no answer or a sliding-scale answer. It leads nowhere.*

Level 2: Learning: Everyone filled out your smile sheet and they liked you and your content. But what happens later is what's really relevant. Approximately two to four weeks after the training, revisit what they learned. This will give workers time to integrate their learning into what they already know. You can measure Level 2 outcomes through onsite observations, focus groups, testing, team assessments, self-assessments, or any other means that will let you know how participants are incorporating the new material into their day-to-day activities. For example, is the newly created list of commonly asked questions and answers posted in plain view? Are calls being answered by the third ring?

Level 3: Behavior: About four weeks later, go through the same process as you did in Level 2. At this point, you want to determine to what extent learners have changed their behavior in the workplace. For example, if your overall goal was to improve customer satisfaction by 15 percent within one year, is there any movement in that direction? Have you decreased the time customers are on hold? Are customer service representatives finding creative ways to satisfy customers? Are they handling irate customers with empathy?

Level 4: Results: Eight to twelve weeks later, you revisit the original goals as thoughts turn to the bottom line. What organizational benefits have resulted from the training? Are you retaining more customers? Are customers recommending you to others? Are customer surveys giving you better results? If you determine that the training was successful but customer satisfaction hasn't increased, what other factors may be contributing to customer dissatisfaction? Were major delivery deadlines missed? Did the product arrive broken? Was there proper technical support?

If you had to identify, in one word, the reason why the human race has not achieved, and never will achieve, its full potential, that word would be *meetings*.

—Dave Barry, Pulitzer Prize–winning
author and columnist

Chapter 8

Virtual Meetings: From Sleep-Inducing to Sizzling

In this chapter
- *Tips for conducting successful virtual meetings*
- *Videoconferences*
- *Telepresence*
- *Teleconferences*

Just as email has changed the way we communicate, virtual meetings are changing the way we meet. Virtual meetings bring teams together into one space to learn, explore new ideas, brainstorm, and make decisions in an immersive and shared environment. Virtual meetings will never completely replace face-to-face (FTF) meetings because there are times when FTF contact is necessary. However, large companies report saving as much as 50 to 80 percent on travel budgets by incorporating virtual meetings into the mix. And there are other company advantages as well, such as:

- Building a global presence
- Reducing your carbon footprint
- Minimizing disruptions in schedules
- Eliminating delays due to transportation problems
- Gaining skills from people who are reluctant to travel or relocate
- Experiencing greater participation because of the ease of attendance
- Saving money

- Conserving energy
- Outsourcing operations
- Increasing productivity
- Reducing chit-chat
- Holding meetings on short notice
- Meeting with clients and customers (both potential and current).

 Factor in the advantages to employees. They avoid schlepping their brief-cases and laptops on no-frills airlines that treat them marginally better than luggage. And they can foster their work-life balance by not being away from the office and home as often.

Tips for conducting successful virtual meetings

While new technology has made it easier than ever to conduct virtual meetings, there is no shortcut to success. You must plan properly, keep participants engaged, and create momentum between meetings.

 Check out Chapter 7, "Virtual Learning: From Enervating to Empowering," to learn about selecting collaboration tools.

 A special thanks to virtual meeting experts Nancy Settle-Murphy, Guided Insights, and Julia Young, Facilitate.com, for graciously allowing me to include in this chapter the following suggestions from their white paper "Planning and Running Effective Remote Meetings." To order the white paper with its full array of tips and techniques, contact Nancy at www.guidedinsights.com or Julia at www.Facilitate.com.

From *Planning and Running Effective Remote Meetings*

Plan a viable agenda or series of agendas

Lay out a series of relatively short agendas that meet overall project objectives. When transitioning from face-to-face to virtual meetings, consider how best to break overall objectives into shorter components, building a series of agendas to get to your end result, rather than attempting one long session. Most virtual meetings should not exceed two hours, or you risk losing people somewhere along the way. Each agenda may involve different people. Some agendas can run concurrently. Some agendas will require a real-time meeting; others may be run asynchronously. Consider all possibilities as you plot your course.

Determine the level of interaction required for different kinds of virtual meetings: communication, data gathering, idea generation, team building, problem solving, decision making. The type of meeting will determine the level of interaction required between participants. This in turn shapes your agenda, pre-meeting activities and the tools you need to keep participants engaged and involved. Kinds of interaction include: listening, reading, asking questions, individual reflection, providing ideas and input, responding to questions, simultaneous brainstorming, drawing on a whiteboard, voting and polling.

Determine what conversations are needed to achieve each meeting objective. Asking good questions and engaging participants in meaningful and productive discussions is a key to all meeting facilitation. For virtual meetings these conversations tend to be more structured to accomplish a lot in a short period of time. If open conversation is needed, allow time for that too. Test questions in advance to make sure they are well-understood to others before you go live. Consider which questions you may want to pose in prework to give people a chance to reflect on possible answers, versus those best asked in the moment. Consider the extent to which participants hear, speak and write in the shared language. Err on the side of asking questions in advance when some or all participants are not native speakers.

Judge the length of time needed for different portions of a virtual meeting. Virtual meetings tend to be more structured and time sensitive. Plan out the appropriate amount of time for each agenda item and let people know ahead of time your plan. Look for opportunities to gather input ahead of a virtual meeting so that voice-to-voice time is focused. Have off-line follow-up possibilities if agenda topics run long. Use web meeting tools to capture input from participants simultaneously and leave time for reading and discussion.

Determine how many people can effectively participate in each kind of virtual meeting. The appropriate number of people depends on the purpose of the meeting (presentation, idea generation, decision-making, etc.), the desired level of participant interaction and the tools available. One-way communication can be to a large audience by audio and/or video conference. Web conferencing tools allow for presentations and simple Q&A to groups of up to 30. Web meeting tools allow for high levels of interaction between participants in groups of up to 30 with brainstorming, organizing and prioritization tools. Online surveys and asynchronous web meeting tools allow for data gathering from a group of several thousand people if need be. The more interactive your meeting type, the more likely people will be to remain engaged.

Identify who needs to be at which meeting. Invite the minimum number of people needed to accomplish your objectives, especially for same-time (synchronous) meetings. Determine what role each person has to play. Look for opportunities to get some people's input ahead of the virtual meeting so that your virtual event has the smallest number of critical participants. Find ways to involve other participants before or after the synchronous meeting, or limit the role of some to note-taking or other forms of listening, to allow key participants to be fully involved in the needed discussion.

Work with a client or meeting "owner" to establish roles and working relationships before, during and after the virtual meeting. Discuss the flow of the virtual meeting with participants, your manager, client or meeting owner. Establish their role in the meeting: when they will present information, when you will ask them to make a decision, when you will seek their input as to what direction to move forward with, when you will check in with them to see if they are getting what they need from the meeting so far. As you cannot read body language in a virtual meeting, plan your checkpoints and what each of you will be listening for during the meeting. Consider using IM or some other means by which you can virtually kick someone under the table or pass them a note to make sure you're in synch.

Use pre-meeting activities and instructions to ready participants for a focused agenda. Pre-meeting activities such as surveys, setting expectations, asking questions, prioritizing agenda items, sharing project updates and other information relevant to the meeting topics help bring participants up to speed before the meeting. This helps you focus meeting time on problem-solving and decision making activities. This can also familiarize participants with the use of certain tools before your meeting.

Use pre-meeting information sharing and data gathering to limit actual meeting time. Look for opportunities for data gathering and information sharing before and between virtual meetings. Since virtual meetings have to be brief and must run on time, you'll want to find ways to avoid having anyone giving presentations or otherwise sending people straight to multitasking.

Use asynchronous activities to manage multiple time zones. The nature of virtual teams is often that they cover many time zones. This can make scheduling a real-time meeting a challenge. Asynchronous data gathering activities such as reading documents, idea generation and surveys can often be conducted asynchronously. An asynchronous brainstorm over a period of several days allows people to ponder a problem, statement or issue and return with new ideas and build on each other's comments for a richer dialogue. In some cases, people will not be able to participate on a call at all; this way, they can participate before or after the actual call.

Construct an agenda that encourages participant input every 10–15 minutes. Assume that participants in your virtual meeting will start to get distracted by what's around them after 10 or 15 minutes or after 3 presentation slides. Design into your agenda ways to engage participants with questions, online idea generation, visualization exercises, etc. more frequently than you might in a face-to-face session.

Construct questions to focus participant input. Use focused questions to keep participants actively engaged during a virtual meeting. Try varying the way you pose questions. In some cases, you might offer a fill-in-the-blank statement. Or you might ask an open-ended question, or ask people for their "top three" of something. Use technology to get everyone involved in answering these questions. This also helps deter them from multitasking. Send people away from meetings with questions to ponder, with an option to check in again later to an asynch conference.

Build in appropriate time for checking in and checking out. Provide time for social interaction at the beginning and end of a meeting—up to a point. Some people may see a social time, albeit brief, as an annoying distraction, while others may see it as critical to build relationships. Using online tools to allow people to check in while others are joining the call helps speed up the check-in time. Online survey tools can also help to quickly gather session feedback. Checking-in activities set the tone of a meeting and allow you to create a friendly atmosphere and establish ground rules. Checking-out activities help make sure that everyone agrees to key decisions, actions, etc. from the meeting, and to establish a shared notion of what's next.

Set measures of success for a virtual meeting. Begin with the end in mind and work with your client to set measures of success for your virtual meetings. These include meeting objectives and specific outcomes, level of interaction and participation, level of participant satisfaction, effectiveness of communication given and received, time management and technology. Measures help set realistic expectations and drive conversation about what to do differently next time. If you're planning a multiple set of virtual meetings, participation at subsequent sessions can also be a good way to gauge success.

Keep people focused and engaged

Establish rapport with a group on the phone. Work the room as people join the teleconference. Repeat instructions and have something for the early birds to do such as a check-in sheet if using web meeting tools. Connect to individuals following up on pre-meeting conversations. Make connections between participants as you introduce them. Build in time for introductions appropriate to the nature of the virtual-meeting and team-building objectives. Add a question to your introductions, either in asynch or synch meetings, which creates some social context for each participant. For example, you might ask what can be seen from the closest window, or a favorite aspect of the current season.

Create checkpoints to facilitate redirection when a meeting goes off course. Check in with participants at least every 10–15 minutes. Use scheduled checkpoints when needed to refocus the group on the meeting objectives. Have a written agenda with detailed times for you to refer to so that you are fully aware if the conversation will prevent you from meeting your objectives. Stick to your stated agenda and keep conversations focused and concise. Make sure to keep a parking lot, just as you might for an onsite meeting, to ensure that questions or issues that can't be covered during the call can be tackled afterwards.

Use collaborative technology to keep people focused and engaged. Use web conferencing and web meeting tools to bring focus to a discussion. Quiet time with everyone typing in ideas, suggestions, questions or concerns is a quick way to get all participants engaged and focus the conversation back to the critical question at hand. Then you can return to a more focused conversation.

Modulate the tone of your voice to replace facial and other gestures. Listen to your tone of voice during conference calls and ask others for feedback. Listen to other people's tone of voice and reflect on how it impacts how you listen to them. Think about how you project and use your personality during face-to-face meetings and how you can use your tone of voice to do this during a virtual meeting. Make notes in your private-agenda copy to smile and breathe.

Build in participation after no more than three slides of a presentation. If you must use slides during a same-time meeting, do so sparingly. Assume that participants will begin to get distracted by what is around them after the third slide of a presentation. Build in ways to engage participants to prevent this distraction. Ask questions, seek comments, conduct a quick poll, call on people by name, ask someone to annotate the slide, pause the presentation and conduct a quick brainstorming activity. If you're using a meeting tool that allows the presenter to control the slide set, it's harder for others to multitask without getting lost later on.

Check in with participants about their level of engagement. Prepare in advance ways to check in with participants about their level of engagement, both as a group and individually. If you wonder whether people are paying attention, ask them. If you find yourself multitasking, ask who else is. Use quick polls to test the temperature of the group. Plan spontaneous check-ins. Be prepared to vary participation methods mid-stream if energy ebbs. For example, if you had planned to have people type in responses at a certain point, try a quick one-word check in from each person before asking them to type. In some cases, you may have to dispense with the typing if you suspect that may stifle verbal participation later on.

Keep track of participants and their level of interaction. Keep a list of participants at hand; check off when you hear from them. In a hybrid meeting, with some people in a room and others offsite, list virtual participants on a flip chart to keep them visible. Notice who is not participating verbally and find ways to include them. Speak to people individually early and often, setting the expectation that you may call on someone at any time. Use attributed online brainstorming and chat tools periodically so that you can see who is entering ideas and who is not.

Ask everyone to stay off mute. Staying OFF mute allows people to readily participate in verbal conversation without a pause to un-mute their phone. This allows for easier conversation and gives the facilitator a greater sense of whether people are engaged and alert. Background noise may necessitate the mute button but generally keep it off. Another benefit: People who may otherwise drift to email will realize their key clicks will be noticed by others are fully participating in the meeting.

Judge the appropriate amount of quiet time when asking for input online. Web meeting tools allow for everyone to participate at the same time in a discussion, idea generation, prioritization or voting exercise. Generally, people prefer to have quiet time to enable them to think about their contributions and read and reflect on the contributions of others. As a facilitator resist the temptation to talk while people are typing. Ten minutes of quiet time is OK. Check in to see if people want more time or are ready to move on. If you suspect some people are finished while others are still working, encourage them to build on others' ideas that are visible.

Test whether silence is a sign of engagement or disengagement. Be attuned to your own sense of whether people are engaged, whether you're getting the responses you are seeking or expecting. When you are unsure, ask the group, consider a quick poll as an alternative to a show of hands, ask individuals about their level of engagement and the pace of the meeting. Build checkpoints into your agenda; consider a pace-maker as one of the group roles. Remember to call on virtual participants in a hybrid meeting where some people are in the same room as you.

Be prepared to interrupt a continual speaker. Thank a person who has spoken up a lot and ask if someone else would like to add something. Go around the virtual table and give each person a chance to speak. You may want to think of a fill-in-the-blank or other simple question to encourage a brief response from each person. Implement a virtual talking stick and a 30-second speaking rule. Switch the conversation to a web meeting brainstorming tool to give everyone a chance to add their ideas and comments simultaneously.

Be aware of language differences. Language differences can affect the effectiveness of your meeting and discussion. Summarize comments to acknowledge contributions and check for understanding. Ask another participant to paraphrase or build off what they have heard. Web meeting tools where people type comments rather than speak them can give everyone time to compose ideas and read others' comments. This technique works for people who are shy or otherwise reluctant to speak up.

Create a virtual parking lot for off-agenda issues. Capture issues and comments that are important but may distract the group from the meeting objectives. Use a shared whiteboard, slide annotation or online flip chart. Acknowledge the comment and move on. Come back to the issues at the end of the meeting. In advance, ask someone else to act as scribe, especially for parking lot issues, actions and decisions.

Maintain momentum between meetings

Expect to increase your level of preparation as a facilitator when managing a series of virtual meetings. Plan for your facilitator's role to extend well beyond the bounds of your virtual meeting time. Build in increased time for communication and coordination between meetings and with participants. Schedule more checkpoints, in-person or by phone, with your client and meeting owner to assess progress and plan next steps. Don't just rely on email for communication.

Facilitate the creation of a plan for communications between meetings. Make sure everyone understands how, when and where to report status; surface issues; ask questions; get help; prepare for the next meeting; etc. Create an online check-in sheet when people visit your web meeting site. Ideally, you will have had a meeting with your client sponsor or meeting owner to determine to what extent the team has a well-thought-out communication plan in place already. Make sure you're not overstepping your perceived bounds. Chances are, your client will be grateful for your offer to help the group create a communication plan that works best for them.

Create venues for meeting asynchronously. Schedule asynchronous team input and activities between meetings to keep team members engaged and aware of progress and process. Avoid long periods of no communication or activity. Use asynchronous web-meeting tools to provide an interactive meeting place. Use check-in sheets or attributed comments so that you know who has participated. Try social networking tools to keep people connected—especially those that alert users when "friends" are doing something new.

Use multiple communication channels to maintain connections between meetings. Combine several methods of communication, including email, web postings, phone calls, web collaboration tools, social software tools, etc. Determine how your group's objectives can be best met by each form of communication.

Check that communications have been received. Discuss email protocol—ask for prompt replies or acknowledgement so that you know that your messages have gotten through. Don't assume that instructions and information have arrived or been read when it is critical to the effectiveness of your next meeting. Follow up with people you have not heard back from.

Keep people engaged if there is a long time between meetings. Encourage people to stay connected, even if you as the facilitator won't have an ongoing role. Give them ideas for interesting and fun ways to stay connected, which might include setting up a chat room, SharePoint site, Facebook area, or shared portal. Make sure the group has agreed upon ways to make periodic check-ins to keep the work of the group in everyone's mind's eye.

Establish action plans and accountabilities for delivering results. Allocate at least 10 minutes before the end of the official meeting time for follow-up and next steps. Create formal action plans. Include specific accountabilities and time frames. Ask for verbal acknowledgement from individuals responsible for specific actions. Make sure action plans are fully understood and agreed to. Confirm action plans immediately after the meeting in an email.

Keep track of deliverables between meetings. Ask participants how they plan to report updates. Encourage them to establish means for regular progress updates. Identify critical activities that others depend on and make sure these are flagged somehow by the group. Work with the team leader or client to ensure action items are completed; know what has been done or not done before the next meeting.

Use shared archives or web portals as a document repository. Create practical ways to share documents and information. If possible, use document archives to avoid multiple copies of documents being circulated at the same time. Use document editing/tracking tools to track changes. Ensure that everyone has access to the documents.

Continuously improve. Make sure that your tools and techniques are working for the group. Stay on the lookout for drifting participants, lower attendance rates, a lack of energy and other signs that may indicate something's not working. Using a similar process, tools or format each time can get stale. And since virtual team members can check out without anyone knowing, it's crucial to find ways to keep people engaged. Challenge yourself to come up with new ways to ask questions, engage participants or achieve outcomes.

 The facilitator should set the ground rules at the outset of the meeting. These can involve asking people to state their names before they speak, not to speak over one another, and anything else that will make the meeting run more smoothly. Also ask participants to turn off all devices that could cause distractions (such as cell phones that play "La Cucaracha" as the ringtone).

 Nearly every type of meeting can be virtual, but not all should be. FTF meetings work best for personnel employment development discussions, key customer prospecting meetings, highly sensitive issues, very personal issues, and some client meetings. If you feel an FTF meeting would work best to build a relationship, you're probably right.

Summary of tips and tricks

In addition to planning a viable agenda or series of agendas, keeping people focused and engaged, and maintaining momentum between meetings, here are a few more tips and tricks:

- When possible have people attend the meetings from their own offices rather than from a conference room (unless they're in a telepresence room). When you have too many people in one room, you hear echoes from the keyboard, and side conversations are a distraction.
- Introduce all participants. If you don't know everyone, ask people to introduce themselves.
- Review items on the agenda (which participants should already have), and remind them how important it is to stick to the agenda.
- If you're using web collaboration tools with a built-in phone, have people wear headsets to cut down on echoes.
- Keep a troubleshooting list handy in case you lose power, a connection breaks, a file freezes when downloading, or anything else unexpected happens.
- Give participants instructions in case you experience technical problems or get disconnected.
- Urge participants to address each other by name when responding to questions or comments. This will avoid confusion during an interaction.
- Build in time for participants to interact, giving the feeling of a more traditional meeting.
- Plan a short break if the conference lasts more than 1½ hours.
- Be attuned to body language if using video.
- At the end of the meeting, summarize the key points, reiterate any decisions, review action items.
- Agree on the date and time for a follow-up conference if one is needed.
- Be sure that someone at each site is in control of the camera so the speaker will always be in view.

Videoconferences

Videoconferencing is a great way to have "face time" and reduce travel budgets. In a videoconference, participants at two or more locations communicate by using audio and video equipment. The content is usually transmitted by an analog or digital phone network, a local area network (LAN), or over the Internet. In addition to holding virtual meetings, you can use videoconferencing to share documents, computer-displayed information, and whiteboards. You'll need a video camera, monitor, microphone, and speaker.

Presentation tips

Before

- Prepare the space to keep the camera from facing bright windows or bright lights.
- Remove unnecessary equipment such as computers, televisions, or anything that would draw attention away from the people at the meeting.
- Test the equipment in advance and have a contingency plan.
- Create an interesting background. A white background can make you look washed out.
- Seat participants as close together as possible so everyone can be seen on camera.
- If you're showing slides, adhere to the guidelines outlined in Chapter 7.
- Plan a 10- to-15-minute break if the meeting will last longer than two hours.

During

- Keep the microphone on mute when having a private conversation or when there are distracting noises.
- Be aware of any habits that will appear exaggerated. These can include but aren't limited to saying "um," fidgeting, and swiveling in your chair.
- Direct your voice toward the microphone.
- Look at the camera, not the monitor.
- Pick up all personal items before leaving the room so it's ready for the next group.

Clothing tips

- Wear conservative colors.
- Avoid white, which tends to look washed out.
- Avoid plaids and thin stripes, which may appear distorted on the screen.
- Leave flashy jewelry for evening wear.

Telepresence

Telepresence is the next best thing to being there; it's like videoconferencing on steroids. You walk into the room and there's a conference table facing high-definition screens that project life-size images of people sitting in a telepresence suite elsewhere in the world. It's so real that after a short time you forget you're not actually together in one room. Nancy Settle-Murphy had this to say about a telepresence meeting she facilitated:

"Walking into the conference room in Marlborough, Massachusetts, with five of us on one side of a curved table, and five of our colleagues across from us in Palo Alto, I felt transported to a different reality. I could really sense the presence of the others—it

Cisco TelePresence System 3000: Office suite. *Courtesy of Cisco Systems*

was a visceral experience in a way that simple teleconferencing cannot touch. I found I could whisper to my colleague at my end of the table, although she was 3,000 miles away, and only she and I could hear our conversation.

"For every one of us in Marlborough, it was an entirely new experience that dumbfounded us. One of my colleagues even balled up a piece of paper to throw it over the table to see if our Palo Alto colleagues could catch it. When they saw he was about to throw something their way, they held up their fingers to symbolize a goalpost. Of course, the ball of paper never left our room, but I think all of us believed that maybe it really would, the experience was that magical. Other than not being able to reach over and touch them, in all other ways it really was just like being in the same room together."

Telepresence systems are expensive to own, but hotel chains such as Taj, Marriott, and Starwood are opening telepresence suites throughout the world that can be rented by the hour. You can start a session with the press of a button, play back the session if you need to clarify something, and record the event to guarantee compliance with regulatory agencies in the case of litigation.

 Consider telepresence to conduct your business meetings, interview potential candidates (see photo on page 57), build relationships when you can't meet FTF, conduct key negotiations, and even hold family reunions. (I recently heard of two families who arranged a marriage for their children. The future bride and groom met via telepresence.)

Next generation

Perhaps younger people are craving more personalized connections. Orbit Social Phonebook is a combination of voice, email, face-to-face, and social networking. It's purported to be the game changer that will leave Facebook and Twitter in the dust. Phonebook provides a list of all your friends in a city, plus everyone who knows them. When you want to chat with a friend, look him up and arrange a virtual face-to-face meeting in a restaurant, bar, or other public place. It's a free app somewhat like telepresence, on a much smaller scale.

Teleconferences

A successful teleconference starts by planning properly, staying focused, having everything on hand that you need, and treating everyone as if they were in the same room. Be on time, be prepared, pay attention, and participate. However, you must be comfortable knowing that you'll be talking with a group that gives you no visual cues or feedback. Here are some guidelines to help you:

 To place conference calls over regular phone lines with no computer or Internet access required, sign up for free service at http://www.freeconference.com.

Tips for the moderator

Send out advance invitations that include the purpose of the call, dial-in number, PIN, name of moderator, start and end times, participants, and agenda topics. Try to limit the number of participants to ten; more than that is unmanageable on the phone.

- Test the equipment several days prior to the actual meeting.
- Conduct a few trial runs with the other locations to ensure that everything is working well and audibility is good.
- Arrive a few minutes early so you can greet each participant. Note when everyone is "present" so you can start the meeting.
- Ask people to introduce themselves so others can hear the voices.
- Discuss the agenda items that you sent prior to the meeting.
- Make sure people stick to the agenda. Keep people on course by being polite but firm.
- Close the meeting by thanking participants for their time.
- If a follow-up call is needed, get a consensus for the date and time.
- Conduct a role call at the end to allow for latecomers.
- State very clearly when the call has ended by summarizing highlights, action items, and follow-up items.

Tips for participants

Know the downsides of using speakerphones, cell phones, cordless phones, computer telephony, and headsets. Although these technologies are wonderful, they can create noise that others will find disruptive.

Do's

- Select a quiet room where there will be no background noise. You don't want people to hear your barking dog or screaming child. That would give the impression that you're sitting there in your pajamas waiting for the call to end.

- Read the agenda beforehand and be prepared to participate actively.

- Say your name before you speak even if you think everyone will recognize your voice. Begin with *This is Marty,* and then speak. When you re-enter the conversation, say *This is Marty* again.

- Come to the call with all relevant documents you need.

- Listen carefully to what others are saying.

- Participate without interrupting.

- Stay on topic and stick to the agenda and anticipated time frame.

- Use the mute button when you're not speaking. You don't want others to hear the tapping of your keys as you multitask or take notes on the computer.

- Turn off the ringer to your second phone line.

- Disconnect call waiting.

- Stay focused. It's easy to drift away or multitask. All too often we hear, "Can you please repeat the question? I wasn't paying attention." It's unprofessional.

Taboos

- Sitting in a leather chair. (When you move around people at the other end may hear what appears to be an embarrassing sound.)

- Shuffling papers, tapping your pencil, chewing gum, munching on chips, or anything else along those lines. The sound will be magnified, indicating that you're not fully engaged in the conversation.

- Breathing heavily into the mouthpiece.

> Unlike in the physical world, setting up a [virtual]
> booth eats all of 30 minutes and takes no sweat.
> —Melanie Lindner, "How to Tackle a
> Virtual Trade Show," Forbes.com

Chapter 9

Virtual Trade Shows: From Humans to Avatars

In this chapter

- *How realistic is a virtual trade show?*
- *Reasons to go virtual*
- *Before the event*
- *During the event*
- *After the event*
- *Event planners are coming aboard*

Does this sound familiar? You attend a live trade show and are away from the office for about a week. When you return, you're inundated with a tsunami of unanswered emails and phone calls. You must take care of everything else that transpired during your absence. You have meetings to attend. And you have too many pressing commitments. So all the good information and hot leads you got at the trade show are placed on the back burner, never to reach a boil.

You can't afford to ignore the virtual trade show market. Businesses of all sizes are trying out the concept as a revenue generator and marketing tool. Virtual trade shows aren't gimmicks; they're game changers. As live trade show attendance continues to plummet, it's expected that within the next several years more than 25 percent of all trade shows will be conducted in virtual environments—adding one more tool to everyone's marketing arsenal. Some companies are testing the waters with hybrid trade shows as a way to increase attendance at a relatively low cost. The virtual component can include an online representation of the event, the ability to watch live streaming video, and an integration of Twitter and Facebook.

When people attend a virtual trade show, they can sit at their computers and be there when it's convenient, 24/7. Travel isn't impeded by inclement weather, which can be a problem for live trade shows during certain times of the year. After the show ends you can keep it online for several months, extending the exposure.

Dan Ziman of Lithium Technologies wasn't sure the topic of customer relationship management would draw enough for a real summit. Lithium's virtual trade show drew more than 2,200 registrants, and about half logged on for a 10-hour event. A quarter of the attendees were from other countries. "We couldn't have accomplished that with a live event," he said.

How realistic is a virtual trade show?

Virtual trade shows can be as realistic as a three-dimensional walk-through of an entire trade show or as simple as a series of pages with each one representing a virtual exhibition booth. Companies can register visitors and give each one an ID number, making it easy for them to receive information. As a visitor, you will:

- Log in, watch the introduction, and get a sense of the event.
- Get a floor map to decide how you want to navigate the show.
- Enter a building that looks like any convention center or meeting place. Your host might even replicate the top floor of the Sears Tower.
- Sign up for the conference sessions you want to attend. (Many are recorded in advance and there's a Q&A at the end. You can watch the recording later on by logging into the session and miss only the Q&A.)
- Enter a conference hall with a podium and audience.
- Browse the exhibition floor.
- Enter booths that reflect the imagery of real-world trade show booths with desks, displays, and representatives waiting to welcome you with demos, giveaways, and prize drawings.
- Listen to live or on-demand presentations from keynote speakers.
- Place literature in your virtual briefcase and download a zip file when you're ready.

Virtual lounge. *Courtesy of ON24*

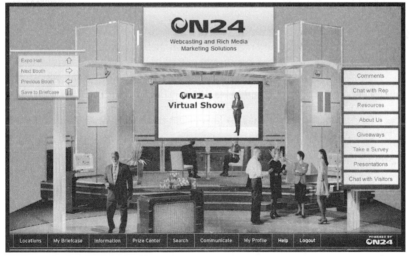

Trade show floor. *Courtesy of ON24*

- See the wizardry of avatars, 3-D graphics, multimedia videos, and slide shows.
- Raise your glass in the virtual networking lounge. Mingle. See if you can add anything to the conversations that are happening. If you want to speak to someone privately, use email or chat.

Reasons to go virtual

In addition to showing the world you're a tech-savvy company, here are just a few reasons to go virtual:

Reduce expenses. Imagine participating in a trade show without the cost of reserving your space, shipping (or renting) your booth and all the materials, flying a crew of people to populate the booth and host the hospitality suite, paying for hotel rooms and meals, and all the other expenses you typically incur at a live event.

Attract more visitors. An attractive booth with wonderful display signs will bring people in. But once they get there, what's next?

- Offer product demonstrations, games, trade-show discounts, and anything else that makes visitors feel involved.
- Offer raffles and surveys to help you collect contact information.
- Offer promotional products as giveaways as well as white papers and other things of value.

Staff your booth. You would never leave your booth empty at a live trade show, so don't leave it empty at a virtual trade show. Instead of standing on your feet for endless hours, you can sit at your computer answering questions and chatting with attendees. Because you're online, you can have several chats at a time and rotate people every one or two hours.

Be sure your company has no firewalls in place that could limit or deny access.

Open yourself up to new markets. Explore new markets without blowing your annual marketing budget. Because of low overhead, you can attend trade shows you otherwise couldn't afford and free yourself from being stuck in the rut of repeating what worked last year or the year before. Change what didn't work from previous shows. Experiment with innovative exhibit ideas.

Set up with ease. You can set up a virtual trade show in a reasonably short time, depending on the software and the site. Most offer instant messaging to chat in real time and some offer Voice over Internet Protocol (VoIP).

Generate exciting leads. You can run analytics and keep track of attendees and companies, making it easy to follow up after the show. Collect valuable leads and have a built-in management system that can track those leads.

Level the playing field. Large companies can pay $100,000 and upward for a live trade show, which is out of reach for many small companies. In the virtual arena, smaller companies can participate and compete as well.

Track every transaction. Every action and transaction can be tracked, reports are transparent, and ROIs can be calculated easily.

 One thing you may miss from a live trade show is not digging your fingers into the candy bowl at the booth.

The obvious downside of a virtual trade show is the lack of face-to-face, on-the-spot meeting opportunities. However, you can learn about products and services, exchange virtual business cards, and make follow-up appointments by phone or in person.

Before the event

Prior to the event, you must establish meaningful and measurable goals, determine the most effective exhibit booth display, select promotional collateral and products, and train your team members to represent your company regarding lead generation and securing sales.

Schedule the event carefully. Timing is everything.

- Be aware of other events in your industry so you don't compete for attendees' time.
- Don't schedule your event too close to major holidays.
- If you have a global audience, be aware of holidays in the countries you're targeting.
- Be attuned to budget cycles in your industry.

Recruit sponsors. Virtual trade shows can be as lucrative for sponsors as live trade shows. Remind prospective sponsors that they can benefit from lead generation, branding, and visibility. Educate sponsors with your marketing materials and a pre-show website.

Optimize your programs. An optimized program will draw the greatest number of attendees. Here are a few suggestions:

- Book speakers early. (The good ones book well in advance.)
- Schedule your best events throughout the day to encourage people to stay longer.
- Plan breaks between events so attendees can visit the exhibit hall.
- Focus on adding value for your attendees rather than selling.

Gaining traction

Following are some suggestions for gaining traction:

- Optimize your trade-show web page for all browsers (including smartphones).
- Prepare still images, podcasts, videos, and multimedia to engage the attention of your visitors.
- Exhibit a warm and engaging person as the face of the company to keep visitors coming back.
- Monitor Twitter, Facebook, and blogs to get feedback on what is and isn't working. This will let you respond immediately to any negative issues.

If your virtual trade show complements a live trade show, plan the exhibition floor layout and booth location to match. Provide online maps of the floor and link each booth on the map to the vendor's virtual booth.

Boost registration. As soon as you've finalized the details, begin registration. Keep the registration process simple.

- Minimize the number of clicks. Include a landing page with a link to the registration. When the registration is completed, have a thank-you page with confirmation appear.
- Include a dynamic description of the event and an audio teaser.
- Remember to include fields for global audiences.
- Ask two or three short-answer questions, if relevant.
- Stay in touch with registrants through a series of three or four different email blasts. (There's a difference between reminding and nagging.)

Market, market, market. Begin marketing your event two months in advance to give attendees time enough to reserve the dates.

- Market the event through website advertising such as banners, video clips, magazines, portals, partner sites, and sponsor sites.
- Use your email newsletters, partner, and sponsor newsletters. Send out press releases and develop articles that correlate with your event topic.
- Post the event on social networking sites.
- Find organizations or associations interested in promoting this event to their members and customers.
- Get your sponsors and exhibitors committed to promoting the event.

 One week before the event, have a "dress rehearsal" so you can make whatever adjustments are necessary. Contact the speakers to reconfirm the dates and times. Recheck all the equipment the day before the event.

During the event

Try these tips when the event is in process:

- Have IT help on hand in the event that Murphy's Law strikes. (You know, if something can go wrong, it will.)
- Assign a moderator to keep sessions lively.
- Conduct polls to gather qualification information.

- Delegate someone to record the speakers and all the events.
- Direct visitors to the marketing collateral.

After the event

No amount of planning or success during the event will be of value if you fail to follow through after the event.

- Hold a leads meeting to divide the leads into hot, warm, and cold. Assign a sales representative to contact the hot leads, send a written message to the warm leads, and add the cold leads to your database to send newsletters or occasional communications.
- Analyze the traffic patterns, what information was viewed most, and the survey results.
- Send "we missed you" emails to all who registered but didn't attend. Encourage them to visit the event online.
- Send "thank-you" emails to all those who attended. Encourage them to revisit the event online to capture anything they have missed. Suggest that they share the link with others.
- Thank all speakers and send a small gift to show your appreciation.
- Keep the event live. (Ninety days is recommended.)
- Create an event audit to justify the next event.

Event planners are coming aboard

Savvy event planners are adding virtual event management to their repertoires. To manage or coordinate a virtual trade show, you should:

- **Become at ease with technology.** Although event planners don't need to program, they do need to learn enough of the technology to exercise a series of tasks. Tasks can include generating carefully timed emails, scheduling and releasing alerts, broadcasting during an event, delivering breaking news, or getting last-minute speakers if necessary. If Murphy's Law should rear its ugly head during a video or web transmission, event planners must have immediate resources available to correct problems.

In real-world trade shows, speakers typically thank the technicians who help their voices to be heard. The same courtesy should extend to the virtual world.

- **Engage your sense of humor.** Your sense of humor will go a long way when dealing with demanding sponsors, exhibitors, and attendees. And when "technology happens," or when any bump in the road threatens the smooth running of the show, your sense of humor can keep you from pulling your hair out.

In the real world you should be quick to apologize for an honest mistake. In the virtual world a smiley icon can do that.

- **Understand the legal ramifications.** Much like in the face-to-face world, legalities are an issue. Event planners must protect their interests, yet keep sponsors, exhibitors, attendees, and speakers happy. In the virtual world, event planners can place disclaimers regarding sponsors, exhibitors, attendees, and speakers. Know when to get an attorney involved.

Part Four

Managing and Working Virtually

GONE ARE THE DAYS when colleagues worked under the same roof or even the same flag. More people than ever are working virtually. This trend has been driven by laptops, email, IM, high-speed Internet access, smartphones, secure networks, and a host of other technologies that have changed where people work and the way they work. Read on for tips and tactics for managing and working virtually and setting up and maintaining virtual team networks.

A number of factors are driving the growth of mobile work including potential cost savings from a reduced office footprint, the need for access to global talent, threats of business disruption, concerns for eco-responsibility, employee work/life balance, and financial hardship to employees caused by the high cost of commuting.

—"Top 10 Myths about Mobile Work," Sun Microsystems white paper, August 2008

Chapter 10

Managing a Virtual Workforce

In this chapter

- *Companies benefit*
- *Communication is key*
- *Hone your management skills*
- *Document the policies and expectations*
- *Establish a comprehensive training program*
- *Performance feedback and appraisals*
- *Manage intercultural teams*
- *From the trenches: In their own words*

Working virtually is here to stay. As commuting times grow, gas prices rise, and technology becomes faster and more reliable, workers and employers are discovering the benefits of telecommuting. It is now possible for anyone with a desk, computer, and telephone to become a virtual worker (also called mobile worker, remote worker, or telecommuter), capable of completing a day's work in bunny slippers. But how do you effectively manage these workers? The answer lies in trust, communication, and striking a careful balance between autonomy and accountability.

Companies benefit

When people work outside of a traditional office, companies benefit. They save on rent, furniture, and facility maintenance, benefit from a wider and more diverse range of talents, have a broader range of influence, reduce absenteeism and increase productivity, increase retention, and much more.

The virtual workplace is a major paradigm shift . . .

From	To
Eyeball management	Trust management
Observation oriented	Success oriented
Fixed-team involvement	Shifting-team membership
Team members dedicated 100 percent to one project	Most team members working on multiple projects
Teams having fixed starting and ending points	Teams forming and re-forming continuously

 I encourage all managers to read Chapter 11, "Working Far from the Mother Ship."

Communication is key

One of the greatest challenges to managers of virtual workers is communication. Lack of communication and miscommunication are ongoing problems even in the traditional workplace. Add distance to the mix, and these challenges are intensified. Virtual workers don't have the

A strong virtual team starts with a strong manager.

Yes, managing a virtual team can be a challenge. But it isn't as difficult as you think if you create a plan and stick to it. Elizabeth Ross, Director of Technology Projects Execution at AMEC Earth & Environmental, has both worked virtually and managed virtual workers. She sees a direct relationship between the strength of a manager and the virtual work experience. In an interview in *CIO* magazine (May 30, 2009), she says, "Managers who know how to manage resources, subcontractors, and the like, can make the situation work, sometimes exceptionally. Managers who don't communicate well, don't know how to manage their own time well, and so on, don't get around to checking in [on] or managing the remote worker very well—if at all."

chance meetings that happen around the water cooler or the cafeteria. When colleagues don't build rapport, it can negatively impact collaborative efforts.

Technical people pose another challenge, as many (certainly not all) aren't natural communicators, and they aren't extroverts. They can remain sequestered in their offices and fail to converse with colleagues. Without regular face-to-face discussions, managers will need to pay special attention to their technical staff to solicit their valuable input.

 Sometimes hiring an outside coach may be the answer. I recently coached a highly technical person who was very shy and hadn't been demonstrating any "people skills." This woman hadn't been interacting with coworkers or her internal clients—other than by sending a few emails or IMs when there were problems. This was hindering her ability to move ahead in the company. As her coach, I helped her to become more conversant using day-to-day conversational skills. She started engaging coworkers in casual conversations, inviting them to lunch, stopping in to chat with clients, and more. She's now becoming a trusted advisor, not just a person who can solve technical issues. And she's looking forward to a promotion.

If you have concerns about managing virtual workers, remember this:

- They typically work longer hours because they don't have to spend time commuting.

- They're often more productive in their own environments without the day-to-day distractions of the brick-and-mortar office.

- They work on their natural clock rather than being forced into the traditional 9-to-5, five-day-a week schedule.

Hone your management skills

If you or someone you know was burned by a virtual worker who disappointed, don't let that jade your thinking. Some people are highly productive amid the hustle and bustle of a busy office environment; others find it easier to concentrate at home. Virtual workers typically appreciate the privilege of working out of a home office and will make a diligent effort to see that they're meeting their responsibilities and beyond. By carefully selecting virtual workers, setting clear expectations, and following up with them in a proactive and positive manner, you can create a successful partnership, one that results in a job well done, happier, more productive employees, and a healthier bottom line.

Select the right people. A virtual team depends on people who can get their work done without having a manager roam the halls peeking into their cubicles. (These aren't the type of people who rush in at 9 and quit sharply at 5.) Take time to discover if an employee has the potential for virtual work. For example, find out if his work environment is conducive to productivity. He may have young children, a barking dog, noisy neighbors, or other distractions. Working virtually is not for everyone; the selection process is key to making it work. There are ten characteristics a virtual worker must have to be successful. Ask yourself, Does this person . . .

1. Have a dedicated workspace?
2. Take work seriously?
3. Work well independently?
4. Accept responsibility for things that don't go well?
5. Respond as a team player in a variety of circumstances?
6. Have excellent communication skills?
7. Ask for help when needed?
8. Suggest ideas?
9. Make decisions collaboratively?
10. Work collaboratively?

Set clear expectations in writing. Defining productivity standards and expectations can eliminate many performance-related issues down the road. As soon as you start telecommuting arrangements, communicate the parameters of the job in writing. You may want to set assignment deadlines, require employees to work a set number of hours per week, state when you will be available for meetings, specify that you will respond to requests within a given period of time, and more.

Foster a sense of "we." Studies continue to show that employees who have strong friendships at work are more motivated, loyal, and productive. In a typical office setting these relationships can form naturally. You go to someone's office and see pictures of his family. You see things on his walls and shelves that mean something special. You get to know colleagues as people outside the office. These types of getting-to-know-you encounters don't happen naturally in a virtual setting. They must be fostered.

To build relationships, there's no substitute for meeting face-to-face. This can be done via technology, but it must be done. Allow time for people to get to know each other, discuss hobbies, community involvements, and things they like to do. If possible, there should be a face-to-face meeting among team members every quarter, even if the meetings are virtual.

Virtual workers must see themselves as part of the overall plan and know how they fit into that plan, or they may lose sight of the team's objectives. Encourage them to work with each other by creating team-oriented tasks that require input from several people.

 Create a periodic e-newsletter or blog. Profile people on the team and include photos of them and their families. Describe their hobbies, interests, volunteer activities, or hidden talents.

Synchronize schedules. Some of your virtual workers may want to work their own hours. A few may like to sleep until noon and burn the midnight oil. Others may want to put in four 10-hour days and have a long weekend. While these people may be happiest working when it best suits them, divergent schedules can erode the goals of a team. Set certain times during each day or week when remote workers need to make themselves available for calls or meetings. Following are a few things to do that will help:

- Maintain a group calendar. This allows team members to coordinate their efforts and not worry about infringing on each other's time.

- Be aware of the holidays in countries where you have workers.

- Understand that if you have virtual workers in different time zones, there are going to be times when group meetings inconvenience some members of the team.

Leverage communication and collaboration technologies. Technology has become so advanced that there's little difference between communicating with someone in the next cubicle, the next building, or another country. In order for your virtual workers to succeed, they must have the right tools. Here are some essentials:

- Good office phone with voicemail system capabilities and caller ID
- Fast, reliable Internet connection
- Virtual Private Network (VPN) to access the corporate network
- Teleconferencing tools
- Presentation-sharing tools
- Email and IM capabilities
- Antivirus software
- Project management tools to let people access information

- Online workspace to collaborate on projects through online file sharing
- Group bulletin boards, discussion areas, and chatrooms
- Web-based groupware and virtual office platforms along with dedicated software solutions to help manage group schedules and shared calendars
- Customer relations management (CRM) tools to keep customer data in order and make sure that all team members are on the same page.

Show your employees that you're invested in their success and they'll be more likely to give you their best effort.

Keep your virtual door open. Let virtual workers know that your virtual door is open. Presence awareness technology will let them know when you're available to discuss progress, answer questions, or chat about their concerns. It can also alert your staff if you're on a mobile phone. Remember to:

- **Touch base regularly.** Let your virtual workers know that they're part of the office and that you're available to help resolve issues and see that things are running smoothly. Use email, IM, and the phone to stay in touch. When your employee feels connected to the office, he'll be a much higher performer.

- **Build trust through availability.** Give virtual workers your cell phone so their calls don't go to voicemail in the event they need you. Go out of your way to deal with issues that would come up naturally if you all worked in one place. Although you must set parameters, virtual workers (especially those in other time zones and countries) need to feel comfortable calling you at odd hours when there's a critical need, even if it's during your dinnertime. Being available demonstrates support and will strengthen the relationship.

 Virtual workers should also feel comfortable collaborating, sharing ideas, and asking each other for help.

 Create time to chat. Chatting isn't the same as communicating. Chatting is personal and is crucial for a team to bond. Even though chatting can't happen organically because virtual teams can't have early-morning coffee or lunch together, there are some things you can do to promote this level of personal interaction. Consider a breakfast where all team members have coffee and bagels while videoconferencing, or order pizza for the group at their various locations and have a virtual pizza party.

Document the policies and expectations

Create a written policy stating who's eligible for virtual work. This document should consist of general descriptions, such as what job categories qualify, what the personal characteristics of a virtual worker must be, and anything else that reflects your company's needs. Describe the equipment and services your company will supply and what the virtual worker must supply. If relevant, include information about insurance and security issues.

Individualize the details. Because virtual workers will be doing different jobs, you'll need to prepare an additional document that outlines in writing what's expected of each person. Meet with each worker and draft a document describing his responsibilities. Here are some things to address:

- **Scope of work.** Although the job may be the same as the person would do onsite, outline the scope of all projects including milestones, deadlines, reporting, and anything else that's applicable.

- **Face-to-face meetings.** State how often the remote worker is expected to visit the home office or participate in videoconferencing.

- **Reimbursable expenses.** List reimbursable expenses. These may include the cost of computers, Internet access, fax machines, pagers, telephones, telephone lines, supplies, and other work-related costs.

- **Time off.** Outline up front what time off means and when it will be taken.

- **Legal issues.** Depending on the type of work, zoning laws may prohibit people from working at home. Check the person's city planning department or by-law office before you forge ahead.

- **How effectiveness will be measured.** Outline how you'll measure the tangible and intangible effectiveness of the remote worker's performance.

- **Escape clause for both sides.** As a manager, you may discover that a virtual worker needs to be brought back in-house because the arrangement isn't working. Or the worker may request to be brought back. Outline some of the details that would lead to either scenario.

Signals of slacking off can include reduced productivity, lack of responsiveness, polished answers to questions, constant technical problems, inventive excuses for missing deadlines or meetings, complaints about workload, and more.

Establish a comprehensive training program

Set up a training program that involves the remote workers and their supervisors.

For the virtual worker

Create an employee training program that includes any or all of the following:

- Expectations for accessibility, accountability, and self-direction.
- If the employee is paid hourly, the hours of work for which he'll be paid.
- Preferred methods of communicating with managers and teammates.
- Expectations for presence onsite and at meetings with coworkers.
- How to prepare progress reports and how often to submit them.
- Tips on time management.
- Guidelines for creating the best home-office working environment.

For the manager

Managers who are accustomed to the traditional office setting must reorient their thinking to learn the following:

- Managing by objectives (MBO). This means learning to work in tandem with your remote workers so you'll both (or all) be in sync. You may wish to prepare an itemized list of what is expected on a weekly, monthly, or quarterly basis.
- Managing for results by establishing quality and quantity norms as well as planning, scheduling, and tracking assignments and milestones.
- Administering flexible work schedules and tracking attendance, personal leave, and vacations.

> ## Teach people what to say.
>
> When someone calls the main office and asks for the virtual worker, you must train people on what to say. You wouldn't say the person works at home any more than you'd say the person's in the restroom. Here's how a typical conversation may go:
>
> Caller: May I speak with Mr. Jones?
>
> Callee: Mr. Jones is out of the office right now. May I have him return your call? [or] Mr. Jones is working at a remote site today. May I have him return your call?
>
> Caller: Sure.
>
> Callee: Please let me take your name, number, and a short message, and I'll have him get back you to as soon as he can.
>
> Then get the message to Mr. Jones immediately.

- Setting expectations for communicating with the virtual worker on a regular basis.

 It may also be useful to train "those left behind" to prevent them from feeling resentful. This will help everyone to work as a team and appreciate each other's responsibilities and challenges.

Performance Feedback and Appraisals

When appraising performance, focus on tangible and intangible objectives. Completing a proposal, for example, is a tangible objective. Ask: Did the employee get the proposal out on time? Was it comprehensive and on target? Did it yield the expected results? A person's work-related characteristics, for example, are intangible objectives. Ask: Does he communicate clearly? Does he take initiative and make decisions on his own? Does he collaborate well? Is he a team player? Does he go beyond the call of duty?

Performance Feedback

Whether an employee works onsite or offsite, he needs ongoing feedback. Don't wait until it's time for the performance review to provide that. The performance appraisal should contain no surprises.

Conduct regular meetings (in whatever form they take) to give feedback. Remember that virtual workers don't have much of an opportunity to bump into you, so make every effort to offer praise and give constructive feedback when they're due. You can do this through email, a short chat on the phone, during a meeting, or whenever the opportunity presents itself.

 As a rule of thumb, put praise in writing and criticize verbally. When you praise someone in writing, the person is likely to read your message many times, print it out, and show it to others. This amplifies the praise. When you criticize in writing, the recipient is also likely to read it many times. This can make him feel worse. When you criticize someone, you owe that person the courtesy of engaging in two-way communication. Do it face to face or on the phone.

Performance Appraisals

Although some companies have one set of performance appraisals for those who work onsite and another for those who work remotely, this is typically not a good idea. You should measure all workers by the same standards and leave no chance for either group to feel that the other is getting preferential treatment. All performance appraisals should . . .

- Outline and prioritize performance objectives.
- Define how performance is measured.
- Specify deliverables and deadlines.
- Create a plan for improvement (courses to take, new skills to learn) based on the input of both manager and employee.

Manage intercultural teams

Today's teams span time zones, geographies, language barriers, and diverse cultures. Stay alert to cultural issues. You may not be able to manage virtual workers in San Francisco the same way you manage those in Singapore. When you manage intercultural teams, make sure you understand the culture. Read books. Take courses. Be attuned to language differences, even if your teams speak English. Learn some of their language.

 Even though the workers you manage may speak English, they'll likely use words or phrases that you're not familiar with. A client recently asked me to facilitate a workshop between engineers from the US and their counterparts from India. Everyone spoke English, but there were differences in expressions between the two groups that were confusing. For example, the engineers from India often used the word *prepone*. (It's a perfectly logical word that hasn't caught on in the US yet. If you want to reschedule a meeting to a later time or date, you *postpone* it. If you want to reschedule a meeting to an earlier time or date, you *prepone* it.)

 Make an effort to become familiar with the official languages of the countries in which you have workers. Even if you communicate with your team in English, it shows respect if you make an effort to learn their language. After all, they've learned yours. And a knowledge of basic expressions will be a great help when you visit *them* on *their* turf.

From the trenches: In their own words

The following is sagely wisdom from my colleagues who are skillfully and successfully managing remote workers. I asked them each the same four questions. Answers are in their own words.

Bard Williams, Director of Marketing, TiVo

TiVo is a pioneer of the digital video recorder (DVR).

Q. How do you build trust?

A. I build trust with a proper introduction and virtual team. "All hands" are essential for the success of introducing remote workers to a cross-functional team. I make sure that the new team member's background and skill sets are broadcast to all. I often use conference calls, or less often, web-based conferences to make the introduction. Usually, I include icebreakers, such as the sharing of personal hobbies or interesting tidbits by the entire team, to unify the team and help engage more folks. Over time, I make sure successes are shared across the team, and I highlight personal achievements to help others remember the value of their team members.

Q. How do you evaluate performance?

A. [I do] quarterly evaluations—usually by phone—that include a self-evaluation and a review of progress on goals and objectives. If there's an issue, I try to deal with it quickly and in person, if at all possible.

Q. What do you find to be the best way for workers to communicate with you and with each other?

A. Regularly scheduled meetings are a must. They add a regularity and formality to the communication and ensure that even if things get crazy, there's always a time to sync. Most cross-team communications happen by phone or email.

Q. How do you facilitate team meetings?

A. Mostly through conference calls, sometimes through web conferencing with Adobe Connect. When possible we have in-person meetings, but we've moved away from that because of the expense and the geographic dispersion of the team.

Charlie Sidoti, Vice President, Risk Control Services, OneBeacon Insurance Group

OneBeacon provides specialty, commercial, and personal insurance solutions through teams of local experts partnering with select independent agents.

Q. How do you build trust?

A. It is not a matter of *building* trust. If the trust has to be built, the relationship between supervisor and remote employee is probably not suitable for a telecommuting arrangement. As a manager, I take a leap of faith when I place someone in that situation. I start with a very high level of trust. If I have reason not to trust the employee, I shouldn't put them in the telecommuting position in the first place. I believe this approach empowers and motivates the employee. It also results in a high level of trust in me from the employee. My experience is that this most often leads to high dedication from the employee. Sometimes the trust is damaged or turns out to be unwarranted. When this happens I manage through the situation. It is easier to manage with a specific set of facts than try to manage a wide array of things that hypothetically could happen because of an assumption that employees with minimal direct supervision can't be trusted. We approach exempt highly skilled positions very similarly to nonexempt lower skill and wage positions.

Q. How do you evaluate performance?

A. This is difficult. The temptation is to focus solely on results because that is what matters. It is easy to convince yourself that an employee who is delivering results (sales, production units, hours, etc.) is by definition performing as desired. Behaviors, however, lead to results and should not be assumed to be there just because the results are. Many behaviors are very difficult to observe in remote employees because of their remoteness. We try hard to ensure that results are in fact repeated because they are based on sound behaviors instead of just luck.

We consciously try to mitigate the remoteness by visiting employees often and forcing them to come into offices on a regular basis. Some argue that this defeats the purpose of having a remote worker, but long-term it helps keep remote employees engaged with our business strategies, corporate and department culture, and their peers. Additionally, if specific desired behaviors are not easily observed because of the employee's remoteness we look for proxy variables that suggest what the behavior was or wasn't. In account files we pay particular attention to meeting agendas, minutes, and correspondence. We continually try to raise the level of file documentation quantity and quality. Documentation files should tell a story of how the employee handled a particular situation or customer engagement. This is a constant battle, because employees consider much of the extra paperwork to be a waste of time. However, it gives the management team a good sense of what is and isn't happening in terms of communications and relationship-focused behaviors.

Q. What do you find to be the best way for workers to communicate with you and with each other?

A. There is no *best* means. The real danger is that we too often over-rely on a single form of communication. It is so easy for managers and staff to default to email, or worse, text messages. The ease of use of these tools is both their greatest benefit and their biggest weakness. We want our staff to select an appropriate communications medium based on nature of content, relationship to individuals involved, time constraints, communication objective, urgency, etc. We encourage staff to use a diversity of communication methods the same way financial planners recommend diversification in an investment portfolio, because in reality different communication tools perform differently.

We want staff to consider not just efficiency, but effectiveness of the communication method selected. For some messages, an email might be more efficient than a meeting. But if the email transmittal method requires three attempts over the course of six months to achieve the intended goal, it probably is not very effective. Scheduling a meeting, which requires more time and effort up front, may actually be the better choice in the long run. With current technology there are many communication options available. We are experimenting with emerging tools such as social networking sites and using brief recorded PowerPoint messages, which we make available to staff on demand. We also supply staff with notecards to encourage them to consider handwritten notes, which can be more personal and memorable to the recipient.

Q. How do you facilitate team meetings?

A. Although it's expensive, we try to get the team together annually for an extended meeting. The physical meeting helps to establish a personal camaraderie that results in more frequent and better collaboration amongst the staff throughout the year. Additionally we have frequent conference calls where we share best practices, successes, challenges, strategy changes, and performance summaries. On a regular basis we also have webcasts where we drill down into specific topics more deeply.

Hal Tugal, Vice President, Engineering, Barry Controls

Barry Controls is a recognized world leader in the design, manufacture, and application of products and systems technology for the control of vibration, mechanical shock, and structure-borne noise.

Q. How do you build trust?

A. It all depends on the person and his or her attitude. If the person is honest, has good integrity, and trusts you, things usually work out well.

Q. How do you evaluate performance?

A. Simply stated, by output—the results one obtains from the person, through sales, analysis, meetings with results, etc. The performance is usually good.

Q. What do you find to be the best way for workers to communicate with you and with each other?

A. Email, conference calls, cell phones, and telephone calls work very well. Online presentations reviewed via PC help quite a lot. The remote person has to have a good PC, printer, and fax, a top-of-the-line Internet connection, and a mobile telephone.

Q. How do you facilitate team meetings?

A. Conference calls and presentation-sharing on a PC.

Candace Toner, CEO, Biomatters, Ltd.

Biomatters is a New Zealand company dedicated to creating software that addresses large existing inefficiencies in biological research in the post-genomic era.

Q. How do you build trust?

A. Trust is established through regular reviews of the output created, and detailed feedback, critique, and analysis. When someone puts in effort and time to produce code or visit a customer, it is rewarding to know that management actually appreciates the time and diligence put into a task, enough so to provide input and guidance. Additionally, timelines set for tasks are no different than those set for being in the office. If there are tasks performed more quickly than originally planned, that is acknowledged and appreciated. If there are delays, then it is not a question of "What else have you been doing?" but rather, "What is there that the team needs to do to get it finished?" There is no reference to or ill feeling about working remotely, and thus the trust is built that the home office is no different than an office down the hall.

Q. How do you evaluate performance?

A. Every employee in the company, regardless of their physical work location, has a set of KRAs (Key Results Areas) that are mutually agreed upon at the beginning of the financial year. These include three areas of measurement—a Performance Plan, Stretch Objectives, and a Career Development Plan. There are shared company goals that get the highest weighting in the Performance Plan KRAs, then group-specific, and finally, employee-specific measures. The employee also provides input into the objectives. Formal reviews are every six months, with less formal feedback on a weekly basis via a shared developer meeting, and if needed, a one-on-one phone call.

Additionally, I created a peer review document that is used by the developers to evaluate each other as a team. This is very effective for building a strong feedback discussion during the annual reviews. Each developer evaluates himself or herself and the totals are tallied. Then every developer evaluates the other in an anonymous format, with the averages taken. My software development team manager sits down in private with each developer and goes over the comparison of how they see themselves versus what the team's consensus is of their performance. There are high points and low points, and it is excellent for coaching the individuals on areas of strengths and weaknesses and for helping them create a personal plan for the year ahead.

I've had some developers join Toastmasters to improve communication skills, take time management courses that they would never normally consider, and get involved in drama and acting courses to help "come out of their shells," all as a result of these managed feedback sessions.

Q. What do you find to be the best way for workers to communicate with you and with each other?

A. For our company, it is definitely via email or chat features. In terms of managing shared workload in the development cycle, we have a number of software tools that we use to manage customer relationships and sales, development jobs, bug fixing, and timelines. These tools are crucial to our performance: TeamCity, JIRA, and Salesforce.com. All of these applications are accessible via secure VPN [Virtual Private Network] from any Internet connection in the world, so everyone can stay in touch and on top of things when away. It's vital to make it easy to stay connected to the heartbeat of the company, not only to ensure a smooth workflow but for employee engagement in the business.

Q. How do you facilitate team meetings?

A. Every week we have a whole company meeting for an hour. There is a regular agenda, and each team leader reports on what has happened in their area for the week. There is an executive summary from me, a technical update from the development team leader, a customer service and support update on questions and suggestions from customers, a market update from our sales team, etc. There is also a specific developer meeting held every Monday for one hour where open and robust debate and discussion is held. We also use the Belbin system for team roles and often refer to this during team creation for projects and during heated discussions.

Mary Ellen Eagan, President, Harris Miller Miller & Hanson (HMMH)
HMMH is an international leader in environmental noise and vibration control, air quality analysis, airport and airspace planning, and climate and energy solutions.

Q. How do you build trust?

A. We encourage interoffice visits by many staff, not just managers, so that the maximum number of people get to know each other by face, not just through voice and email. This gives opportunities to socialize a bit outside the project teams. "Management" also visits branch offices regularly to discuss strategic issues, business development, and just to check in with employees, so that visits from "the home office" do not have a negative connotation that evokes a response of *uh-oh* as soon as a branch hears I am visiting. We also don't deliver significantly bad news by email or even by phone if at all possible.

Q. How do you evaluate performance?

A. We don't track financials by geographic location except for tax purposes where gross receipts or profits are required by state. Performance is judged at the individual level compared with each person's goals, responsibilities, and metrics, which are consistent company-wide. Practice areas (markets served) are much more of a focus than branch-office performance at a physical location. Our philosophy is that we're all in it together, with common resources and objectives, and we downplay (and try to eliminate as much as possible) differences among offices.

Q. What do you find to be the best way for workers to communicate with you and with each other?

A. We use email heavily and provide both laptops and PDA equipment for frequent travelers. We allow network access via VPN and encourage everyone to stay in touch no matter where they are. We also have two regular company-wide meetings totaling about 1½ hours, for which attendance is mandatory, to discuss scheduling, make announcements, identify business development leads, and present topics of varying types (technical and administrative). We have a pretty sophisticated network and interoffice connectivity system that facilitates data transfer and file sharing.

Q. How do you facilitate team meetings, when appropriate?

A. We use WebEx or regular teleconferences. The conference-room cameras haven't caught on so much, but they are available. We stop short of a full AV "virtual" meeting. For major projects using interoffice teams, we sometimes ask staff to travel to the office where the project is being headed to work in person for a week or so with the rest of the team.

Jeff Teisch, Managing Director, Brown Brothers Harriman (managing Global Technology organization)

Brown Brothers Harriman, offering a range of international investment banking services, is the oldest privately owned bank in the United States.

Q. How do you build trust?

A. Building trust between workers that are not in the same location is no different than building trust between workers at the same location. It is your ability to accomplish and follow up on what you have agreed to that your employees will appreciate. Being a person of your word is what is most important in building trust with your employees.

Q. How do you evaluate performance?

A. In order to accurately evaluate an employee's performance, you must first agree on the goal that they will be working towards. Discrete, measurable goals are the best way to accomplish this. Some of these goals will be in the form of a mutually-agreed-upon project plan. These plans could span weeks, if not months, and have significant milestones and deliverables along the way. Ensuring that employees adhere to the project plan is the best way to evaluate performance as well as to make adjustments, if required, throughout the project. It should not matter which location an employee works at as long as the desired outcome has been achieved.

Q. What do you find to be the best way for workers to communicate with you and with each other?

A. There are several ways of communicating with remote workers, and technology has helped to improve these methods of communication. Email is the most common method of communication in corporations today. Any employee can stay in touch with what is going on if they have access to their corporate email system. Technology exists that will allow employees to access their business email from any Internet-capable device so that they no longer need to be at an employer's location to remain on top of things at work. Further extending the reach of email are handheld devices that allow you to access your corporate email anywhere you travel and at any time of day. (This depends on your carrier and service plan; this coverage could extend worldwide.)

Instant messaging is also popular among employees who would like to use electronic means of communication but prefer the benefits of a more interactive conversation. For remote users, it does not matter where you are. As long as you have access to your company's system, you will be able to use email and instant messaging products to stay in touch. In addition to these communication vehicles, collaboration tools exist so that employees can easily refer to and share all relevant documentation.

Q. How do you facilitate team meetings?

A. Utilizing a phone conference service, whether it is in-house or managed externally, is the best way to facilitate a team meeting. Conferencing services allow multiple people to share information in a manner that all involved may hear. This is a great method to use when conducting a status meeting. Videoconferencing systems take this method of communication one step further and allow you to see the person or people that are in attendance, which helps provide a more effective means of communicating.

Tom Gardam, Director of Test Engineering, Pegasystems

Pegasystems is the industry leader in Business Process Management (BPM) software solutions.

Q. How do you build trust?

A. 1. Build and sustain a weekly engineering rhythm with a weekly goals process. Tie weekly goals to quarterly goals, which you present to the whole team in person every quarter.

Wednesday = Mid-week check

Thursday = Set goal for next week

Friday = Close the week

Monday = Demo the results

Repeat every week.

2. Insulate the remote teams from the daily distractions of the onsite HQ [headquarters]. Control and qualify the flow of work.

3. Defend the team and let them know when you do.

4. Face time. Visit the offshore team regularly. Work with them in a workshop setting. Make them "your team," not a remote faceless software factory.

5. Reward all sins of commission and punish people who suffer in silence. Never accept the "we are waiting for guidance" excuse—the team should make proposals.

6. Choose your leaders carefully and groom them. Allow them to make the on-the-ground decisions. Avoid remote management of granular tasks. Give the leadership team SMART [Specific, Measurable, Attainable, Realistic, Time-bound] goals, and let them figure out how to get them accomplished.

7. Be energized and enthusiastic—prizes, praise, and competitions may seem tacky in the US, but offshore they are a very good thing.

8. Be respectful of time differences. Lead by example—if you work unsocial hours then your leadership team will do the same.

9. Be very aware of family commitments—especially in India, where family is king. If possible meet the parents of the leads who work for you.

Q. How do you evaluate performance?

A. 1. Performance is measured at the process level, weekly goal performance level, and individual staff level.

2. Build value chain maps of the core processes used. (Establish the ratio between value-add time and time spent waiting for each major process—publish this in percent form and improve on it.)

3. Staff are measured using a process called Role Value Utilization (RVU). This picks four key competencies necessary within the offshore organization overall and then weights each competency based on role. Every month the leads grade their teams (1–5) for each competency area. This is averaged across a quarter and rolled up into a percent value. The target is 90 percent RVU. If staff fall short of that target two quarters in a row then they are managed out by the leads. This way the leads control their team. The leads themselves are assessed by the onshore managers' view of their entire team and their team's weekly goal performance.

4. Establish a "continuous improvement" mindset.

Q. What do you find to be the best way for workers to communicate with you and with each other?

A. 1. See points 1 and 3 in "How do you build trust?", above.

2. Make sure that the onshore contact is not a bottleneck. By growing the offshore leads you can avoid "issue Ping-Pong" between offshore and onsite teams.

3. Institutionalize knowledge transfer. Make sure to publish a quarterly curriculum of weekly team seminars. Each week have a different theme and different presenter. Finish with a quiz and prizes for the group!

4. Try to use technology to get around written language issues. For example, use Snagit AVI [Audio Video Interleave] screen capture to record UI [user interface] bugs rather than have the team try and write down what they see.

Q. How do you facilitate team meetings, when appropriate?

A. See points 1 and 3 in "How do you build trust?", above.

A lot of managing an offshore team is similar to managing any team. The things you do are things any good manager should do. However, the difference with offshore is that there is much less leeway for doing it badly. If you don't manage an offshore team and you don't have an offshore leadership team you can trust, then it is almost impossible to see what is going on.

I think of flexible hours and telecommuting as making better use of our overall resources. In effect, we have people that cover for us around the clock. It's a benefit to the company more than anything else.

—Mike Natan, CIO,
OneBeacon Insurance Group

Chapter 11

Working Far from the Mother Ship

In this chapter

- *What it takes to be a virtual worker*
- *Draft a proposal*
- *For better or for worse*
- *Invest in good furniture*
- *Create your own environment*
- *Find time to exercise*
- *Minimize distractions*

Whether you consider yourself a virtual worker, telecommuter, remote worker, or mobile worker, it all boils down to the same thing: You're working far from the mother ship. Your manager and teammates may work at other local offices, in other cities or states, or in other countries.

What it takes to be a virtual worker

Working virtually can be a rewarding and challenging experience, but it's not for every person or every job. For example, programmers who customize databases can work virtually. IT people typically cannot; they must be onsite to troubleshoot. Many people would like to work at home even one or two days a week, but few are suited to do it on a regular basis. A successful virtual worker is:

- Self-motivated and self-disciplined
- Able to work independently without supervision
- Highly organized, with good time management skills
- Adept at multitasking
- Confident in decision-making abilities
- Diligent about meeting deadlines
- Able to work under pressure
- Able to troubleshoot basic problems
- Resourceful
- Capable of quickly grasping and applying new concepts
- Able to use and adapt to mainstream technology.

Draft a proposal

Remember that working virtually is a privilege, not a right or entitlement. It's rare to find a job that starts out as a telecommuting gig. It's more likely that you'll first have to demonstrate your productivity and trustworthiness. Once you've done that, create a compelling business case. Focus on what this arrangement will do for your company, not on what it will do for you. Your manager doesn't care that you want to be there when the kids get home from school. Present a proposal you've thought through carefully. Here are some steps to get you started:

Consider the arrangements that will best meet your needs and the company's needs.

- How many days or hours per week are you proposing?
- What part of your job can you do easily, or better, at home?
- What compromises are you willing to make?

Identify potential difficulties and offer solutions.

- How will this arrangement impact your relationship with your col leagues and supervisors?
- How will you keep in touch with your team and the home office?
- What equipment will you need?
- What equipment do you already have?
- Will you suspend working at home if you're needed at the office?
- How will customers or clients interact with you?
- How will you get and give support and feedback?

Stress the ways in which your telecommuting can benefit the company.

- Will you work longer hours because you won't be commuting?
- Will your absence allow more spaces and resources to be available for others?
- How much more productivity do you anticipate because of fewer distractions?

When you're ready to present your proposal, ask for a meeting with your manager. Listen to what she has to say. If she's skeptical, revise your proposal, suggest a trial period, or try again at a later date.

For better or for worse

Following are a few of the great and not-so-great things about working virtually.

For better

Working virtually can mean anything from working in your home office with your cat on your lap to working in a satellite office to working on the beach in Bora Bora (although the last is quite unusual).

Eliminate commuting costs. The most obvious and coveted benefit of not going to the office each day is not having commuting costs. You save the price of gas, wear and tear on your car, or train and bus fare.

Gain additional hours each week. You free up commuting time that can include hunting for your keys, trudging to and from the parking lot in bad weather, waiting for a bus or train, and other unexpected delays. Given that the average commute is estimated to be about one hour each day, this can free up five hours a week.

Accommodate other obligations. Early birds and night owls both can accommodate their needs with optimum schedules to meet the kids at the bus stop or take elderly parents to doctors' appointments.

Save on the cost of clothing. Although you may not choose to work in your bathrobe and bunny slippers, you'll certainly need a simpler wardrobe.

- Don't become sequestered and work nonstop. If you let it, telecommuting can interfere with your normal family life. Make every effort to spend evenings and weekends with your family and friends.

- Your office-bound coworkers don't want to hear that you're working on the beach or enjoying the sunny day working on the back porch. Always give the impression you too are slaving away at your desk.

Dispelling the myths.

No longer do smart businesspeople think that virtual workers . . .
- Sleep until noon, then meander to their computers in their PJs to type like compulsive monks.
- Suffer from low productivity and lack of discipline.
- Can be productive only when other team members work in the same office.
- Must be technically savvy.
- Jeopardize their chances for career advancement.
- Live a lonely and isolated existence.

For worse

Working virtually may seem like a fuzzy-slippered fantasy, but it does have its pitfalls. Here are a few:

Technology happens. When you have trouble with hardware, software, or your Internet connection, perhaps there's no one around to help. (The bright side is that when you have to rely on yourself, it's amazing what you can do and learn.)

You may wear a cloak of invisibility. Out of sight is sometimes out of mind. You may find out about relevant events too late. You don't learn of people's promotions, bereavements, and the like. You may be out of the loop on certain meetings because people forgot to include you.

You may not get the most from meetings. When you're teleconferencing, you don't get to participate in the after-meeting discussions. People may refer to visuals that you're not able to see. People may forget you're in a different time zone. You may have received the wrong dial-in code (perhaps two numbers were transposed). Your connection may not be working optimally, so you miss certain key points. People may mumble or talk softly, and you can't keep asking them to speak up. Organizers may show up late and you're stuck listening to a Beethoven concerto in its entirety. And you don't get to sample the free food.

You miss the day-to-day social interaction. You have to work harder to form personal relationships. There's no small talk around the vending machine, you miss the immediate nonverbal feedback, you can't stop by someone's office to chat, and you miss the office gossip.

Family and friends may not understand that you're working. Not all family members (those living with you and those living nearby) may understand that you're working. It's important to set boundaries, as we discuss later in this chapter.

 Don't share your computer with family members. This isn't the computer on which your children should be playing video games or going on Facebook.

 Secure all confidential records and make sure that unauthorized people don't have access to your computer or your files.

Invest in good furniture

Good furniture and lighting will improve your performance. Here are some guidelines:

Desk   The recommended height is 26 to 29 inches from the floor. You'll be most comfortable when the work surface is slightly above your elbow. Have enough surface area so you don't feel cramped.

Chair   Look for a chair that has a sturdy base with four or five legs on freewheeling casters. It should also have armrests to help relieve pressure on your wrists. When seated, adjust your chair so your feet are flat on the floor.

Lighting Poor lighting can cause eyestrain, headaches, and fatigue. Use indirect, ceiling-mounted, or ambient lighting in combination with a desk lamp. Track or ceiling lights should be slightly behind you. Position your monitor to reduce glare. Avoid reflections from windows or overhead lighting. Adjust blinds and curtains as necessary.

Electricity Cover cables to avoid accidents. Use a state-approved surge protector, and don't overload electrical outlets. Make sure that electrical enclosures such as switches, outlets, receptacles, and junction boxes have tight-fitting covers or plates.

 Prevent falls or slips by making sure floors are level and free of protrusions, loose tile, or worn or frayed seams, and carpets are well-secured to the floor.

Understand what your employer will provide, what you must buy, and what will be reimbursable (such as pens, paper, staples, paper clips, and the like). Not all companies will pay for your home equipment,

Set up a dedicated work area.

It's critical to physically separate your professional life from your personal life so you can work without distractions. This will help to put you in the right frame of mind when you're at the "office." Your office space can be a separate room, the corner of a room, an alcove, or whatever space you can allot for yourself. If you don't have a dedicated work area, your business and personal life may become blurred, leaving you distracted and disorganized. Don't share your space with family members.

Secure your password.

Security is more important than ever. You must safeguard your password. Many people choose passwords that are easy to remember such as their cat's name, their spouse's name, or a favorite vacation spot, but passwords like these are surprisingly easy to guess. Here are two easy tips for creating complex passwords from memorable information:

- Deliberately misspell words. (Your favorite vacation spot of Aruba may become ArBBA.)
- Substitute numbers or special characters for letters. (Randy can become r@nd3.)

especially if they provide office space. Some will, however, provide a laptop, smartphone, and other necessities. Regardless of whose equipment you use, you and your manager need to figure out how you'll protect your computer from hackers, spyware, and viruses.

Create your own environment

Does your office need an extreme makeover? Does it need a minor makeover? Your work environment impacts the quality of your work, so surround yourself with things that are important to you such as your favorite colors, family photos, souvenirs from a trip, books you enjoy, and the like. Here are a few other suggestions:

- Organize your supplies in attractive-looking baskets.
- Play tranquil music.
- Turn on a tabletop waterfall.
- Light scented candles.

Dress to go to the office. When you go to a traditional office you get dressed in business clothes—however dressed up or dressed down those clothes may be. The same thing applies when you work from home.

Green your office.

When you work from home you're already green. There are lots of things you can do to be even greener and in some instances save money:

- Turn off your computer at the end of each day. Even in sleep mode, it uses electricity.
- Switch off the chargers for your mobile phone, batteries, camera, and other equipment when you're not using them.
- Install energy-efficient, compact fluorescent bulbs. They use 75 percent less energy and last ten times longer than traditional bulbs.
- Install videoconferencing facilities by getting a webcam and signing on to Skype instead of going to meetings, when appropriate.
- Use the reverse side of 8 ½" x 11" paper.
- Print on draft quality for most documents.
- Recycle your printer cartridges.
- Keep a bin near your desk for recycling.
- Shred documents you no longer need. Bring the shredded paper to a shipping company (such as your local UPS store) for use as packing material.
- Get off junk mail lists.
- In the winter, turn down the heat and wear an extra sweater.
- In the summer, open a window instead of using air conditioning.

When you get dressed, you put yourself in the right frame of mind and gear up for the workday.

Create a daily schedule. Start your workday with a ritual. Yours may include taking a shower, getting dressed, eating breakfast, and planning your day. Create a start and end time just as you would in a traditional office setting. Your schedule may vary day to day, but whatever it is, stick to it and let coworkers know your hours.

When it's time to quit, turn off your equipment, close the door, turn on the radio or TV, take a walk, pick the kids up from school, change your clothes, and "go home." This will help you to avoid burnout or become a workaholic.

Be part of the team. Out of sight is out of mind. Stay connected to the mother ship so your manager and coworkers view your efforts at your office in the same way as they view those of the people they see each day. Here are a few ways to stay connected:

- Submit regular progress reports.
- Contact coworkers when you need help or can offer help.
- Be available for meetings and luncheons if you're near enough.
- Chip in for the occasional gift for a coworker.
- Adapt your schedule to the time zones of others, if possible.
- Adhere to core start and finish times, when possible.
- Communicate by phone, VoIP, IM, email, videoconferencing, and whatever other methods will make you part of the team.

 If you're ill or will be out of the office for personal reasons, be sure to let your manager and teammates know in advance.

Be your own cheerleader. Because people don't see you on a regular basis, you have to blow your own horn in a tactful way to demonstrate your accomplishments and productivity. You can do this by sending to your manager and teammates a weekly list of what you've accomplished, what challenges you've faced and overcome, what you'll be doing the following week, and what help you may need from them.

Create your own water cooler. Unless you like working in isolation (and very few people do), create your own team. It's energizing to be around and communicate with other people.

- Participate in traditional office activities when you can.
- Join social networking groups and participate in chats.
- Bond with colleagues through live networking groups that meet periodically.
- Take your laptop and go to a coffee shop that has WiFi. (If you're going to sit there for a long period of time, make sure you purchase something, even if it's just a cup of coffee.)
- Meet a friend or colleague for lunch.

Set expectations with family and friends. Let family and friends know that although you work at home, you have the same time constraints and responsibilities as people who go to the office. Occasional intrusions may be unavoidable, but you can minimize them by letting everyone know during which hours you are and aren't available. Also let them know what questions, special needs, or favors may be critical enough to warrant interrupting you. You may experience some teasing from people who are unfamiliar with telecommuting about "not having a real job." Take it in stride!

Schedule visits to the office. No matter how much technology keeps you in touch, it's important to meet with your colleagues face to face. If you're nearby, join the group for luncheons, important meetings, and other activities where you can interface. If you're across the country or across the globe, make an effort to schedule a meeting at the beginning of the fiscal year. If you wait, these trips have a way of "falling off" the budget.

Find time to exercise

Telecommuting can take a toll on your health because you're not getting the type of exercise that moving around the traditional office provides: walking up and down stairs, walking to meetings, walking to the copier, and more. Take a short exercise break every hour. Stretch, move, and get the blood circulating. Here are some exercise tips for people in reasonably good health:

Breathing. With your eyes open or closed, concentrate on breathing. Take 5 to 10 long and deep breaths, inhaling through your nose and exhaling through your mouth.

Eyes. At least once every hour look away from your computer screen and focus on an object 15 to 20 feet away. A wonderful exercise for eye relaxation is to rub your hands together briskly until your palms feel warm. Make shallow cups and gently place your palms over your eyes. Without pressing on your eyes, make sure no light enters. Hold your palms over your eyes for 30 seconds. For a little variety while your eyes are covered, roll both eyes to the left and back to the middle. Do this 5 times.

 Don't forget to blink. Studies have shown that when people are talking, they blink an average of 22 times a minute. When they're using a computer, they blink an average of 7 times a minute.

Hands and wrists. Every 15 to 30 minutes, stretch your arms out to your side and over your head. Massage your hands and wrists to improve circulation. Don't forget to massage the spaces between your fingers and the area around your nails. Flex your fingers and do wrist stretches frequently.

Neck. While breathing deeply, tilt your head toward your left shoulder, then toward your right shoulder. Then, with your head in a forward position, drop your chin to your chest and slowly raise it back up.

Arms and back. Hold your right elbow with your left hand. Gently push the elbow toward your left shoulder. Hold the stretch for five seconds. Repeat this exercise with the left elbow. Interlace your fingers and lift your arms over your head until your elbows are straight. Press them as far back as you can without causing discomfort.

Note: Report any work-related injury or musculoskeletal disorder to your supervisor immediately.

You never have to feel guilty about not being glued to your desk all day. If you take a look around a traditional office, you'll find that most people don't work all day long. They're chatting, grabbing a cup of coffee, lingering in the kitchen area, talking in each other's cubicles or offices, and generally moving around.

Allow yourself a few indulgences, but be sensible. Avoid the temptation to make regular refrigerator runs, take a nap, laze on the couch, or watch TV. You could wind up an unproductive, oversized couch potato.

Minimize distractions

Many people who work in brick-and-mortar office settings complain about the endless distractions they deal with each day. If you think this problem will be solved by working virtually, think again. Working virtually can have its own distractions, and it's up to you to minimize and eliminate them so they don't interfere with your work.

Telephone calls. Telephone interruptions are probably the biggest problems faced by those who work in virtual offices. Here are a few suggestions:

- Maintain a phone number exclusively for work, and don't give it out to family and friends.
- Get caller ID so you know who's calling before you answer.
- Create an appropriate, businesslike outbound message on your answering machine.
- Contact the National Do Not Call Registry at https://www.donot call.gov to minimize telemarketing calls.

Email. While email will help you stay connected, it can be a huge distraction if you're not diligent. Here are some tips for keeping email under control:

- Set up separate email accounts for business and pleasure.
- Use email filters to sort and keep track of email. You can opt to ignore emails that aren't directly related to work.
- Be responsive to emails from colleagues so they know you're there and being productive.
- Be selective as to how many groups or lists you join. Joining even a few can dramatically increase the number of emails you get each day.

✓ Check out Chapter 14, "Email Savvy."

In summary . . .

- Set up a comfortable work space that will help you to be productive.
- Work at your desk, not in bed or on the couch.
- Get to the tasks at hand, and don't procrastinate. (You can rearrange your sock drawer in the evening.)
- Stick to a relatively consistent work schedule.
- Don't let friends or neighbors distract you.

Go back to working in a traditional office if working virtually isn't for you.

Our team is well balanced. We have problems
everywhere.

—Tommy Prothro, American
football coach

Chapter 12

Go, Team!

In this chapter

- *Select a cohesive team*
- *Form, storm, norm, and perform*
- *Manage a team*
- *Dynamic meetings*
- *Appreciative inquiry (AI)*
- *Document lessons learned and best practices*
- *Why teams fail*
- *Team-building activities*
- *Team recognition*

The older generations tended to be individual contributors, not team players. They grew up in homes with patriarchal leaders. The father was the breadwinner and head of the family. The mother assumed a domestic role and supported the father in his decisions. While the father and mother undoubtedly had their own private conversations about family decisions, what the father said in front of the children ruled.

The younger generations are growing up differently. Both parents may work, both assume domestic roles, and both share openly in decisions. These generations also participate in group activities and team sports at school. A team-approach mindset is familiar to them.

Select a cohesive team

Every project is different, and selecting the appropriate team is the cornerstone of a project's success. Although you may be tempted to assemble teams you've relied on in the past, you must ask if they are the right people for the project at hand. There's a synergistic magic that happens when all parts of a team galvanize to create something that is greater than the contributions of each individual. Following are some team roles:

Guidance team. When the project is large, it may require a guidance team. The guidance team will support the team's activities, secure resources, appoint the project leader and team members, and clear paths in the organization.

Team leader. This person will run the team, assign administrative details, arrange logistical details, facilitate meetings, oversee the preparation of reports and presentations, and ultimately create channels to enable the team to do their jobs. The team leader must understand the scope of the project, demonstrate strong leadership skills, and have the ability to keep projects on schedule.

Quality advisor. Important in technical and scientific environments, this person has expertise in special areas and is versed in quality improvement. The quality advisor will train the team in the use of certain pieces of equipment, offer advice, and "get his hands dirty" when the situation warrants.

Team members. They are the bulk of the team, the people who will carry out the assignments. They can be of various ranks, trades, professions, shifts, classifications, or work areas, and may be internal or external to the company.

Form, storm, norm, and perform

Forming, storming, norming, and performing are the four stages in a model of group development introduced by the psychologist Bruce Tuckman in 1965. Tuckman asserted that these four stages are necessary and inevitable in order for a team to grow, face challenges, tackle problems, find solutions, plan work, and deliver results. His model has become the basis for subsequent models that are still used in today's business environment.

Forming. During this early stage, team members get to know each other, exchange some personal information, and form alliances. They learn

> ### Create a mission statement.
>
> Successful teams start with a vision and a sense of purpose. A brief, well-crafted mission statement focuses on the critical project objectives and inspires team members to work toward the common goal.
>
> - Keep it brief, between one and four sentences.
> - Use clear language that can be understood by all team members.
> - Tell why the team exists. Be specific to the project at hand.
> - Distribute the mission statement to all team members.

about the opportunities and challenges, agree on goals, and begin to tackle the tasks. There's typically lots of anticipation and optimism. No one has offended anyone at this stage.

Storming. The honeymoon is over. Although necessary to the growth of the team, this stage can be contentious, unpleasant, and even painful to team members who are averse to conflict. Tolerance of all team members and their differences needs to be emphasized. The team addresses issues such as what problems they are really supposed to solve, how they will function independently and together, and what leadership model they will accept. During this stage, team leaders or managers should be accessible and may need to offer guidance in decision-making and professional behavior.

Norming. This is the time for team members to adjust their behavior toward each other as they develop work habits that make teamwork seem more natural and fluid. Team members often work through this stage by agreeing on rules, values, professional behavior, shared methods, working tools, and even taboos. Team members begin to trust each other and are expected to take more responsibility for their decisions and their professional behavior. As issues arise, teams may bounce back and forth between storming and norming.

Performing. By now, team members should have become interdependent, self-directed, motivated, competent, autonomous, and able to handle the decision-making process without too much, if any, supervision. Dissent is expected and allowed as long as it's channeled through means acceptable to the team.

Manage a team

Every sports team has a coach whose role it is to strategically position the players, train them, coach them, bolster their morale, and motivate them to become winners. There are many similarities between coaching a sports team and managing a company team. Both must be positive, upbeat, and have a can-do attitude that will ripple down through the entire team. When the team wins, the coach is a hero; when the team loses, the coach is a zero. Following are some ways to become the hero.

Roles and goals

- **Establish clearly defined roles.** Every team member should know what's expected of him (down to the smallest details) and how his role fits into the team's overall mission.

- **Set and share common goals and objectives.** A team without a shared objective is merely a collection of people. Share the short- and long-term goals with the entire team. Let them know that the goals are realistic and attainable and how they fit into the larger company strategy. (Too many teams work in a vacuum and don't realize how they impact the rest of the company.)

 Be aware of cultural differences in the way global teams function. For example, in some cultures decisions are made by consensus only; in others, by executive rule. Also, verbal and nonverbal cues are strongly influenced by culture. Become familiar with the cultural backgrounds of your team members.

Communication

- **Hold team meetings.** Review the projects and the progress at team meetings. This keeps people informed, provides them with the information needed to take on a task or project, and resolves any issues that have surfaced.

- **Build fun into the agenda.** When you have teams that are assembled for long periods of time, have a potluck lunch, host a dinner at a local restaurant, take the team to a sporting event. When you add fun to the mix, you have a stronger team. (Learn more about team-building events later in this chapter.)

- **Include icebreakers.** Quick icebreakers are especially important for newly formed teams or virtual teams that don't know each other very well. Icebreakers help people to relax and add enjoyment to what can otherwise be a boring meeting. Ask team members to briefly discuss what hobbies or sports they like or something else others may not know about them. You can find lots of ideas for icebreakers online.

- **Acknowledge that you may not have all the answers.** Encourage your team to try new and creative approaches. Of course, not all approaches will work, but give people the leeway to try what's reasonable. You'd be surprised at how innovative and intuitive some people can be.

- **Be available.** Your team needs to see you around, not behind closed doors. Be approachable. Listen to their concerns. Give advice when needed or when asked.

- **Delegate.** You don't see pro coaches making touchdowns or hitting home runs; the team players do that. Delegating doesn't merely mean divvying up the tasks. It means developing your team members, building skills, and fostering self-esteem.

- **Foster teamwork.** A team isn't about stars. It's about a group of people working together toward a common outcome.

- **Keep channels of communication open.** Maintain open communication between you and each team member and encourage them to keep open channels among themselves. Use email, voicemail, meetings, and whatever works for the issues at hand.

- **Encourage growth.** Members come to the team with a variety of skills. Encourage them to develop new skills to increase their versatility, flexibility, and add value to the team.

 Check out Chapter 13, "What's the Best Communication Method?" and Chapter 10, "Managing a Virtual Workforce."

Recognition

- **Celebrate milestones.** You can celebrate a milestone with something as simple as a pizza party or an announcement in the company newsletter.

- **Mark achievements.** Although you want to promote teamwork, some people will shine and deserve special recognition. (Learn more about recognition later in this chapter.)

Don't just manage—be a role model and be part of the team. Never ask team members to do something you wouldn't be willing to do yourself, and pitch in when time pressures become overwhelming.

Dynamic meetings

According to Les Giblin, best-selling author of books about people skills, "It is a proven fact that from 66 to 90 percent of all failures in the business world are failures in human relations." Dynamic meetings can strengthen relations and relationships. When a meeting is necessary, well-planned, and well-conducted, it can be magical. It can bring out the best in every team member—the best ideas and the best decisions.

Before the meeting

- **Schedule your meetings at appropriate times.** You know what's appropriate for your group, your organization, your clients, and the like. For example, if your group has flextime, arrange an important meeting during the hours everyone is in the office. If you have remote workers, consider their time zones.
- **Pick a suitable place.** Don't try to squeeze 15 people into a room the size of a closet.
- **Prepare a realistic agenda and distribute it in advance of the meeting.** List the date, time, place, purpose, participants, roles, impending decisions, how people can prepare, and whatever else is relevant.
- **Be attuned to team members in other countries.** Rotate the times of your meetings so you inconvenience some of the people some of the time, not all of the people all of the time.

During the meeting

- **Make sure your meetings start on time.** Even the laggers will be there on time when you have a reputation for starting on the dot.
- **Use parliamentary procedures.** If this is a formal meeting, parliamentary procedures dictate the system for making motions, seconding motions, and more.
- **If the meeting is small or informal, make sure people know each other.** Start with a role call, or ask participants to introduce themselves.

- **Create an all-inclusive environment.** Create ground rules at the outset of the meeting to make sure everyone feels comfortable speaking up without fear of mockery, condemnation, or reprisals.

- **Minimize distractions.** Shuffling papers, having side conversations, text messaging, ringing cell phones, and other things along those lines are distracting.

- **Stick to the agenda.** No matter how interesting a diversion may be, stick to the agenda. If the group veers too much, bring it back to focus. If issues arise that aren't on the agenda, "park" them. If time allows you can address them at the end of the meeting. If time doesn't allow, discuss how best to handle those items.

- **Involve people in the group.** Even if you're doing a presentation, make it interactive.

 As a participant, never interrupt anyone, even if you disagree strongly. Make a note of what's been said and return to it later. When you speak, make sure you're brief and make a relevant contribution.

- **Create a plan of action.** What are the outcomes? Who has to do what as a result of the meeting?

- **End on time.** It's important for people to leave on time so the meeting doesn't negatively impact the rest of their day. If you complete all the items on the agenda, end the meeting early. There's no reason to fill time because you planned a one-hour meeting and covered everything in 40 minutes.

After the meeting

- Distribute the meeting notes as quickly as possible.
- If there's a speaker, always extend a warm thank-you.

 Virtual meetings are the lifeblood of remote teams. Check out Chapter 8, "Virtual Meetings: From Sleep-Inducing to Sizzling," for tips and best practices.

Appreciative Inquiry

Appreciative Inquiry (AI) is a methodology used to bring about purposeful change. It was developed by David Cooperrider and his associates at the Weatherhead School of Management at Case Western Reserve

University in the mid-1980s. In a nutshell, AI allows people to master their successes, learn from positive experiences, and focus on what works. Green Mountain Coffee Roasters, British Airways, the US Navy, Yellow Roadway (formerly Roadway Express), Hunter Douglas Windows, Save the Children, Habitat for Humanity, United Religions Initiative, McDonald's, GTE Wireless, and countless others businesses and organizations have used AI to facilitate team building, product development, core business design, mergers and acquisitions, focus groups, process improvement, strategic planning, labor-management relations, joint ventures, customer relations, and more.

After his company started using the AI methodology, GTE Wireless President Tom White said, "What I see in this meeting are zealots, people with a mission and passion for creating the new GTE. Count me in. I'm your number one recruit, number one zealot." People cheered. Within fourteen months GTE's stock had risen significantly, morale had increased, and union-management relationships were stronger. GTE won an award from the American Association for Training and Development for the best organization-change program in the country. So if you have doubts about the effectiveness of AI, remember that it was the backbone of the change in GTE's corporate culture.

Both the typical problem-solving approach and the AI methodology have a place in bringing about change. Think of AI as another tool to broaden the conversation. Notice the difference in the two approaches and image the types of conversations each will lead to:

Typical problem-solving approach. A manager calls a meeting with his team to discuss a problem. He puts the problem statement on a PowerPoint or whiteboard and people discuss options. Morale is low. The mood is negative. People are edgy. Questions may be, "What's the problem?" "What's wrong with . . .?" "Whose fault is it that?"

AI approach. Given the same scenario, the manager focuses on what the team is doing well and discusses those positive aspects that need to be strengthened. Morale is high. The mood is positive. People are at ease. There's no blame. Questions may be, "What possibilities haven't we thought about?" "What's the most productive way to . . .?" "What do you appreciate about . . .?"

Four stages of AI

The following are the four stages of the AI process:

1. **Discover.** This is the stage during which you discuss when you, your team, or your company were at your best. Ask a series of open-ended questions that encourage storytelling: "Describe the time you felt the most . . ." Prompts can continue with "What made that experience possible?" "What did we do as individuals [as teams/as a company] to help bring that about?"

2. **Dream.** This stage is about envisioning the process as it would work in the future. "Describe what that might look like a year from now." "What would it look like if . . .?" "If . . . didn't exist, what would . . . look like?"

3. **Design.** During this phase, groups analyze the input from the discover and dream phases. They use their findings to design a roadmap of actions and resources from inside and outside the group. This is more of an activity than a process of questioning.

4. **Destiny.** This involves a strong top-down commitment; it's where the rubber meets the road. Groups of people make a commitment to follow the roadmap. Questions may include, "What should we set as our priorities?" "What should our focus be over the next [time frame]?" "Who from outside the group would be interested in working on . . .?" "How will we measure success along the way?" "How will we know when . . . has changed [improved]?"

 AI is a continuous process. The destiny step leads to new discoveries that start the process anew.

Turn negatives into positives.

Try this at your next session to bring about change. Divide people into groups and present a scenario. For practice, imagine that you're embarking on a new project and you're asking the team to come up with a unique approach to solving a problem.

1. The first person makes a suggestion.

2. The next responds by saying, "Yes, but . . ."

3. Then the next person adds to that another "Yes, but . . ."

4. Keep that going until everyone on the team has had a turn, or until you've had six or seven "Yes, but . . ." statements.

Then repeat the scenario with one slight change: "Yes, and . . ."

1. The first person makes a suggestion.

2. The next responds by saying, "Yes, and . . ."

3. Then the next person adds to that another "Yes, and . . ."

4. Keep that going until everyone on the team has had a turn, or until you've had six or seven "Yes, and . . ." statements.

Notice the difference when you switch to a more positive conversation. People get excited and want to contribute. They create a positive energy. Google "Appreciative Inquiry" to learn more about how companies are using this process for more productive outcomes.

Document lessons learned and best practices

If you're a golfer, have you ever taken a mulligan—a do-over? If so, hopefully you didn't make the same mistake on the next shot. You can't take team mulligans, but you can prevent future teams from making the same mistakes multiple times. You can also help them to benefit from your successes by recording lessons learned, which lead to best practices. Why don't companies do this more systematically? Because once the project is over, everyone is ready to move on to other projects.

Lessons learned

Lessons learned reflect the 20/20 hindsight that teams frequently have after completing a project. They should include detailed information about behaviors, attitudes, approaches, forms, resources, or protocols. They should incorporate what went right and what went wrong.

To assure that team members are prepared for a productive lessons-learned session and the meeting results in actionable outcomes, set ground rules. Otherwise the meeting can turn into a gripe session. (See the Appreciative Inquiry section earlier in this chapter for suggestions on keeping it positive and not playing the blame game.) Ask everyone to come prepared with notes and be willing to participate. The facilitator can ask leading questions such as, "What went well during the alpha test that we should do again?" "What went wrong during the alpha test?" "How can we prevent this from happening again?"

Best practices

The process of creating best practices can be as simple as having team members maintain ongoing logs—jotting down successes and failures and sharing them at team meetings or during certain milestones of a project. Team members can record their observations in notebooks or databases and post them in hallways, project war rooms, or on internal blogs or wikis. For example:

- If quality was an issue, a best practice could be to create step-by-step checklists.

- If people were thwarted by complex document formats, a best practice could be to prepare templates.

Craft the repository of best practices in such a way that anyone reading them will have a clear sense of the context, how and why they were derived, and how, when, and why they're appropriate for other projects. This is a big step in lean transformation.

Why teams fail

In this virtual world, it's nearly impossible not to be part of a team. Projects are too big, too complex, and too involved for one person to do it all. If your company is experiencing failing teams, it's up to the manager or team leader to identify the reasons why so you can take corrective action. Here are some of the reasons teams fail:

A team isn't the optimum way to organize the effort. Many companies function in a team environment and often form teams when just one or two people can get the job done more effectively.

Lack of trust among members. When team members don't want to share their vulnerabilities or trust each other's judgments or competencies, the end result is a noncohesive group of people, not a team. They don't share knowledge and resources, there's poor coordination and cooperation, communication channels are closed, and there may even be sabotage.

Fear of conflict. You've probably heard the expression that a couple isn't truly married until they've had their first fight. The same is true of teams. If team members avoid conflict at any cost, they're unproductive. They must be open enough to engage in civilized, unfiltered, and passionate dialogue. If they don't, tension mounts, anger builds, and the success of the team is severely compromised.

Wrong mix of people. For a team to be successful, it needs the right mix of skill sets and personalities, with leaders and followers. When a manager knows the abilities and natural tendencies of people, he can ensure a much better chance for success. For example, when one member assumes a very dominant role, others may feel stifled. Conversely, when there's a weak leader or none at all, the team will flounder.

People are being pulled in too many directions. Many companies function by putting out one fire after another. If team members are pulled off projects because of other pressing priorities and they aren't properly replaced, the best-laid plans go awry.

Too many I-guys. Belonging to a team means being part of something that's larger than you. Even though you have a specific function or belong to a certain department, you're unified with everyone else in the group to accomplish your company's overall objectives.

Unproductive meetings. Meetings are one of the most critical aspects of a team's success. They're the time for initiating strategies and innovative solutions, solving problems, identifying lessons learned, brainstorming, and solving problems.

Lack of role clarity. When roles aren't clearly defined, the result can be confusion and conflict. You may have some members shouldering too big a share of responsibilities who find themselves maxed out; others may be carrying too light a role. It's up to the manager or team leader to define the roles of each team member.

Lack of accountability. Accountability is the linchpin. If one person on the team doesn't meet expectations, the entire team can fail. One of the best ways to create accountability is to develop shared accountability among team members. Some companies form small accountability groups in whom team members can confide their struggles, weaknesses, and insecurities. Accountability groups provide mentorship, keeping in mind the goals and growth the team intends to achieve.

Poor planning. Planning might include the basic techniques of Six Sigma, a management strategy first developed in the 1980s at Motorola to eliminate defects and maximize efficiency. Six Sigma's DMAIC methodology has five components: Define, Measure, Analyze, Improve, Control. Even with a strong plan, a project will undoubtedly require adjustments along the way. That's to be expected.

Losing focus on the business objectives. To quote an old expression, "If you don't know where you're going, any road will get you there."

Lack of time management skills. A team must budget its time wisely to work smarter, not harder. It should define concrete goals and meet them on time. If extenuating circumstances prevail, the team must create a new schedule.

Economic conditions or faulty company policies. Teams are only as good as the frameworks within which they operate. Despite a team's best efforts, when economic conditions shift, the team's processes must shift. When the team has been handed poor forecasting models, poor foresight, and a weak analysis of external environments, that can also lead to failure.

Team-building activities

In sports, camaraderie on the playing field is critical to a successful team. In business, however, time is money, and managers don't often think of building camaraderie. When people don't get to know each other, team bonding and team building are less effective.

There's a big distinction between team bonding and team building. *Bonding* means sticking together, getting along, and sharing. *Building* means achieving goals, setting milestones, and creating a continual process for improving.

Managers should create opportunities for team members to bond and build. One way is to sponsor a *well-thought-out* team-building event. *Well-thought-out* are the critical words. Too many companies sponsor team-building events that are fun—but they're merely team-bonding events. They offer an immediate boost to employee enthusiasm and increase morale during the event, then employees return to the status quo and don't apply the valuable knowledge they acquired. Follow these two steps to ensure that the event has a positive and long-lasting impact.

Step 1: Planning the event. Determine what activities are appropriate for the situation and the members. Managers must understand the issues, the culture, and expected outcomes. Members should enjoy the activity, learn from it, and be able to incorporate what they learned into their workday.

Step 2: Planning the follow-up. After the event, schedule a meeting to capture the lessons learned to determine how teams will implement them. Then keep the ball rolling by re-creating the atmosphere from the event in the workplace. This maintains the spirit and changes relationships and behaviors. Keep the follow-up going until the team has truly become viable and productive. If you ignore this step, people will return to business as usual. You won't have solved your problems, employees will become jaded about such events, and you'll have wasted a lot of time and money.

 Check out http://www.businessballs.com/teambuilding.htm for lots of team-building games and exercises.

 Check out the sections on ROI, ROE, and the Kirkpatrick model in Chapter 7, "Virtual Learning: From Enervating to Empowering."

Team recognition

Think back to when you were a kid. Did your parents ever tell you that they'd give you money or buy you something you valued if you got better grades on your report card? If so, chances are you tried a little harder and your grades improved.

When employees are asked what type of recognition they want most, it's not always money. More often, it's knowing they're valued and appreciated. When people feel valued, they're more positive, productive, innovative, and upbeat. Here are a few ways to reward excellence:

Company-wide recognition. Post a note on the bulletin board, send a company-wide email, recognize someone in the company newsletter, organize a luncheon or dinner. Recognition in front of peers encourages other teams to perform at peak efficiency.

Handwritten note. Send a handwritten note to each team member expressing appreciation. Include a copy of the note in the employee's performance file.

Time off. If a team finishes a project ahead of time or on time and on budget, give each member time off. It can be a discretionary day or even a few hours. In this way people can go to the beach on a sultry summer day instead of calling in sick.

Draw from a gift bag. Have each team member draw from a gift bag that can include dinner for two at a restaurant, a gift card, or even cash. When you put chain restaurants and chain stores in the hopper, virtual workers can participate as well.

Applaud their efforts. At a staff meeting, recognize accomplishments by giving the team a round of applause—even a standing ovation.

Elect the team to a "wall of fame." Post the team photo on a wall designated for high achievers.

Part Five

Potpourri for Today's Workplace

THIS SECTION IS an informative potpourri of topics that didn't fit elsewhere, yet they add depth to this book. Whether you're part of a multigenerational workforce, lead an intercultural team, work or manage virtually, seek meaningful employment, or simply need to get up to speed on the hottest buzzwords in the modern workplace, the chapters that follow will give you a competitive edge. Read on for tips, tricks, and techniques you can put to use right away.

The biggest problem with communication is the belief that it has actually occurred.

—Newt Gingrich, 58th Speaker of the House of Representatives

Chapter 13

What's the Best Communication Method?

In this chapter

- *Two-way communication*
- *Face-to-face*
- *Phone call*
- *Instant messaging*
- *One-way communication*
- *Email*
- *Texting*
- *Letter*
- *Handwritten note*

Communication has led to many inventive ideas throughout the years. Native Americans sent smoke signals and runners from village to village. Paul Revere rode on horseback from town to town to warn his countrymen that the British were coming. African tribes beat deep-sounding drums to send messages through dense jungles. Throughout the centuries people have found ways to communicate through whatever means were available. With so many means available today, it's important to determine what works best and when.

 The best way to communicate isn't what's best for the sender—it's what's best for the recipient.

Case in point:

I had an appointment to meet a client in downtown Boston one morning at 9:00, so I called the day before to confirm. On the morning of the meeting the weather was dreadful. I knew that the heavy rain and fog would make driving slow, so I left very early. When I arrived at my client's office around 8:50, she looked at me quizzically and asked, "What are you doing here? Didn't you get my message?"

What she did:

She was working late the night before hoping to finish something in time for our meeting. Realizing she wouldn't be ready, she shot off an email at 10:30 p.m. letting me know we had to reschedule. (I have a life and don't read email at 10:30 at night.) I left very early in the morning without having checked my email; therefore, I didn't get her message.

What she should have done:

She should have phoned me in addition to sending the email (thereby covering all the bases), so I would have known not to drive in.

 Ask your clients, customers, or colleagues how they prefer to communicate. This sends a message that they're important.

 Good grammar and punctuation are analogous to good manners. When you don't speak and write properly, your audience has to work double-time to decode your message. In this age of "instant everything," communicating clearly is more critical than ever.

Following are some examples to help you determine when to use two-way or one-way communication and the most appropriate way to deliver the message.

Two-way communication

Give careful thought to the "conversations" that would benefit from two-way communication. Too many important messages are dashed off hurriedly via email and other means of one-way communication, and they suffer as a result.

Face-to-face

When you let technology do your talking, many things fall through the cracks. There's nothing to take the place of face-to-face (FTF or F2F) communication to see someone's nonverbal cues and to establish and build relationships. FTF is appropriate when . . .

- You need to criticize someone's job performance. (Two-way communication will give each person a chance to have her say.)

Factors in determining the best means of communicating.

There are a number of factors that will determine the most appropriate communication method:

- Is the content confidential?
- Is speed an issue?
- Is cost an issue?
- Is a certain type of feedback needed or required?
- Do you need one- or two-way communication?
- Is your communication formal or informal?

Advantages of written communication

- Allows you to formulate your message, rethink it, revise it, and hold off sending it until you're sure it's what you want to say.
- Keeps a permanent record so you don't get into the "he said/she said" scenario.
- Lets you communicate with large numbers of people through a single transmission.
- Passes on information as it was written rather than as someone remembers it.

Advantages of verbal communication

- Gets immediate feedback in situations where you're not sure the other person will understand your message or your intent. (You learn a lot from body language as well as from words.)
- Creates an open exchange when there's a topic that may be easily misunderstood.
- Gets you off the hook if you lack sterling grammatical skills. For example, if you don't know the difference between *who* and *whom*, you can say the word quickly and the listener won't hear the difference.
- Engages in a personal exchange.

- You want to chat with someone in your office in order to establish a relationship. (This can be done at the water cooler, cafeteria, coffee machine, or any other place that's reasonable.)
- You want to brainstorm. (Virtual meetings can be an option for those who aren't physically present.)
- You want to build rapport with a potential customer or client.

The digital disadvantage

In "Why Gen-Y Johnny Can't Read Nonverbal Cues" (*Wall Street Journal*, September 4, 2009), Emory University English professor Mark Bauerlein writes, "We live in a culture where young people—outfitted with iPhone and laptop and devoting hours every evening from age 10 onward to messaging of one kind and another—are ever less likely to develop the 'silent fluency' that comes from face-to-face interaction. It is a skill that we all must learn, in actual social settings, from people (often older) who are adept in the idiom. As text-centered messaging increases, such occasions diminish. The digital natives improve their adroitness at the keyboard, but when it comes to their capacity to 'read' the behavior of others, they are all thumbs."

Phone call

We now have land lines, mobile phones, and VoIP, making it easy and relatively inexpensive to send and receive calls from nearly anywhere. Next to FTF communication, the phone is still the one way to stay connected and have meaningful conversations. People can get aural cues from your tone, inflections, rhythm, speed, volume, and pitch. A phone call is appropriate when . . .

- Someone responds to an email with several questions about the email you sent. (It's time for a two-way conversation.)

- It's the day of a meeting and you just found out the meeting will be preponed (moved from 9:30 to 9:00). You must let one person know of the change. (Consider sending an email as a backup.)

- You want to schedule a meeting with one person. (It's much easier to schedule a meeting when you both have your calendars in front of you. Otherwise, there's a lot of back and forth as to who can and can't make certain dates and times.)

- You need to criticize the performance of someone. (Two-way communication will give each person a chance to have her say.)

- A situation is complex or confrontational and you need to engage all of your people-reading skills.

Instant Messaging

Businesses are starting to embrace instant messaging (IM) as a means of real-time communication facilitated by special software. IM is appropriate when . . .

- You're part of a remote team working under a tight deadline. All team members need to "chat" each morning about the progress of the project. (IM is quickly replacing email and the phone. You can have several screens up and several different people "talking." The session can be saved and used to track the project.)
- You work a help line or customer support line and need to get information from coworkers in order to answer customer questions. (You can find out who's live and get immediate answers.)
- You need to have a casual conversation with someone. (The phone would also work if you don't need to document the conversation.)
- You need to ask a colleague a simple question, such as when a report will be ready.

One-way communication

One-way communication is very practical when you don't need immediate feedback or interaction.

Email

Email is a serious business communications tool and you should treat it with the same respect as any other document you write. Just because the computer screen doesn't have the weft and feel of a sheet of paper, that's no excuse to abandon the good habits you learned for the print medium. Email is appropriate when . . .

- You're sending a follow-up reminder about a staff meeting to be held the next day.
- You want to praise an employee for a job well done. (Send your message to the group and anyone else who needs to know.)
- You want to send a press release about your company. (An email will pique the interest of the journalist or publication and control the flow of information. However, journalists may want to verify facts, ask you questions, and hear your tone of voice, so consider sending an email and following it up with a phone call.)
- You're sending your manager your weekly or monthly status report.
- You're sending an attachment.
- You need to forward a document to someone else.
- You need to create a paper trail.

Check out Chapter 14, "Email Savvy," to become a smart communicator.

Texting

Text messaging, or texting, is a quick, quiet, and easy way to send a person-to-person message from your cell phone to someone else's cell phone, handheld computer, pager, or email. When you're stuck in a meeting or other place where you don't want to interrupt, you can stay in touch silently. Texting is appropriate when . . .

- You're sending information such as offers and product updates to your customers' phones (with prior permission, of course).

- You need to keep in contact with employees who are traveling and have heavy meeting schedules.

- You want responses to quick questions.

- Traditional marketing and advertising methods are not longer effective and you want to capitalize on this rapidly growing form of market penetration.

- You need to send an address or phone number but realize the person at the other end may not have a piece of paper handy or be in a place to write. The text message records that information for later use.

 With messages typically limited to 160 characters, there's no room for small talk. You must get to the point quickly.

 Check out Chapter 15, "JTLYK (IM and Texting)" to see many of the new abbreviations.

Letter

There's nothing to express sincerity like a letter. Letters are making a comeback for people who want to stand out from the masses. That's because emails and other forms of e-communication have become all too impersonal and commonplace. Letters are appropriate when . . .

- You're sending promotional materials.

- You want to recap the details of an important meeting with a key client/customer.

- You're a small business and want to welcome a new family to the neighborhood (perhaps enclosing a discount coupon).

- You want to make a candidate a formal job offer.

- You're sending a cover letter with a paper resume. (Use the letter to spark interest in your special skills, explain an anomaly, note a special link to the company, or anything else that will enhance your resume.)

- You want to present yourself as someone worthy of the same respect that you're giving the recipient.

- You're involved in fundraising. Aside from FTF or talking on the phone, letters are about as personal as you can get with a donor (or prospective donor).

- You want to thank a customer who has made a major purchase or has sent a referral your way.

- You want to thank someone for a business favor.

- You're communicating with someone from the older generation who appreciates letters.

 Perhaps you recall when e-cards were all the rage. You'd receive an e-card for everything from your birthday to the winter equinox. The use of e-cards has declined dramatically because they express ease in sending, not in communicating a sincere message. There's nothing that expresses sincerity like a paper greeting card.

Handwritten note

When was the last time a business associate sent you a handwritten note? It was probably too long ago to recall. If you've gotten one lately, you undoubtedly remember exactly who sent it, when, and why.

Compare that to email. When you send someone an email, she'll read it, then most likely delete it. When you send someone send a handwritten note, she'll read, it, most likely place it on her counter or desk, and think of you whenever she looks at it. A handwritten note is personal and shows sincerity. Would you rather be deleted or remembered? Those three- to five-sentence notes can make a mighty impact. Send a handwritten note when . . .

- You want to thank a prospective employer for an interview. (A typed letter will also work if you have poor handwriting.)

- You're sending an expression of sympathy.

- You want to send someone a warm, sincere thank-you.

- You need to apologize to someone and FTF isn't an option.
- You're sending a colleague a newspaper or magazine article that may be of interest (this is great for networking).
- You want to express congratulations for an achievement of a customer or business associate.
- You received a gift or were a guest in someone's home.

 A handwritten note is a very strong tool that's vastly underused in virtually every service-oriented business. It's a "ping" that's likely to echo back to you in some way soon.

In conclusion, it's critical to remember that communication styles differ from one generation to the next. To quote my friend and colleague Suzanne Bates, President and CEO of Bates Communications, "We have to be better than we are at getting to the point and we absolutely must embrace the many channels of communication available to us today. The message needs to be clear and very, very timely. And it needs to arrive in a channel that your people are actually monitoring. If you think you need to communicate something today, it was probably yesterday. Rumors flying? You don't have until Tuesday to respond, because people are already talking—digitally. They no longer have to hide in the bathroom to gossip. They can do it via computer. So you must reach them that way, too."

> Email technology is marching forward too fast for social rules to keep up, leaving correspondents to police themselves and sometimes commit gaffes that would make Miss Manners wince.
>
> —Jeffrey Blair, columnist

Chapter 14

Email Savvy

In this chapter

- *Do's*
- *Taboos*
- *Handheld computers and the changing face of email*

Good manners (such as the commonly forgotten words *please* and *thank-you*) go a long way toward good relationships. Just how important are good manners? A client of mine purchased a company in Ireland. Before too long, the Irish managers were complaining that they felt the Americans were rude. Not knowing why they were perceived as such, the Americans invited a group of Irish managers to the US to mend fences. When asked to elaborate, the Irish managers mentioned examples such as the following:

- The Americans don't say *please* or *thank you.*

- They shoot off emails with brusque messages such as "I need the report by next Friday."

- They don't include salutations or closings.

Because a few common courtesies such as those were missing, the Americans were construed as rude. Following are do's and taboos that will keep you from being construed as rude and get you the results you expect from your email exchanges.

Do's

A lot of email savvy and etiquette is common sense. Because emails are so quick and easy, however, people often get sloppy and write them without thinking. Here are a few things to think about:

Let the *From* line contain your name. Make sure your name or company name appears in the *From* line so readers know an email is from you. Too many people use a random array of alphanumerics that have no meaning.

Create a compelling subject line that delivers your bottom line. During the email workshops I facilitate, I hear from people who are deluged with a tsunami of emails. Some get as many as several hundred a day. Most of these people don't read the majority of their emails. If you want your message to stand out, create a compelling subject line—one that will deliver the message at a glance. Subject lines such as *Hi, Meeting, Call me,* and so forth, tell the reader nothing, and the email may not get opened.

Instead of writing . . .	Write . . .
Profit report	12% profit expected for Q1
Staff meeting	Staff mtg rescheduled to May 2 at 2:00
Hi	Thanks for sending the report so quickly

 If your message has multiple topics, consider sending multiple messages, each with a "bottom line" subject line.

Say it in the subject line. When the message can fit in the subject line and you know the person well, say it in the subject line and don't bother writing in the text box. This is an incredible time saver and gives your reader an instant message.

 Here's how I used this method recently in an exchange with a colleague. We rescheduled a meeting through a series of subject lines without either of us having to go into the text box.
> What time will you be here tomorrow? —Pat
> I'll be there at 3:00. —Sheryl
> Can you come here at 2:30 instead?—Pat
> Yes. See you at 2:30 tomorrow. —Sheryl

 Beware of using !!! or ??? at the end of your subject line. Some people feel that several exclamation or question marks are distracting and unnecessary.

Emphasize mutual connections. If you were referred to the reader by a mutual connection, put the connection's name in the subject line. This will increase the odds of getting a reply. You may say, for example, *Referred by Bob Gandler.*

Ask yourself the questions your reader will have. Put yourself in your reader's head and ask *who, what, when, where, why,* and *how.* Answer his questions. This way he won't have to come back to you for clarification and you can get the response you want in a timely manner.

Send one email for each topic. My workshop participants often complain that readers don't answer their messages, or they send only partial answers. Perhaps that's because the sender included too many topics in one email. Readers can't digest too many disparate thoughts. Here are a few suggestions:

- If your message contains several topics about a variety of issues, add an introductory sentence or two letting the reader know what's in the text.

- If the topics are substantial or completely unrelated, split them into separate emails, each with an appropriate subject line.

Highlight the "ask." If you're asking for something or there's an action item or next step, make that clear. If you bury your request in the body of the message, the reader may not read it. Consider putting the request in a headline or on a separate line. You may label it *Next Step, Action Requested,* or anything that will get the request to pop out.

 With so many people reading emails on handheld computers, consider putting *Action Requested* at the beginning of the subject line. This will let the reader know immediately he's being asked to do something.

Respond within 24 hours. We live in a very dynamic society and people expect responses immediately. If they didn't mind delays, they'd send snail mail. If you aren't in a position to act immediately, reply with "Sorry, I won't have that information until early next week. I'll send it to you then."

Set up an auto-response when you'll be away from the office and won't be checking messages. This lets people know they shouldn't expect a reply until you return. If you can, leave the name, phone number, or email address of someone to contact in your absence. Remember to change your message when you return.

When returning from a trip, review your messages from the *most* current to the *least* current. Many people view the oldest messages first, figuring that those senders have been waiting the longest for a reply. But it's more advantageous to read your email from most to least current. That way you won't waste time worrying about problems that have already been solved or questions that have already been answered—and you won't be wading through hundreds of emails the day you come back from vacation.

Know when to stop. Don't continue a stream of messages beyond the necessary point. It's fine to send a quick *thank-you* or *I look forward to it,* but know when to stop. Here's a needlessly protracted exchange through a series of subject lines a client shared with me:

> James: Do you have the report ready?
> Bobby: You should have it by tomorrow morning.
> James: Good, looking forward to seeing it.
> Bobby: You'll like the findings.
> James: I hope so.
> Bobby: Until later . . .
> James: Until later . . .

Use salutations and closings. Would you ever pick up the telephone without saying hello or hang up without saying good-bye? Would you ever send a letter without a salutation or a closing? Of course not. So why would you send an email without a salutation and a closing? After all, email is a serious business communications tool that deserves the same respect as any other form of communication. Popular salutations and closings include the following:

Salutations	Closings
Hi,	Best regards,
Hi Bob,	I'll see you tomorrow,
Dear Mr. Smith,	Thanks for your help,
Good morning,	Have a nice weekend,

Include a signature block. Your signature block should include your name, phone number, email, website, and any other information you want to share. Following is an email I received from a client. (I changed the name of the sender to protect the guilty.)

> Hello Sheryl,
> I hope this message finds you well. Please call me to schedule a phone conversation with one of our business leaders on conducting some type of solution for a group of folks that are struggling with the creation of business letters both in letter format and via email. Is there a good time in the upcoming weeks when we could talk this through? Looking forward to hearing back from you.
> Sincerely,
> Ann Onymous

This client had just moved to another city and wanted me to call her, yet she didn't provide me with her new phone number. I had to search on the Internet to find it. She should have included her number as part of her signature block.

 Here's the signature block I use to conclude my messages. In addition to including contact information, I display my tagline.

> Sheryl Lindsell-Roberts, Principal
> Sheryl Lindsell-Roberts & Associates
> www.sherylwrites.com
> sheryl@sherylwrites.com
> 508-229-8209
> You make more dollars when you make more sense!™

 A few things to remember:
- If your phone number spells out your company name (such as 800-SPEARCO), include the numerals in your signature block because you can't dial letters from a mobile phone.
- Don't include the URL of your blog. Many email providers may see it as spam and block your messages.

Provide ample white space. Always remember that people don't read, they scan. You must make key information pop out at a glance. Here are some ways to do that:

- Break paragraphs into about eight lines of text and leave a line space between each paragraph.

- Leave one line of white space above and below bulleted and numbered lists.

- If you have something critical such as a deadline or effective date, put it on a separate line with white space above and below.
  Deadline: May 25

- Make important information stand out.
  Date: June 5
  Time: 10:00–11:30
  Place: Conference Room B

Use *To, Cc,* and *Bcc* appropriately. When sending an email to multiple readers, always determine each reader's significance with regard to the message. Choose from the following options carefully, because each has its advantages and pitfalls:

To: Use when all readers are of equal importance and it's critical for everyone to know who received the message.

Pitfalls: Everyone can see everyone else's email address, anyone viewing your list can harvest the names and sell them, and too many names can be daunting.

Cc: Use when one person is your primary reader (his name is in the *To* field), and you want him to know of others you're copying. Before you cc

---

Be sure you put the correct address in the To, Cc, or Bcc fields.

A client of mine, whom I hardly know, sent me an email sharing the details of a horrific divorce she was going through. When I tactfully (if there was such as way) brought this to her attention, she realized that she'd sent it to the wrong Sheryl. She was mortified. It's easy to start typing an address and click on the wrong name. Always double-check. For example, my husband's email company address is jroberts@company.com. He works with a gentleman whose email address is jroberto@company.com. They invariably get each other's messages.

---

anyone, ask yourself this question: Would you gather these people in a room to deliver the message? If not, perhaps they shouldn't be cc'ed.

Pitfalls: Just as when you use *To*, everyone can see everyone else's email addresses, anyone viewing your list can harvest the names and sell them, and too many names can be daunting.

Bcc: Use when you don't want the primary reader to know you're sending a blind copy to another, you have a large distribution list and you don't want too many names in the other fields, you want to protect the privacy of your readers, or you want to prevent people from harvesting the names.

Pitfalls: When you use *Bcc* it may look like you're going behind someone's back. Use it sparingly.

 I use the *Bcc* list when I send out my monthly communication tips. This protects the names and addresses of the people on my list, and there's no indication that anyone else received the message.

Signal the importance of your message. Remember, what's important to you may not be important to your reader. If you signal everything as being a priority, you become like the little boy who cried wolf. When something is truly important, people will ignore your signal of priority. Use high, medium, and low priority realistically. When something is purely informational, start the subject line with *FYI*.

Be savvy when it comes to privacy issues. Email and privacy are mutually exclusive. Just as a pedestrian passing the mailbox outside your home can reach in and intercept your mail, hackers, criminals, company administrators, and the government can intercept your email. Also, you don't know what system your email is passing through or what system other people's emails are passing through.

Email has raised a lot of issues about privacy, and many cases have been brought before the courts. The Electronic Communications Privacy Act (ECPA) upholds a company's right to monitor its email, so it's prudent not to send anything that you wouldn't want posted on the company's bulletin board. Here are some cases in point:

- A large entertainment company was in the midst of bankruptcy proceedings. Vast numbers of files were confiscated. Among those files were incriminating email messages that weren't meant for the public eye. This led to the dismissal of several high-level executives.

- An employee of Morehouse College received a wedding photo of a gay couple as part of a chain email. She forwarded the photo on, along with her own disparaging comments. Stating that "those who cannot embrace the Morehouse code of ethics will be sanctioned accordingly," Morehouse president Robert Franklin fired the employee.

- A noted New York columnist opened a bluntly critical email message from a young female colleague. He responded with a barrage of sexual and racial epithets that got him suspended for two weeks.

Inform people of a change of address. The late comedian Rodney Dangerfield did a spiel that went something like this: "When I was a young boy my parents sent me off to school one morning. When I arrived home, the house was empty. The furniture and the people were gone. My parents had moved and left no forwarding address."

In the email world, people tend to disappear without a trace as well. Whenever you change your email address (whether you've changed jobs or service providers), let those you correspond with know your new address. After all, when you move your office or change your phone number, you let people know.

Break the chain. Chain letters, scams, and jokes are rampant in the electronic world; they contribute dramatically to information overload. When you receive jokes, hoaxes, surveys, bogus warnings, recipes, promises of financial rewards, petitions, cute clip art, and more, don't open the emails and don't pass them on. In addition to being annoying, the messages may include viruses.

Be cautious of sending attachments; they must be in a format people can read. Not everyone can open all attachments. Some may be too large and others may be written on software that recipients don't have. Also, people reading on handheld computers can't read large attachments on a small screen. To make it easy for your recipient, summarize the gist of the attachment in a brief opening paragraph so he can get the important information quickly.

Delete the email history unless you need it for a specific reason. One reason to leave the history (trailer) is that you or your correspondent may have to refer back to something. Another is that you may want to bring someone else into the conversation who needs to become familiar with what has transpired.

Managing your email efficiently.

Following are some ways to manage your email more efficiently:

- **Use folders.** Set up folders for your needs. You may have a folder for regular correspondents, e-newsletters, and anything that makes sense for the way you conduct business.
- **Open each message only once.** Decide if you'll put it in a folder, respond to it, file it, forward it, print it, delete it, or not answer. If the message requires that you do something, add it to your "to-do" list or folder.
- **Close your program when you don't want your attention diverted from what you're doing.** When you're concentrating on a project or something that needs your full attention, those cues letting you know that you just received a message can be distracting.

 Attachments are baggage, and several airlines are charging for too much baggage. Send attachments only when necessary.

Proofread carefully. Although spell checkers work well, don't turn on your computer and turn off your brain. Use proper spelling, grammar, and punctuation. You often send emails to people who don't know you. What type of impression do you want to make?

Taboos

With the advent of email, we can embarrass ourselves in front of a group or even a worldwide audience. The following guidelines can help avoid that.

Responding to all. Don't respond to all unless it's *absolutely necessary* that everyone sees your response. It's likely that only the sender needs your reply.

 One of my clients is the HR director of a company of about 150 employees and was planning the company summer outing. She sent out the invitations and asked people to RSVP. About 100 people replied to all. Only *she* needed the headcount.

 When responding, make sure you change the subject line to reflect your "bottom line" message to your reader. Maintain a thread to continue the conversation if it's ongoing. A thread may be *June 16 meeting . . . ABC contract . . .* or whatever will identify the continuation of your message topic.

Sending Rambograms. *Rambogram* is a term I coined to refer to a message that's crude, rude, lewd, or thoughtless. The next time you're tempted to send a gruff, ill-tempered, or snippy email in the heat of the moment, pause, take a deep breath, and think again. You don't want to be like Attorney B in the following story (condensed from an article in *The Boston Globe*):

Attorney A was miffed when Attorney B notified him by email that she'd changed her mind about working at his law firm after having accepted the position verbally. Here's the gist of the messages they exchanged:

> **Attorney B:** The pay you are offering would neither fulfill me nor support the lifestyle I am living.
>
> **Attorney A:** Given that you had two interviews, were offered and accepted the job . . . I am surprised that you chose an e-mail and a 9:30 PM voicemail message to convey this information to me. It smacks of immaturity and is quite unprofessional. Indeed, I did rely upon your acceptance by ordering stationery and business cards with your name, reformatting a computer and setting up both internal and external e-mails for you. . . . I sincerely wish you the best of luck in your future endeavors.
>
> **Attorney B:** A real lawyer would have put the contract into writing and not exercised any such reliance until he did so.
>
> **Attorney A:** Thank you for the refresher course on contracts. This is not a bar exam question. You need to realize that this is a very small legal community, especially the criminal defense bar. Do you really want to start pissing off more experienced lawyers at this early stage of your career?
>
> **Attorney B:** bla bla bla

Attorney A was so incensed that he started circulating the exchange of emails. The messages traveled through cyberspace across the country and to all continents. Attorney B was professionally blacklisted. She's now working by herself in a space in Boston where she takes court-appointed cases. That's how viral email can be.

Assuming the recipient actually received (read) your message. There are a lot of reasons your recipient may not have read your email. Perhaps it went into spam. Perhaps there were so many messages in his inbox that he missed it. Perhaps it went to someone else. And perhaps it wasn't delivered.

If you think messages can't float around cyberspace for long periods of time, think again. Three months after one of my dear friends died, I got an email from her asking me to meet her for lunch. After I got up from having fainted and regained my composure (exaggerating, of course), I looked at the date. She'd emailed me six months before she died. That message was floating around cyberspace for nine months before it landed in my inbox.

Using email for personal business. Your company provides you with an email account to conduct company business, so send personal messages sparingly. No company will mind if you send personal emails occasionally, but keep them to a minimum.

Using return receipt requested. Requesting a return receipt for every email you send will annoy most readers. Instead, you may try saying in the text, "Please let me know you received this."

Using all caps or no caps. Sending a message in ALL CAPS is the digital equivalent of yelling at your reader, and all caps are hard to read. (I don't know why that terrible button was put on computers in the first place.) And sending a message with no caps is considered lazy (unless you're ee cummings).

Including anything that may be ambiguous or subject to interpretation. For example, the terms *today, tomorrow,* and *yesterday* are relative to when your reader opens the message, not to when you sent it. And expressions such as "next Friday" may be confusing. If you send someone a message on Tuesday saying "I'll call you next Friday," it's not clear if you mean the next Friday to come (the end of the current week) or the Friday of next week.

I called a friend and invited her to my home. She responded with the following email:
Hi Sheryl,
Thanks for the invitation. We'd love to come.
Our grandson is crawling. Can't wait to see him.
Regards,

I didn't know if she meant that she was planning to come and she was also letting me know that her grandson is crawling. Or if she was expressing regrets because she was going to see her grandson (who lives in another part of the country). As it turned out, she was declining my invitation.

Handheld computers and the changing face of email

The groundswell of handheld computers (PDAs, smartphones, and others) is rapidly changing the face of email. No longer are users viewing messages on large monitors or subject lines in fields of 35 to 40 characters. Monitors have given way to two-inch screens; subject lines, to fields of a few words.

Instant messaging and emailing are morphing as users incorporate IMing and texting abbreviations into emails. I'm not recommending that you start using these abbreviations quite yet, but know what they mean when you see them. Some popular abbreviations include @ (at), BFN (bye for now), CID (consider it done), CU (see you), FYI (for your information), HTH (hope this helps), IOW (in other words), L8R (later), NRB [date] (need reply by [date]), NRN (no response necessary), PLS (please), THX (thanks), TBA (to be announced), YW (you're welcome), and many more. Here are some tips to help you communicate more effectively with PDA users.

 Check out Chapter 15, "JTLYK (IM and Texting)," for a more complete list of abbreviations.

Subject lines

Many handhelds and phones display only a few words in the subject line. That very valuable real estate will determine whether the intended receiver reads your message. Conventional wisdom has told us to write compelling subject lines. However, with such a limited field of view, it becomes a matter of what to skip, what to abbreviate, and what to start with. Here are a few suggestions to grab interest or deliver the message at a glance:

Hosting a seminar
> *Weak:* ABC Company to host sales seminar
> *Strong:* Increase sales in 30 days

Rescheduling a meeting
> *Weak:* We need to reschedule the March meeting
> *Strong:* March mtg to be rescheduled

Calling attention to information

Traditional ways of calling attention to information have included boldface, bullets, tabs, and more. Some of these methods don't always survive the trip through cyberspace and show up as gobbledygook on handhelds and phones. Here are some options:

- Instead of using bullets, consider using asterisks (**), greater-than symbols (>>), hyphens (--), or other characters.
- Instead of boldface, include some other way to emphasize the text. You may write **Deadline: May 5****. If the bold doesn't appear, the reader will still see **Deadline: May 5**.
- Instead of tabbing, use the space bar.

Copying and pasting

If you copy and paste from another format (such as an Excel spreadsheet), some handhelds display the word *Insert* instead of the file that was pasted. Consider sending the file as an attachment.

A lot of fellows nowadays have a B.A., M.D., or Ph.D.
Unfortunately they don't have a J.O.B.
—Fats Domino, singer, pianist,
and songwriter

Chapter 15

JTLYK (IM and Texting)

In this chapter

- *IM etiquette*
- *Texting etiquette*
- *Pulling from the Scrabble box*
- *Emoticons :-)*

Instant Messaging (IM) and texting are somewhat controversial in business, but many companies are seeing the benefits, one of which is the ability to communicate with colleagues, customers, and clients simply and quickly.

IM Etiquette

Just as everyone is starting to get the hang of email etiquette (okay, so not everyone), along comes another technology we need to think about. IMing can be a wonderful communications tool, or it can be a way for people to embarrass themselves a hundred times faster than ever before.

Don't barge in. Always introduce yourself, especially when starting to IM with a new contact. Before beginning a conversation, ask the recipient if she has a minute to chat with you. Being online doesn't mean the person at the other end is waiting for you. When you start a conversation, ask yourself the following: How would I approach the other person verbally? Where might be a good place to start the conversation? You may say, "Is this a good time to discuss the Berger contract?" or "Will you be at Bob's 2 PM mtg?"

Also, be respectful of coworkers. If they set their default message to read *busy*, perhaps it's a sign that they're working on a priority project and want to be interrupted for urgent matters only. Conversely, if you're on a priority project or tight deadline, set your default to *busy* so your colleagues will know you're not ignoring them.

Write carefully and thoughtfully. Never write anything in an IM you wouldn't want posted on a billboard. Your message can be saved, forwarded, and used against you. This isn't the place to reprimand an employee, blame a colleague, write IHMB (I hate my boss), or otherwise criticize, condemn, or complain.

Think short. Remember, the key word is *instant*, so be brief. If you're writing a lengthy response, let the recipient know beforehand so she doesn't think you're ignoring her while you're keying in the message. And send the message all at once, rather than a sentence or two at a time.

 If your conversation is going to be long-winded, pick up the phone.

Be sensitive to other people's typing skills. You may be a whiz at keying in 100 words per minute, but not everyone else is. Be patient when waiting for a response from the hunt-and-peck crowd.

Multitask realistically. Do you think you can talk on the phone and IM at the same time? Few people can multitask and remain on task. Besides taxing your communication skills, one or more of your messages will suffer. In the business world, this can be dangerous, especially with clients, customers, or vendors.

Avoid sloppy writing. Even though IMs are meant to be casual, never abandon good habits, especially in business situations.

- Don't use all caps.
- Don't use all lowercase.
- Check for typos.
- Show your good manners by saying THX (thanks) and PLS or PLZ (please).
- End your message appropriately. Sign off with TTYL (talk to you later), CFN (ciao for now), TAFN (that's all for now), EOM (end of message), or something along those lines.

Phrases such as CUL8R (see you later) may be subject to misinterpretation. Do you mean see you later today, later this week, later this year, or later in this lifetime? If you're using that expression for more than a casual sign-off, be more specific.

Use abbreviations and emoticons with care. DGOBWA [Don't go overboard with abbreviations]. Learn some of the popular ones later in this chapter.

Alert people when you're away. IMing doesn't involve a ring or busy signal the way the phone does. When you're on an extended phone call or when you're away from your computer, consider leaving a default message that says, *Sorry, not available now* or *I'm away from the computer. Back at noon.*

Be considerate about inviting others into a session. IMing is a wonderful way for team members to communicate in real time. Before you invite one or more people into a multiparty session, ask those already in the session for their approval.

Don't hide behind IM. IMing isn't intended to replace emails, face-to-face communication, or phone calls. Don't be an IM coward and use the technology to break up with your boyfriend or girlfriend, chastise a colleague, terminate an employee, or be confrontational.

Texting Etiquette

According to a survey by the Pew Research Center, those born after 1980 send more texts than any other generation. However, many people from the older generations use texting as well. It's important to apply the same degree of etiquette when texting that you would with any other form of communication and to be aware of the commonly used abbreviations. See the list of abbreviations later in this chapter.

Texting doesn't replace the subtleties of face-to-face meetings or phone calls, and it doesn't build business relationships. It's about communicating briefly and quickly.

Do's

- **Keep messages brief.** Verizon suggests that anything over 160 characters should be an email. Ask yourself, Would I call this person to give her the message? If the answer is no, don't send a text.

Unless your spouse, significant other, or partner is expecting a baby momentarily, turn your phone off during meetings. When you're speaking on the phone or texting, you're not engaged with the people in your group. And be sure to turn it off in public places such as movie theaters, restaurants, museums, and concert halls.

- **Use texting for quick business messages.** For example, you may write, "JTLYK will B late 4 sales mtg. L8R." [Just to let you know, I'll be late for the sales meeting. See you later.]

- **Limit abbreviations.** A few common ones are fine such as L8R (later), BTW (by the way), and EOM (end of message), but too many may be confusing, such as IM TTLY BRD RT NOW (I'm totally bored right now).

- **Think about the tone of your message.** What may seem completely innocent to you may be misinterpreted by the recipient.

- **Be attuned to people's schedules.** Just because you're awake and working in the wee hours of the morning doesn't mean others are.

- **Double-check the recipient's number before you hit "Send."** You'd be pretty embarrassed if you inadvertently sent a colleague a love note intended for your boyfriend or girlfriend.

Taboos

- **Texting while driving.** It's bad enough to talk on the phone while you're driving, but pounding out a message is just plain dangerous. And in many states, it's illegal.

- **Texting while in the presence of other people.** This is especially rude when you're sharing a meal in a restaurant and on other social occasions.

- **Texting to dump your boyfriend or end your marriage.** Britney Spears ended her marriage to Keven Federline with the text message "I H8 U, loser!" Canada's MuchMusic channel caught Federline's reaction on film.

I was having dinner at a posh restaurant. Sitting at the table next to me were three very well-dressed patrons, each talking on cell phones during much of the time. When they weren't talking on their phones, they were texting and laughing at their messages. Perhaps they weren't enjoying each other's company. Another time I was at the Metropolitan Opera in New York, and someone's phone rang in the middle of the performance. The person answered in a rather loud voice, having absolutely no regard for the performers or the audience. Know when to turn off your phone.

Pulling from the Scrabble box

Your friends may be conversant in this new language, but don't assume your business associates are. Don't overuse abbreviations, or your message will look like a bowl of alphabet soup. Here are some commonly used abbreviations:

AAMOF as a matter of fact

AFAIK as far as I know

AFK away from [computer] keyboard

AIM AOL Instant Messenger

AM away message

ASAP as soon as possible

A/S/L age/sex/location

ATM at the moment

B back

BBL be back later

BBS be back soon

BC because

BCNU be seein' you

BEG big evil grin

BFF best friends forever

BFN bye for now

BFO blinding flash of the obvious

BG big grin

BI buddy icon

BL buddy list

BMG be my guest

BRB be right back

BTA but then again

BTDT been there, done that

BTW by the way

C see

CFN ciao for now

CID consider it done

CSG chuckle, snicker, grin

CTRN can't talk right now

CUL see you later

CUL8R see you later

CYL catch you later

DHTB don't have the bandwidth

DQMOT don't quote me on this

EOM end of message

4 for

FAQ frequently asked questions

F2F face to face

FTF face to face

FWIW for what it's worth

FYA for your amusement

FYI for your information

G2G got to go
GAL get a life
GL good luck
GMTA great minds think alike
GRA go right ahead
GW good work

HAND have a nice day
H&K hug and kiss
HT hi there
HTH hope this helps

IAC in any case
IAE in any event
IDK I don't know
IHMB I hate my boss
IK I know
IKWUM I know what you mean
I LV U I love you [or] I'm leaving you
[quite a difference]
IM instant message
IMHO in my humble opinion
IMNSHO in my not so humble opinion
IMO in my opinion
IMS I'm sorry
IOW in other words

JIC just in case
JK just kidding
JTLYK just to let you know

K OK
KIS keep it simple
KWIM? know what I mean?

L8R later
LOL laughing out loud

MHBFU my heart bleeds for you
MYOB mind your own business

NBD no big deal
NP no problem
NRN no response necessary
NSFW not safe for work

OBTW oh, by the way
OH offhand
OIC oh, I see
OTL out to lunch
OTOH on the other hand
OTP on the phone

PLS please
PLZ please
PMFJI pardon me for jumping in
POC point of contact
POS parent over shoulder
POV point of view

R are
ROTFL rolling on the floor laughing
RSN real soon now
RUOK? are you okay?

SLAP sounds like a plan
SN screen name
SO significant other
SYS see you soon

2 to
TAFN that's all for now
TBA to be announced
TBH to be honest
THX thanks
TIA thanks in advance

TNX thanks	**WRT** with respect to
TTBOMK to the best of my knowledge	**WTG** way to go
TTFN ta-ta for now	**WU?** what's up?
TTYL talk to you later	
TY thank you	**Y** why
	YCQMOT you can quote me on this
U you	**YOYO** you're on your own
UN username	**YT?** you there?
	YW you're welcome
WB welcome back	**YWSYLS** you win some, you lose some
WE whatever	
WFM works for me	

 Be wary of creating your own shortcuts because they may be misunderstood. When I was facilitating my email workshop, a participant shared that he'd created *F/U* as a shortcut for "follow up." Someone read the message quickly, misinterpreted the abbreviation (you can guess what she thought), and reported his "foul language" to HR.

Emoticons :-)

The advent of the emoticon dates back to the early 1980s and has been credited to Carnegie Mellon professor Scott Fahlman. On an electronic bulletin board where students and faculty posted opinions, he suggested using :) to indicate jokes and :-(to indicate serious comments. (The latter quickly grew into a sign of discontent.) Fahlman's symbols caught on, and soon computer enthusiasts were working on an extensive list of new emoticons.

Because IMs and texts are short messages without much context, these little symbols may help to explain your emotions or intentions. Emoticons are especially useful when you want to clarify your true meaning, such as when saying something tongue-in-cheek. They're more appropriate for personal communication than for business. For an extensive listing of neat emoticons and graphics, check out http://messenger.msn.com/Resource/Emoticons.aspx. Here are just a few that are commonly used:

:-)	smile	:-@	angry	:-(	sad
:-S	confused	:-$	embarrassed	8-)	rolling my eyes
:-O	shouting	:-X	lips are sealed	:-|	expressionless
:-8	screaming	]:-)>	devilish	~&:-(	having a bad hair day

Reading nonverbal cues.

The digital natives of the younger generation use their thumbs to punch out text messages faster than a woodpecker uses its beak to peck a hole in a tree. Are they (the younger generation, not the woodpeckers) losing the ability to read nonverbal cues—facial expressions, body language, and other wordless signals? When they're texting during a class, slouching over their phones at the dinner table, or answering a text in the middle of a theatrical performance, are they really communicating?

Anthropologist Edward T. Hall found that diplomats entering foreign countries could be entirely fluent in the native language but nonetheless flounder from crisis to crisis because they failed to decode the nonverbal components of communication—"the unspoken signals and assumptions that flow from human psychology and national character, elements critical to success in business."

BTW: A smiley face doesn't count as communication. YCQMOT.

Don't forget Wingdings. In Microsoft Word, you find them by pulling down the Insert menu and clicking on Symbol. They include ✂,☛,☑,✐,☺, and many more.

> The difficulty is not to affect your reader, but to affect him [or her] precisely as you wish.
>
> —Robert Louis Stevenson, British writer

Chapter 16

Write It So They'll Read It

In this chapter

- *Plan to write*
- *Write strategically*
- *Proofread carefully*

Does your writing shout "Read me"? Does it get the attention it deserves? Do you get the action or responses you expect? If not, that doesn't mean you were born without the writing gene. The good news is that everyone can learn to write clearly, effectively, and strategically. This chapter outlines how.

Plan to write

One of the secrets of good writing is to plan. Planning is the most important part of any project, and this applies to writing as well.

Know your audience. Why is it so easy to send a message to a friend or colleague? Because you know him. You know his preconceived ideas, level of expertise, probable reaction to your message, reaction to slang or jargon, and so on. This same logic applies to any written message. You must see your target so you know where to aim. Fill in these blanks for every message you write. And that includes emails.

My primary reader is _____ and my secondary readers are_____.

My reader needs to know _____ about the subject.

The benefit to my reader is _____.

My reader will be [responsive/neutral/unresponsive] to my message.

After reading my message, I want the reader to _____.

Identify your key issue. Put on your advertising cap and ask yourself this: If your reader forgets just about everything you write, what's the one point you want him to remember? Then distill this key point into one sentence. This step is critical to delivering a clear and targeted message.

Ask yourself the questions your reader will want answered. Newspaper reporters use the questioning approach to guide readers through stories. Here are the questions someone invited to a meeting may ask:

Who else will be there?
What is the agenda?
When is the date?
Where is the meeting?
Why am I being invited?
How can I contribute?

Write strategically

When you write strategically, rather than generically, you keep the reader and your intentions in mind.

Write dynamic headlines that shout "Read me!" Have you ever noticed how newspaper headlines jump out to tell a story? All your business documents—letters, email messages, reports, handbooks, and anything you write—should tell your story. Remember that people don't read, they skim. You want your readers to notice your key issues at a glance. Here's an example of how headlines can tell a story. If people read these headlines and not the accompanying text, they can still get the key information.

Evacuation drill: [date] [time]
To prepare, find emergency routes on bulletin boards
Proceed to the nearest stairway, then leave the building

Helpful generic headlines can include:

Action requested
Next step
Deadline: [date]

Meeting information
    Date:
    Time:
    Place:

After completing your headlines, go back to fill in the supporting text. It's like filling in the blanks.

 You don't have to start your writing at the beginning of the document. Fill in the headline that's the easiest, then go to the next. Your opening and closing will be an outgrowth of what you write.

Sequence for the needs of your reader. When your reader will regard your message as good or neutral news, put the bottom line at the beginning. After all, your document isn't a joke where you put the punch line at the end. When your reader will view your message as negative, you don't want to hit him between the eyes with bad news. Try to maintain goodwill. Here are a few things to consider:

- Offer options, if you can.
- Change the order so you sandwich the bad news between an upbeat opening and a friendly closing.
- Give a reason, if that's appropriate.
- Make lemonade by trying to find something positive.

Design for visual impact. When your document has a strong visual impact, it's readable.

Limit sentence length. As a general rule, limit sentences to 20 to 25 words. Use long sentences for detailed explanations and short sentences for emphatic statements.

Limit paragraph length. Limit paragraphs to approximately eight lines of text. When paragraphs are long and dense, the reader may skip over them. When they're short and choppy, he won't see the connections between ideas.

Prepare bulleted and numbered lists (when they're appropriate).
- Use bulleted lists for items of equal value.
- Use numbered lists to prioritize information.

Use charts, tables, and figures.
- Use pie charts to show percentages of a whole.
- Use line charts to show trends.

- Use bar charts to show relationships between two or more variables.
- Use tables to simplify difficult information.

Use lots of white space.

- Leave 1- to 1½-inch margins on the top, bottom, and sides of hard copy.
- Leave a one-line space between paragraphs.
- Leave a one-line space above and below bulleted and numbered lists.

Eliminate the flotsam and jetsam. You've undoubtedly heard the expression KISS, which stands for *Keep it short and simple*. Eliminate any words or phrases that don't add value.

Simple: The problem started after I . . .
Wordy: The problem started to happen right after I . . .

Simple: We considered the following:
Wordy: We gave consideration to the following:

Simple: Please send us your ideas and suggestions.
Wordy: I would greatly appreciate any ideas or suggestions you may have.

Write	Instead of
apply	make an application
as soon as	at the earliest possible date
breakthrough	new breakthrough
concluded	arrived at the conclusion
consensus	general consensus
development	new development
essential	absolutely essential
experimented	conducted experiments
fact	true fact
factor	contributing factor
first	first and foremost
fundamentals	basic fundamentals
invite	extend an invitation
loan	temporary loan (otherwise it's a gift)
opposite	completely opposite
recommend	make a recommendation
result	end result
status	current status
truth	honest truth

Imagine that every word you use will cost you $100. Eliminate all that aren't necessary without making your sentences curt.

Use positive words and phrases. Presenting yourself as an optimist is a winning strategy. Sometimes it's a matter of saying what you can and will do, rather than what you won't do.

Positive: I hope you'll be pleased with the results.
Negative: I hope you won't be disappointed by the results.

Positive: You can charge orders of $10 or more.
Negative: You can't charge orders under $10.

Note: When you express your thoughts in the negative, do so for strategic reasons.

Use the active voice. When you write a sentence in the active voice, you make the subject the "doer." (In a sentence that is a command, you can infer the subject or doer from the context—you won't see the subject, but it's there. The subject is the person to whom you're speaking.)

Active: Please visit our website for additional information. (Doer is inferred.)
Passive: Additional information can be found on our website.

Active: The team must submit the report by June 15.
Passive: The report must be submitted by June 15.

There are some instances when you may want to use the passive voice. But do so strategically, as in the following examples:

- The law firm was established in the early 1900s. (You want to place the focus on the action, not the actor.)

- Mistakes were made. (You want to hide something or protect someone.)

Use *you* and *your* more often than *I* and *me*. Notice how often the words *you* and *your* are used in advertisements. Advertisers know the importance of speaking directly to the reader.

Reader focused: You'll be happy to hear . . .
Writer focused: I'm happy to tell you . . .

Reader focused: You'll be receiving . . .
Writer focused: I'll be sending you . . .

Proofread carefully

Imagine the following scenario: The new CEO of a major corporation walks into his first board of directors meeting. He wants to dazzle the board. He's wearing a $2,500 dark pinstriped suit, a white silk shirt with diamond-studded French cuffs, highly polished Italian leather shoes, and everything else that says "classy." He sits down, crosses his legs, and (oops!) you notice that he's wearing one black sock and one brown sock. What does that do to his classy image? Every time you think of Mr. CEO, you'll snicker and recall his mismatched socks.

Now imagine yourself working hard to prepare a document. Any errors, no matter how few, are your mismatched socks—what your readers will remember. Here are a few things to focus on:

- Check the spelling of personal names.
- Verify middle initials.
- Check the spelling of company names.
- Double-check all numbers.
- Check days and dates against those on the calendar.
- Check spelling, grammar, and punctuation throughout.

Eliminate any ambiguity, anything that may be misinterpreted. According to urban legend, years ago J. Edgar Hoover (who served as the head of the FBI under many different presidents) asked his secretary to type a memo on internal security. When proofreading the memo, Hoover wrote "Watch the borders" across the top of the page. He wanted his secretary to widen the margins, but instead she typed his words directly into the document. Government officials receiving the memo then alerted the Border Patrol to watch for unusual activity along the Canadian and Mexican frontiers.

 Although spell and grammar checkers are wonderful tools, don't turn on your computer and turn off your brain. (I mentioned that in Chapter 14, but it's worth repeating.)

Proofreading checklist

Keep this checklist handy and review it before you send or distribute any document:

- ☐ My subject line and headlines are informative and will spark my reader's interest.
- ☐ My message is sequenced for the needs of my reader.
- ☐ My document has visual impact including:
  - o Ample white space throughout
  - o 1- to 1½ -inch margins on the top, bottom, and sides
  - o Sentences limited to 20–25 words
  - o Paragraphs limited to 8 lines
  - o Bulleted and numbered lists, when appropriate
  - o Tables and charts, when appropriate
- ☐ The tone is appropriate:
  - o Reader-focused
  - o Short and to the point (KISS)
  - o Positive words and phrases
  - o Active voice
  - o "You" approach
- ☐ Spelling, grammar, and punctuation are correct, and the document makes sense.
- ☐ I didn't put down my cup and leave coffee stains on the paper.

Remember, in this virtual world, clear and concise communication is more important than ever.

> Words are, of course, the most powerful drug
> used by mankind.
> —Rudyard Kipling, British writer

Chapter 17

·············

Lexicon of Today's Business Buzzwords

New technology gives rise to new terminology. The following is a handy list of some of the basic and not-so-basic buzzwords in today's workplace—many of which can already be found in *The American Heritage® Dictionary*. Read on to bone up on the words you need to know as you meet, tweet, train, team, and talk your way to the top.

aggregator
   A program or website that collects feeds from various sources, such as websites, blogs, and news services. Subscribers can view the content of multiple sources all in one place. The Drudge Report and Google News are examples of news aggregators.

app
   Short for *application*. Used informally to refer to a computer program that helps the user accomplish a specific task.

asynchronous learning
   Learning in which interaction happens intermittently and students can participate on their own schedules. Examples of asynchronous learning events include online discussion groups and self-paced courses offered over the Internet.

avatar
   The incarnation of a Hindu deity in human or animal form. Used in the computer sense to mean a cartoon drawing, photograph, icon, or other image by which a person represents her virtual identity, as in a chatroom or interactive online game.

baby boomers
People born from 1946 to 1964. Also called boomers.

blog
A website of logs (*web* + *log* = *blog*) maintained by a person or company. Blogs display the postings of one or more individuals in chronological order and may include commentary, descriptions of events and products, or other material such as graphics and video.

blogosphere
The interconnected community of all blogs on the Internet and the people who create, write for, and maintain them.

cloud
A wireless network that offers coordinated Internet service. Cloud providers deliver common business applications online that are accessed from a web browser. Cloud users can "rent" computing services as needed.

contingent workers
Temporary employees or consultants paid by the hour or by the project. They get no benefits.

CPC
Cost per click. CPC advertisers pay for each time that a user clicks on their ad and is directed to their website.

CPM
Cost per thousand. CPM advertisers pay a fixed amount for every thousand impressions, or loads, of their ad.

crowdsource
To ask a group of people online to handle tasks traditionally performed by employees, or to outsource tasks over the Internet to a community of people in the form of an open call. A marketing firm asking the public to contribute suggestions for a company name is an example of crowdsourcing.

defriend
Also *unfriend.* To remove someone as a friend on Facebook.

digital dashboard
A software tool used by managers or executives to assess progress in various areas and to track the overall performance of a business. Digital dashboards allow users to consolidate data into simple graphic formats such as graphs, pie charts, and maps.

fan
  Someone who connects with you through your Facebook page.

FiOS
  Fiber-Optic Service. A data communications service provided by Verizon that uses fiber-optic cables to transfer data.

friend
  Someone who connects with you through your Facebook profile.

follower
  Someone who opts to get your tweets.

FTP
  File Transfer Protocol. Any of various communications protocols designed to transfer files over the Internet.

Gen X
  Short for *Generation X.* People born from 1965 to 1980.

Gen Y
  Short for *Generation Y.* People born from 1981 to 2000.

human capital
  The skills and knowledge gained through education and experience that help employees perform their jobs.

insource
  To complete tasks or functions in-house, as by bringing in contingent workers. (The opposite of *outsource.*)

intexticated
  Prone to compulsive texting.

microblog
  A blog containing very brief entries. Twitter is considered a microblog because each post is limited to 140 characters.

mistweet
  A tweet sent in error on Twitter. A mistweet can be worse than an email sent in error because it's likely that more people will read it.

onboarding
  The process of acquiring, accommodating, and assimilating new team members, whether they come from outside or inside the organization.

outsource
  To subcontract an operation to a third-party contingent worker or an outside supplier.

PDA

Personal digital assistant. A handheld computer or other digital device used to manage personal information. Most PDAs can be synchronized with personal computers and can connect to the Internet through wireless networks.

phat

Slang for *excellent* or *first rate.* So if a young person says you're phat, that doesn't mean you should head to the salad bar.

ping

Slang for "to contact someone." You might say, "I'll ping you in the morning."

podcast

A series of audio or video digital-media files that are distributed over the Internet by syndicated download to portable media players and personal computers.

retweet (RT)

On Twitter, to forward a message you've received to your followers.

RSS

Really Simple Syndication. A protocol used for distributing news briefs as well as notifying people of new content as it becomes available on websites.

SEO

Search engine optimization. The process of improving the volume or quality of traffic to your website or blog.

sexting

Sending sexually explicit photos, especially by cell phone.

social media

The online tools that enable people to communicate and share information over the Internet. Social media forums include blogs, social bookmarking, photo and video sharing, collaborative websites such as Wikipedia, and more.

social network

An online community whose members interact around shared interests, concerns, and activities and offer one another mutual support. LinkedIn, Facebook, and Twitter are popular social networking sites.

synchronous learning
Learning in which a group of people learn the same things at the same time.

thought leader
A person who is widely recognized for her innovative and influential ideas. This term can also apply to a business.

360-degree assessment
A diagnostic tool for gathering information about employees by soliciting feedback from the people who work with them, such as managers, peers, direct reports, and customers. 360s are used to supplement other means of assessment and are intended to help employees realize their full potential.

traditionalists
People born from 1927 to 1945. Also called *builders, pre-boomers, veterans, silents,* and *seniors.*

tweeple
People who use Twitter. (It's better than calling them twits.)

tweeps
People who follow you on Twitter.

tweet
A message sent on Twitter.

24/7
24 hours a day, 7 days a week. For example, you may hear companies say that they provide tech support 24/7.

twesume
A resume condensed into a maximum of 140 words to post on Twitter.

Twuffer
For use on Twitter, a program that allows you to create a list of tweets for future posting and to schedule their release dates.

unfriend
Also *defriend.* To remove someone as a friend on Facebook.

virtual office
Office space and services that can be rented by the hour, week, month, or longer. Virtual offices offer a professional image in a businesslike setting. Facilities may include a reception area, kitchen,

photocopier, fax, and other office equipment. A receptionist is often on hand to answer the phone and route calls.

virtual office assistant

A skilled, independent professional who works from a remote location for a person or business to provide any of various services such as customer support, bookkeeping, desktop publishing, Web page design, and Internet marketing.

virtual team

A group of geographically dispersed individuals working together through communication technology. They have independent performance goals and a common purpose for which they're accountable.

Vodcast

Short for *video podcast*.

VoIP

Voice over Internet Protocol. A technology that involves digitizing audio data and allows telephone calls to be made over the Internet at low cost.

WiFi

Wireless Fidelity. A popular wireless networking technology that uses radio waves to provide high-speed Internet connections.

wiki

A collaborative website that allows users to edit its content. The most popular wiki is Wikipedia, an online encyclopedia.

YouTube

A video-sharing website owned by Google that allows users to upload videos and watch videos posted by others.

Index

A

abbreviations
  instant messaging and, 254, 257, 258, 260–262
  texting and, 254, 259, 260–262
address, change of, 250
Adobe (company), 31
advertising, 37, 40
affiliate marketing, 37–38
age differences. *see* generational differences
Aitken, William Maxwell, 105
application letters, 54–56
Appreciative Inquiry (AI), 223–226
asterisks, use of, 52, 255
asynchronous communication, 139, 165
attachments, email and, 250, 251
attire, proper business, 109–111, 169
audition interviews, 58
aural learning style, 124
auto-response, email and, 246
avatars, 120, 173

B

baby boomers, 64, 67, 73
bar charts, 129
Bates, Suzanne, 242
B2B (business to business) sites, 19
B2C (business to consumer) sites, 26
Bcc, use of, 248–249
Becker, Dennis and Paula, 126
behavioral interviews, 58

benefits, employee motivation and, 71–74
Berg, Paula, 18
blended learning, 132–134
blogs and blogging
  content, creating good, 32–36
  cultural differences and, 94
  dialogues or monologues, 32, 47
  etiquette for, 38–39
  job hunting and, 45
  marketing strategy and, 36–38, 40–42
  mistakes, avoiding, 37
  overview, 30–31
  profiting from, 37–38
  started, getting, 31–32
  updating, 11, 35–36
Bloom, Eric, 121
body language, importance of, 91, 95–97, 143
Boeing (company), 31
boldface, use of, 52, 255
bookmarks and bookmarking, 29
boomers. *see* baby boomers
brand management
  blogs and, 40
  employment and social networking, 45
  establishing, 5, 7–8
Brogan, Chris, 3
Browne, Cathy, 49
bullets, use of, 52, 255, 266
businesses. *see* companies

About the Author

Sheryl wears a lot of hats, just as you do. First and foremost, she feels blessed to have a wonderful husband, two sons, and three grandchildren. They complete her life and bring her immeasurable joy.

She feels fortunate to have a job that would be her hobby if it weren't her profession. For 25 years Sheryl has been the Principal of Sheryl Lindsell-Roberts & Associates. Between helping clients with marketing campaigns, coaching, and facilitating business writing, technical writing, email, and presentation workshops, she's written 24 other books.

When Sheryl's life gets more hectic than it needs to be, her warm-weather nirvana is her 30-foot sailboat—*Worth th' Wait*. She and her husband, Jon, are aboard every weekend the temperature rises above 60 and the seas aren't too treacherous. (They've also been out there when they were too treacherous, but not by choice.) She doesn't bring a suitcase stuffed with clothes because there isn't room to put too much. She's learned to minimize. All she needs is sunscreen, a few pairs of shorts, some T-shirts, a good book, and her sea legs. Sheryl believes that everyone needs a nirvana—a time when the past is cut off and only the present exists—even if it's a spot under a tree or the corner of a room.

When Sheryl isn't working or sailing, she's traveling, painting (watercolors and oils, not walls), gardening, photographing nature, reading, skiing, kayaking, and working out at the gym. She tries to live each day to the fullest! For more information about Sheryl, please check out www.sherylwrites.com.

Other books by Sheryl Lindsell-Roberts

Speaking Your Way to Success

You *can* speak your way to success, and this book will teach you how. In her signature no-nonsense style, Sheryl delivers guidelines for today's professionals on making conversation, asking for a raise, winning contracts, working a room, and much more.

Mastering Computer Typing, Revised Edition

Appropriate for self-instruction or classroom instruction, this book can teach you to type efficiently and accurately in 24 hours. Fully updated to meet the needs of today's professionals, it includes timely information on email, blogs, texting, and instant messaging.

Strategic Business Letters and E-mail

Sheryl walks you through an extensive array of letter-writing experiences, showing you how to write with confidence and maximum effect. This book contains hundreds of model letters as well as tips on using e-mail effectively.

135 Tips on Email and Instant Messages

Learn how to use electronic communication to advance your career and expand your social network. With special sections on blogs, chatrooms, and texting, this book is packed with essential advice for anyone who communicates electronically.

135 Tips on Writing Successful Business Documents

Whether you work for a large corporation or a grassroots organization, this book will teach you to compose business documents that people will read and act on. Part One explains business-writing basics. Part Two gives examples of specific documents, from press releases to storyboards to resumes.

More Praise for *New Rules for Today's Workplace*

"Smart, direct, concise, and readable."
— Steve Bardige, Sr. Director, EMC Analyst Relations

"I just love Sheryl's style and common-sense tips. She always has a way of taking the intimidation out of new challenges by giving people reasons to embrace change with steps they can learn and do. *New Rules for Today's Workplace* is a must-read. Sheryl shows the reader how to use today's hottest business techniques to enhance proven best practices in a multigenerational workforce. This book is replete with simple strategies that force you to know and satisfy your audience in a highly competitive marketplace. The tech-savvy choices can seem endless. *New Rules* helps you choose what's realistic for you through understanding the what's, why's and how-to's."
— Paula Camara, Senior Management Advisor, Massachusetts Small Business Development Center at Clark University

"It is not easy in today's fast-paced, diverse, and virtual workplace to have your messages consistently understood. Sheryl is one of the few people who knows how to help business professionals get their point across in a concise, professional manner. She is one of the best business-writing and marketing-communications workshop presenters with whom I have ever worked. Her passion for business writing and communications spills over to her workshop participants who rave about her programs, and spills over further into this book. Sheryl understands and captures the essence and importance of clear, concise, and appropriate communication in today's often off-the-cuff, harried work environment."
— Karen Cronenberger, Employers Association of the NorthEast

"This is a book that every company's leadership team should own. Whether you're a boomer, a Gen Yer, or from another country, you'll take away valuable insights into how to use the 'virtual world' to survive and succeed in the 21st century."
— Joe Curtin, Director of Recruiting, Training and Development, Roche Bros. Supermarkets

"It's been very scary how quickly technology has changed the way we communicate in business. Social media and social networking are a whole new world of connecting. This book is a lifejacket for any person who is dreading the inevitable move to 'virtual' anything. The information in Part One alone bridges the gap from 'what was' to 'what is' in the latest and best communication channels. Thank you, Sheryl. It's just in time!"
— Linda J. Jackson, Assistant Vice President and Training Manager, Workers' Credit Union

"Sheryl's book arrives at a time when top talent is being discovered by online networks and virtual communities. Companies need not only to be able to take a dip into that talent pool, but to increase their tolerance for an organization of virtual staff that is not bound by location or geography. As good as that sounds, the hard part comes when we ask our traditional management staff to manage, develop, and assimilate their virtual staff into intact teams. As always, Sheryl is here to help and make this transition easy by breaking it into simple steps and techniques. This book takes you on a virtual journey from leveraging the social networks, building trust virtually, and delivering feedback all the way to the lexicon of today's business buzzwords. This is a back-pocket book for managers and employees of all generations!"

—America Glaude, Leader of Learning and Organizational Development, OneBeacon Insurance Company

"Prior to meeting Sheryl I struggled through my responsibility of writing investment research. My research colleagues would edit my work regularly and provide a litany of corrections and changes. I knew their suggestions improved the paper, but I did not understand what I was doing wrong. After working with Sheryl for a very short time, I became a confident writer and have published numerous investment white papers that drove tangible results and received high acclaim. The evolution of today's workplace has reached escape velocity. It is easy to see why many business veterans, relying on obsolete ideas and methods, struggle to keep pace. *New Rules* lays out the means for professionals of all stripes to catch up, communicate, and thrive in today's virtual environment."

—Robert Graves, CFA, Vice President, Strategic Relations, Columbia Management

"In today's corporate world, virtual communication and cross-national teams have become commonplace. Sheryl's book serves as an excellent guide to the new reality, addressing the most important topics and giving specific advice on how to be successful. Anecdotes and personal experiences make the highly informational content an easy read. I found the chapters about various kinds of virtual communication especially interesting as they teach how to use those mediums efficiently as well as in an ethnic- and gender-sensitive manner. This is a great book for those in fast-track careers who want to proceed as experienced communicators and broaden their reach."

—Alicja Januszewicz, Global Compliance Training and Development, Boston Scientific Corporation

"I'm going to tether my copy of *New Rules* to my desktop and buy copies for colleagues. I've only had it for a week and I've already got it tabbed and earmarked for quick reference. This book is jam-packed with helpful tips, checklists, and reminders on a wide variety of workplace topics. I'm keeping it within arm's reach."
—Karen Kathryn Keefe, Organization Development Consultant

"Follow the advice in Sheryl's introduction: 'Don't share this book—you may never get it back!' You'll want it as your constant companion to help you navigate the ever-expanding virtual world with grace, confidence, and ease. When someone marvels at your proficiency, point them to Sheryl's trustworthy guidance in *New Rules for Today's Workplace*, and you'll have a BFF (Best Friend Forever)."
—Sue LaChance, Director of Organizational and Leadership Development, Constant Contact

"This book is a useful and practical primer on navigating the maze of 'virtuality' in today's workplaces."
—Stephen R. Langlois, Executive Vice President, LPL Financial

"This is a must-have guide to succeed in the virtual world. The great hot tips, reminders, cross-references, and comments from Sheryl are indispensable to every businessperson."
—Susanne Morreale Leeber, CCE, IOM, President & CEO, Marlborough Regional Chamber of Commerce

"It is not easy being a virtual worker in today's society. Whether you are managing or part of a virtual team, *New Rules for Today's Workplace* is the definitive guide. There is something for everyone—the experienced virtual worker, those new to telecommuting, and the manager of virtual teams. This is a must-read."
—Mitch Morrison, Sr. Technical Trainer, The TJX Companies Inc.

"Once again, Sheryl Lindsell-Roberts has provided invaluable insight and business savvy with her new book *New Rules for Today's Workplace*. Whether you're an employee, small business owner, or COO of a major company, the techniques and strategies she details are just what we all need to be successful in the modern workplace. This book will become a prominent part of my reference library."
—Paul Papierski, Learning and Development Specialist & Coach, American Cancer Society

"*New Rules for Today's Workplace* is that rare type of encyclopedic resource manual sought by new entrants into the workplace and those seasoned veterans wondering, What has changed and how do I adapt? Sheryl acknowledges the 'elephants in the room' and provides guidance for dealing with the smallest to the largest office pachyderm. Her expertise is straightforward, commonsensical, and clear, presented with the tone of a trusted friend sharing inside advice—with an addictive dash of humor. She efficiently defines her audience in the introduction of the book, but doesn't take into account the larger group of cultural anthropologists who will be enthralled. This book will provide a slice of history into the modern office of the 21st century."

—Alex Quigley, Manager, Engineering Operations &
Organizational Development, Pegasystems Inc.